AF701404

Food Law for Public Health

FOOD AND PUBLIC HEALTH SERIES

Edited by Jonathan Deutsch and Nicholas Freudenberg

1. FOOD LAW FOR PUBLIC HEALTH
   Jennifer L. Pomeranz 2016

Food Law for Public Health

Jennifer L. Pomeranz

OXFORD
UNIVERSITY PRESS

OXFORD
UNIVERSITY PRESS

Oxford University Press is a department of the University of Oxford. It furthers the University's objective of excellence in research, scholarship, and education by publishing worldwide.

Oxford New York
Auckland Cape Town Dar es Salaam Hong Kong Karachi
Kuala Lumpur Madrid Melbourne Mexico City Nairobi
New Delhi Shanghai Taipei Toronto

With offices in
Argentina Austria Brazil Chile Czech Republic France Greece
Guatemala Hungary Italy Japan Poland Portugal Singapore
South Korea Switzerland Thailand Turkey Ukraine Vietnam

Oxford is a registered trademark of Oxford University Press in the UK and certain other countries.

Published in the United States of America by
Oxford University Press
198 Madison Avenue, New York, NY 10016

© Oxford University Press 2016

All rights reserved. No part of this publication may be reproduced, stored in a retrieval system, or transmitted, in any form or by any means, without the prior permission in writing of Oxford University Press, or as expressly permitted by law, by license, or under terms agreed with the appropriate reproduction rights organization. Inquiries concerning reproduction outside the scope of the above should be sent to the Rights Department, Oxford University Press, at the address above.

You must not circulate this work in any other form and you must impose this same condition on any acquirer.

Library of Congress Cataloging-in-Publication Data
Pomeranz, Jennifer L., author.
Food law for public health / Jennifer L. Pomeranz.
p. ; cm. — (Food and public health series)
Includes bibliographical references and index.
ISBN 978-0-19-022725-8
I. Title. II. Series: Food and public health series.
[DNLM: 1. Legislation, Food—United States. 2. Food Industry—legislation & jurisprudence—United States. 3. Nutrition Policy—legislation & jurisprudence—United States. WA 697]
TX359
363.8′561—dc23
2015020261

For Jeremy and Julia

CONTENTS

ACKNOWLEDGMENTS

Several people were essential in supporting my career: Harold B. Pomeranz, the Honorable G. R. Smith, Michelle M. Mello, and Kelly D. Brownell. I learned a great deal from each one of them and am grateful for their encouragement, thoughtfulness, and mentorship. I wish to thank Nicholas Freudenberg and Chad Zimmerman, without whom this book would not have been possible. Additionally, I would like to acknowledge all the people out there working to improve our food environment in support of public health.

ABOUT THE AUTHOR

Jennifer L. Pomeranz is a professor of public health law and policy at New York University in the College of Global Public Health. Previously she was the Director of Legal Initatives at the Rudd Center for Food Policy and Obesity at Yale University. She is internationally renown for her work on food law for a public health audience. Professor Pomeranz received her Bachelor of Arts from the University of Michigan and her Juris Doctorate from Cornell Law School. After practicing law for five years, she earned her Master of Public Health from the Harvard T.H. Chan School of Public Health.

1

Background: United States Government

Introduction

This book covers a wide range of topics related to how the law impacts food in the United States. The law is created by the government and thus it is important to understand the structure and function of government entities within the United States. This chapter discusses the structure and function of the federal, state, and local governments, while the remainder of the book delves further into the government's role as a regulator, educator, purchaser, and purveyor of food. Chapter 2 explains how the U.S. Constitution is the backbone of all other law in the country. Because this book is about food law, it is important to point out that the terms "policy" and "law" are not interchangeable. Rather, policy is the intent behind a law, a concept that guides government action. A government's desire to pass a certain law is based on a policy objective—what the government wants to achieve by passing the law. However, many use the word policy to include law. The CDC defines policy as "a law, regulation, procedure, administrative action, incentive, or voluntary practice of governments and other institutions."

The U.S. Constitution established three branches of the federal government: the executive, legislative, and judicial. Each branch shapes policy in its own way. The Constitution also established state governments. The term "federalism" describes the division of authority and the relationship between the federal and state governments. All 50 states have their own state constitutions and state governments that generally mirror the federal system with the same three branches. Each branch of government and state governments are discussed in this chapter.

Federal Government

THE EXECUTIVE BRANCH

The federal executive branch is made up of the U.S. President, Vice President, and the executive administration, which consists of the Cabinet, agencies and departments described below.[1] The President is the "chief executive" of the United States and shapes policy through his or her administration and through communication with the public. The President's State of the Union Address is a formal communication between the President and Congress in which the President reports on the current conditions and provides policy proposals for the upcoming legislative year.[2] In the modern age, however, this address is delivered to the nation and the President sets the national agenda publicly.

The President also issues executive orders, which are directives to the federal government. For example, President Clinton issued Executive Order 12898 on February 11, 1994,[3] requiring all federal agencies to address environmental justice by remedying the health, safety, and economic consequences of environmental problems that disproportionately hurt historically disadvantaged communities.[4] Through this order, the President established an interagency working group to develop an environmental justice strategy and provide guidance to the agencies.[5] This was a historic moment for the environmental justice movement.[6]

The President has influence over other government entities through his or her power to appoint the heads of executive administrative agencies, the Supreme Court Justices, circuit court judges, and district court judges. Two executive agencies that have authority directly related to food are the United States Department of Agriculture and the Department of Health and Human Services. These agencies and others are discussed further below.

Finally, although not formerly part of the executive branch, the President's spouse, traditionally known as the First Lady because they have always been women up to this point, typically takes up an issue of civic importance. Depending on the personality of the First Lady, this can set the national agenda for policy. Dolly Madison has been referred to as "the first First Lady" because she created the modern conception of what it means to be First Lady.[7] Eleanor Roosevelt is often cited as the most influential and popular First Lady in modern American history. Michelle Obama took up the issue of childhood obesity,

---

[1] U.S. Constitution. Art II, Sec. 1(1).

[2] Colleen J. Shogan, Thomas H. Neale. *The President's State of the Union Address: Tradition, Function, and Policy Implications.* Congressional Research Service. January 24, 2014.

[3] Executive Order 12898 on February 11, 1994 http://www.archives.gov/federal-register/executive-orders/pdf/12898.pdf

[4] U.S. Department of Justice. Attorney General Holder Marks 20th Anniversary of Historic Executive Order on Environmental Justice. February 11, 2014. http://blogs.justice.gov/main/archives/3553

[5] Executive Order 12898 on February 11, 1994 http://www.archives.gov/federal-register/executive-orders/pdf/12898.pdf

[6] U.S. Department of Justice. Attorney General Holder Marks 20th Anniversary of Historic Executive Order on Environmental Justice. February 11, 2014. http://blogs.justice.gov/main/archives/3553

[7] Public Broadcasting System (PBS). Significant First Ladies. http://www.pbs.org/wgbh/americanexperience/features/photo-gallery/dolley/

through her "Let's Move!" campaign.[8] This effort incorporates issues related to food policy, corporate social responsibility, and physical activity.

Executive Branch Administrative Agencies

There are three types of federal agencies. Most federal agencies are housed in the executive branch of the federal government. Within this group, there are Cabinet agencies and independent agencies. The heads of 15 executive departments make up the President's Cabinet, including the Secretaries of Agriculture, Commerce, Defense, Education, Energy, Health and Human Services, Homeland Security, Housing and Urban Development, Interior, Labor, State, Transportation, Treasury, and Veterans Affairs, as well as the Attorney General (housed in the Department of Justice). Other agencies, such as the Environmental Protection Agency and the Federal Trade Commission are independent agencies, meaning they are independent of Cabinet departments but not independent regulatory agencies. The third category is "independent regulatory agencies," which are agencies established to be independent of the President, and include for example, the Federal Communications Commission, the Securities and Exchange Commission, and the Consumer Product Safety Commission.[9] The White House often exercises direct control over the executive branch agencies and independent agencies by issuing executive orders and by the President's control over the Office of Management and Budget (OMB). The OMB is unique in that it is specifically dedicated to furthering the priorities of the administration and it oversees the interworking of the other agencies.

The majority of administrative agencies fulfill their mission as designated by an Act of Congress. These agencies can act only within the confines of their legislative grant of authority. Congress generally enacts a law, called legislation, on a topic and directs the appropriate administrative agencies to fill in the details through regulations. The majority of administrative agencies enact regulations through a process called Notice and Comment Rulemaking, as specified under the Administrative Procedures Act.[10] The notice and comment process begins when an agency is given authority by Congress to develop a regulation to carry out the intent of the legislation passed by Congress. The agency will propose a draft version of the regulation by publishing a notice of its intent to pass the proposed regulation. The notice is published in the Federal Register with a time period for interested parties to comment on the agency's proposal. Any interested party may comment on the proposed regulation. The agency must review and respond to the comments and the agency typically revises the proposal based

---

[8] Let's Move! http://www.letsmove.gov/

[9] 44 USC § 3501(5).

[10] 5 USCS § 553.

on this process. The agency ultimately publishes its final rule which becomes a binding regulation. Final regulations have the full force and effect of law.

The primary administrative agencies dedicated to food issues are outlined below. Each agency's main programs are described in this chapter so the responsibilities and authority of each agency are clear. These programs are fleshed out in further chapters.

United States Department of Agriculture

The United States Department of Agriculture (USDA) was founded in 1862 under President Abraham Lincoln. At that time, about 50% of all Americans lived on farms, compared with about 2% in the 21st century.[11] The functions of the USDA traditionally related to fostering and promoting America's agriculture and protecting livestock, but the functions of the USDA have expanded dramatically. The USDA oversees farming; conservation; food safety and labeling for meat, poultry, and eggs; research, economic, and educational programs; rural development; nutrition assistance programs; dietary guidelines; and the marketing of agricultural products.

The USDA is responsible for issuing the Dietary Guidelines for Americans. This started as a voluntary effort in 1894 and became Congressionally mandated in 1990. The USDA and other government and nongovernment entities rely on the dietary guidelines for a wide variety of nutrition and food programs.

The USDA's Farm Services administers what is colloquially referred to as the "Farm Bill." Congress reauthorizes the Farm Bill every five years or so, starting with the first, the Agricultural Adjustment Act of 1933; the most recent Farm Bill is the Agricultural Act of 2014. Two of the more controversial provisions of the modern Farm Bills include commodity supports and nutrition programs. The Commodity Program provides income, support, and a safety net to farmers who grow the major commodity crops, which include wheat, corn, soybeans, cotton, and rice. The Farm Bill also reauthorizes the Supplemental Nutrition Assistance Program (SNAP), which was formerly known as the Food Stamp Program. In fact, the nutrition programs make up the largest portion of the farm bill. In the Agricultural Act of 2014, 80% of the Farm Bill was allocated for nutrition assistance. [12]

The USDA's Food and Nutrition Services administers the USDA's nutrition assistance programs, including the National School Lunch Program, National

---

[11] U.S. Department of Agriculture Celebrates 150 Years. http://www.usda.gov/wps/portal/usda/usdahome?navid=USDA150

[12] U.S. Department of Agriculture. Economic Research Service. Agricultural Act of 2014: Highlights and Implications. http://www.ers.usda.gov/agricultural-act-of-2014-highlights-and-implications.aspx#.U3tpqnbGyd4

School Breakfast Program, SNAP, and the Special Supplemental Nutrition Program for Women, Infants, and Children, among many other programs. It is noteworthy that of the aforementioned nutrition assistance programs, only SNAP is funded through the Farm Bill. This has led to divergent interests and differing ideas regarding nutritional guidelines for SNAP as opposed to the other programs. The USDA administers many other nutrition programs, including for child and adult care facilities, emergency food assistance, and for Indian reservations.[13] These programs are examined in Chapter 4.

The USDA's Food Safety and Inspection Service (FSIS) regulates the safety and labeling of meat, poultry, and liquid, frozen, and dried egg products.[14] FSIS and the Food and Drug Administration (FDA) agreed to a memorandum of understanding in which the two agencies divide authority over food. The FDA is responsible for the safety and labeling of all processed food and beverage products, including milk and eggs in their shell.[15] However, the USDA's Agricultural Marketing Service is responsible for establishing quality and marketing grades and standards for dairy products, fruits and vegetables, livestock, meat, poultry, seafood, and shell eggs.[16] The USDA's food safety authority is discussed further in Chapter 5.

Department of Health and Human Services

The Department of Health and Human Services (HHS) is a vast agency with many subparts. Two agencies within HHS that have particular authority over food include the FDA and the Centers for Disease Control and Prevention (CDC). The U.S. Surgeon General is also part of HHS and the position is described below.

The Food and Drug Administration

Congress granted the FDA its modern powers under the Food Drug and Cosmetic Act of 1938 (FDCA). The FDA received increased authority to address food safety and prevent foodborne illness through the Food Safety Modernization Act 2011 (FSMA). The FSMA provides the FDA with the authority to protect the public from being exposed to food that "will cause serious adverse health consequences

---

[13] U.S. Department of Agriculture. Food and Nutrition Services. Programs and Services. http://www.fns.usda.gov/programs-and-services.

[14] Renée Johnson. *The Federal Food Safety System: A Primer.* Congressional Research Service. January 17, 2014.

[15] Renée Johnson. *The Federal Food Safety System: A Primer.* Congressional Research Service. January 17, 2014.

[16] Renée Johnson. *The Federal Food Safety System: A Primer.* Congressional Research Service. January 17, 2014.

or death."[17] Thus, the Act provides the FDA with the authority to inspect food facilities, obtain industry food safety plans, and issue mandatory recall orders if the food company fails to voluntarily recall unsafe food upon the FDA's request.[18] The FDA also has the authority to issue civil monetary fines in the context of food safety.[19] These issues are discussed further in Chapter 5.

The FDA is also responsible for the labeling of all food not under the jurisdiction of the USDA, which comprises the vast majority of food available for sale in the country. Congress passed the Nutrition Labeling and Education Act of 1990 (NLEA), which gave the FDA the authority to require factual nutrition information and ingredient lists on food packaging. The NLEA also provided the agency with the authority to regulate health- and nutrition-related claims on food packaging. It prohibits misbranded food, which is defined as food having a false or misleading label, food that is not properly identified, food that is missing required disclosures or nutrition information, or food labeled with health and nutrition claims that are not made according to specific requirements.[20] The FDA's final regulations pursuant to the NLEA were enacted in 1993. In 2014, the FDA proposed revisions to the NLEA to update disclosure requirements, primarily the Nutrition Facts Panel. These developments are discussed in Chapter 6.

It is important to note that the FDA has less authority to address labeling violations than food safety issues. Although the FDA was granted extensive authority under the FSMA, the FDA's primary method of addressing food labeling violations is to issue warning letters to food companies that violate the FDCA.[21] The FDA sends a letter warning the company that it violated the FDCA and notes an expectation that the company will resolve and correct the violation. For example, Coca-Cola created a carbonated beverage called Diet Coke Plus, which was a soft drink with added vitamins. This product violated the FDA regulations prohibiting the fortification (or addition of nutrients) to soft drinks and candy.[22] The FDA sent a warning letter to Coca-Cola explaining its violations of the FDCA, recommending the company take prompt action to resolve the violations, and seeking a responsive letter.[23]

Like other administrative agencies, the FDA enacts regulations through Notice and Comment Rulemaking under the Administrative Procedures Act.[24]

---

[17] 21 USCS § 342.

[18] Food and Drug Administration. Background on the FDA Food Safety Modernization Act (FSMA). http://www.fda.gov/Food/GuidanceRegulation/FSMA/ucm239907.htm

[19] 21 USCS § 333.

[20] 21 USCS § 343.

[21] J. L. Pomeranz. A Comprehensive Strategy to Overhaul FDA Authority for Misleading Food Labels. *American Journal of Law & Medicine*. 2013;39: 617–647.

[22] 21 CFR § 104.20(a).

[23] Coca-Cola Company (The) December 10, 2008. http://www.fda.gov/ICECI/EnforcementActions/WarningLetters/2008/ucm1048050.htm

[24] 5 USCS § 553.

The FDA also issues less formal guidance documents. These do not have the full force of law and are not required to go through Notice and Comment Rulemaking, although the agency sometimes does accept comments on them. Guidance documents provide information to the food companies on the "FDA's current thinking on a topic."[25] Companies are prompted but not required to follow the advice in guidance documents and the FDA is not required to enforce any violation of the suggestions in a guidance document. In the food context, the FDA has issued guidance on a wide array of issues, such as records maintenance, reducing toxins in food, prevention of foodborne illnesses, and distinguishing between food and dietary supplements.[26]

Centers for Disease Control and Prevention

The Centers for Disease Control and Prevention (CDC) monitors, tracks, and prevents disease; works with communities on public health efforts; engages in scientific research; awards and administers grants; and promotes healthy and safe behaviors. In the area of food, the CDC is responsible for identifying, tracking, monitoring, and investigating foodborne illness outbreaks.[27] As discussed further in Chapter 5, the CDC coordinates national efforts and works with state and local health departments on investigations, prevention and control strategies, and evaluation of foodborne outbreak responses.[28]

Surgeon General

The Office of the Surgeon General is housed in the Office of the Assistant Secretary for Health within HHS. The Surgeon General is known as the "nation's physician" and has an influential voice when it comes to matters of public health.[29] The Surgeon General is appointed by the President with the advice and consent of Senate. The first Surgeon General served from 1871 to 1879. Surgeons General have shaped the nation's policy through reports on selected health issues. One notable report, the Surgeon General's Report on "Smoking and Health," in 1964

---

[25] Food and Drug Administration. Guidances. http://www.fda.gov/regulatoryinformation/guidances/

[26] Food and Drug Administration. Food Guidance Documents. http://www.fda.gov/Food/GuidanceRegulation/GuidanceDocumentsRegulatoryInformation/default.htm

[27] R. Johnson. *The Federal Food Safety System: A Primer.* Congressional Research Service. January 17, 2014.

[28] Centers for Disease Control and Prevention. Division of Foodborne, Waterborne, and Environmental Diseases. http://www.cdc.gov/ncezid/dfwed/orpb/

[29] R. Voelker. What does the U.S. Surgeon General mean to the health of the nation? *JAMA.* 2008;300(16):1869–1872.

is widely considered a watershed moment in tobacco control.[30] In 2001, Surgeon General David Satcher issued the Surgeon General's Call to Action to Prevent and Decrease Overweight and Obesity, and in 2010, Surgeon General Regina Benjamin issued the call to action, The Surgeon General's Vision for a Healthy and Fit Nation, in an effort to strengthen the recommendations of the 2001 decree. Both reports examined obesity in broad terms, discussing food as one of many issues. In December 2014, the Senate confirmed Dr. Vivek Murthy as the next Surgeon General of the United States. Dr. Murthy stated that he will focus his role on addressing obesity, mental health, smoking, and health care delivery.[31]

The Federal Trade Commission

The Federal Trade Commission (FTC) is an independent federal agency and has authority over false, deceptive, and unfair marketing of consumer goods, including food.[32] The FTC and FDA divided the responsibility over food marketing pursuant to a Memorandum of Understanding, under which the FDA has primary authority to regulate food labels and the FTC has primary responsibility for food advertising via all other media.[33]

The FTC operates pursuant to the Federal Trade Commission Act, enacted in 1914. Most federal agencies may engage in Administrative Procedures Act rulemaking as a matter of course, but Section 18 of the Federal Trade Commission Act imposes additional rulemaking requirements on the FTC that make it very difficult and time-consuming for the agency if it seeks to enact a regulation.[34] Rather than engage in rulemaking, the FTC frequently brings individual cases against entities that violate the FTC Act. The FTC has more authority to address individual transgressions than the FDA. For example, unlike the FDA, the FTC does have the authority to require that food companies turn over documents substantiating a health or nutrition-related claim in advertising material, called "substantiation documents." The FTC also may issue civil monetary fines, although it usually settles its cases without fining the offenders. The FTC's regulation of food marketing is discussed further in Chapter 7.

---

[30] R. Voelker. What does the U.S. Surgeon General mean to the health of the nation? *JAMA*. 2008;300(16):1869–1872.

[31] Tanya Somanader. The Nation's Doctor: Dr. Vivek Murthy Is Confirmed as Surgeon General. December 15, 2014 http://www.whitehouse.gov/blog/2014/12/15/nations-doctor-dr-vivek-murthy-confirmed-surgeon-general

[32] 15 USCS §45.

[33] Federal Trade Commission. Enforcement Policy Statement on Food Advertising. May 1994. http://www.ftc.gov/enforcement-policy-statement-on-food-advertising.

[34] J. Pomeranz. Federal Trade Commission's Authority to Regulate Marketing to Children: Deceptive vs. Unfair Rulemaking. *Health Matrix: Journal of Law Medicine*. 2011;21:521.

Legislative Branch

The legislative branch of the federal government is composed of two separate governing bodies or chambers: the Senate and the House of Representatives, elected from the states. Each state has two senators who serve six-year terms each. Conversely, each state has a different number of representatives in the House of Representatives, depending on the state's population. The states are divided into districts, from which a representative is elected and serves a two-year term. Both senators and representatives work on congressional committees and pass federal laws.

The legislative branch enacts law, called legislation, through a process whereby one or more Congress persons proposes a bill, which encompasses a policy objective that they would like to see become law.[35] Congress members sponsor the bill, introduce it to the other members of the Senate or House to garner their support, and then the bill goes to a committee where experts revise the language. The bill is brought back to the House or Senate floor, where it is debated. If the governing body passes the bill, it gets approved and sent to the other chamber. So if the bill started in the House, the Senate must now undertake the same process and pass the identical bill. Once it passes both the House and the Senate, the bill goes to the President to sign. The President can sign the bill and then it becomes law. If the President does nothing, the bill automatically becomes a law. Alternatively, the President can veto the bill. If the legislature still wants the bill to become a law, Congress can hold another vote and override the President's veto with a two thirds vote of both the House of Representatives and the Senate. A comparison of legislation and regulations can be found in Table 1.1.

Congress has shaped food policy in a multitude of ways. Congress passed all the federal laws related to food and under which the federal administrative agencies function, such as the Farm Bills, the Nutrition Labeling and Education Act, and the Food Safety Modernization Act. Congress is also responsible for granting and defining the boundaries of federal administrative agencies' authorities. Each law defines the actions permitted to be taken by the authorized agency. Federal agencies cannot act outside the scope granted to them by Congress. Congress is also responsible for funding the agencies. Therefore, the political leanings and practical considerations of Congress are integral to the reach and success of the federal agencies' missions. As discussed in Chapter 2, Congress also passes laws directly regulating commerce, taxing businesses and products, and granting financial resources to communities for public health support.

---

[35] Office of the Clerk. Kids in the House. How Laws Are Made. http://kids.clerk.house.gov/grade-school/lesson.html?intID=17

TABLE 1.1
Comparison of Federal Agency Regulation and Legislative Law-making Processes

Regulation	Measure of Comparison	Legislation
Federal administrative agency	Responsible Entity	Congress: both the House of Representatives and the Senate must agree
Draft regulation	Name Prior to Enactment	Bill
Notice and comment rulemaking	Process for Enactment	Bill becomes a law
The responsible federal agency has experts on each topic.	Expertise	Sent to committee with experts on the staff; Sponsoring legislators may have experts in their office.
Legally binding	Force When Enacted	Legally binding
Relatively easier	Relative Ease of Amending	Relatively more difficult
Initially the President to shape the direction of the agency; meetings with agency leaders to shape regulations	Lobbyists' Primary Influence	Representatives and/or Senators to shape their political agenda and the legislation itself

Judicial Branch

The Judicial Branch refers to the U.S. court system. Courts are made up of judges who hear both criminal and civil cases. The topics of this book only pertain to civil cases, which involve disputes between two types of parties: the plaintiff who brings the action and the defendant, against whom the action is brought. The process of being involved in a lawsuit is called litigation. The U.S. system of law is based on the common law tradition. This tradition originates from England and is premised on the notion that judges interpret and apply the law to the facts of a case to come to a decision about the dispute. The judges write down their decision to create case law, which has the full force of law for subsequent cases that arise in that court's jurisdiction.

The U.S. system is premised on the theory that everyone should have their day in court, but in reality most cases settle before a trial occurs on the merits of the individual case. A plaintiff usually seeks damages in the form of money or an injunction, which is a request to stop or refrain from acting in a certain manner. One hallmark of litigation in the United States is the discovery process, under which the parties exchange documents relevant to the case. Through the discovery process, parties learn information about the other party's position in the case. A judge (or a panel of judges) always presides over a case, but at the trial level a judge or jury may determine which party's view of the facts is accurate. A judge's final determination of a case is called a judgment and a jury's final determination is a verdict.

The federal court system is described here, and the state court systems are described below. The federal courts hear disputes between private parties, between the government and private parties, and between various government entities, such as a dispute between two states. In civil matters, a plaintiff brings a lawsuit against a defendant in district court, where most federal cases originate. There are 94 federal judicial districts, with at least one in each state, the District of Columbia, Puerto Rico, and the U.S. territories of the Virgin Islands, Guam, and the Northern Mariana Islands.[36] After the original trial takes place in a district court, the party or parties that are unhappy with the decision may appeal the case to a circuit court. Twelve circuit courts sit above the district courts and are roughly divided according to region of the country. These are intermediate courts. If a party or parties are dissatisfied with the judgment at the circuit court level, they may seek to appeal the case to the United States Supreme Court, which is the highest court in the country. The Supreme Court has nine Justices, including one Chief Justice and eight Associate Justices.[37] There are no term limits for Supreme Court Justices, so they are said to be appointed for life, or until they retire. If a party seeks review by the United States Supreme Court, it must file a writ of certiorari, and the Supreme Court determines whether it will accept or reject the case. The Supreme Court does not hear the vast majority of cases that seek its review.

The Supreme Court's judgments are the law of the land, meaning that all other federal courts and state courts must abide by its determinations. The Supreme Court interprets the constitutionality of laws and actions taken by the government and private citizens. It decides issues of constitutional significance that shape the future direction of the country. As we will see, some Supreme Court cases that are not directly related to the subject of food nonetheless have broad significance for public health and food law and policy. Because the Supreme Court rarely accepts cases for review, influential law is created by the circuit courts. If a district court has to address an issue that its circuit court has not addressed, it might look to other circuit courts for a persuasive indication on how it should interpret the law.

It is noteworthy that if Congress disagrees with the judiciary's interpretation of a federal law, Congress can amend the law to further define its expectations. If Congress disagrees with the Supreme Court's interpretation of the U.S. Constitution, it must pass a constitutional amendment to alter this understanding. It is very rare for Congress to pass and ratify a constitutional amendment. There have been 27 constitutional amendments since the Constitution was ratified, and one of these has been repealed. It is more common for Congress to amend a law to respond to a misinterpretation by the Supreme Court.[38] Therefore,

---

[36] U.S. Courts. District Courts. http://www.uscourts.gov/FederalCourts/UnderstandingtheFederalCourts/DistrictCourts.aspx

[37] 28 U. S. C. §1.

[38] For example, see, ADA Amendments Act.

the Supreme Court's interpretation of the U.S. Constitution is usually final unless a subsequent Supreme Court changes course and reinterprets the clause.

State Government

The U.S. Constitution envisions that all powers not delegated to the federal government are reserved for the states. As discussed in Chapter 2, state laws may not conflict with or violate federal law. State and local governments are considered the primary regulators of public health and safety.[39] State governments are generally structured like the federal government. The Constitution does not mention local governments, but to varying degrees individual states delegate their authority to their political subdivisions—such as counties, cities, and towns.

There are two types of relationships states establish with respect to local governments. The first, called "Dillon's Rule," provides a narrow interpretation of a local government's authority. Under Dillon's Rule, local government may engage in an activity only if it is specifically sanctioned by the state government.[40] The majority of states are generally organized according to Dillon's Rule. The second type of relationship is described by the term "Home Rule," under which a state delegates broad power to local governments to create local autonomy.[41] The inflexibility of Dillon's Rule led many states to adopt Home Rule in the early 1900s to give greater authority to locales and limit the degree to which a state can interfere with local affairs. Many states use a mixture of each type of delegation. These relationships are defined by the state's constitution and/or statutes enacted by its legislature.

The executive branch of state governments is led by the governor and each state has a governor whose position replicates that of the U.S. President. Where local governments exist, they have an executive branch head who is usually a mayor of the city or town. States and some local governments also have executive branch administrative agencies, such as departments of health, education, and transportation. Governors and mayors may appoint the heads of these executive branch agencies and also issue gubernatorial or mayoral executive orders.[42]

Each state has a state health agency. These are structured differently across the country, but all are led by a state health official, sometimes referred to as a state health secretary or commissioner of health.[43] In the majority of states the

---

[39] *Jacobson v. Massachusetts*, 197 U.S. 11 (1905).

[40] National League of Cities. Local Government Authority. http://www.nlc.org/build-skills-and-networks/resources/cities-101/city-powers/local-government-authority

[41] National League of Cities. Local Government Authority. http://www.nlc.org/build-skills-and-networks/resources/cities-101/city-powers/local-government-authority

[42] M. Gakh, J. S. Vernick, L. Rutkow. Using Gubernatorial Executive Orders to Advance Public Health. *Public Health Report*. 2013;128(2): 127–130.

[43] Association of State and Territorial Health Officials. Profile of State Public Health, Volume Three. 2014. http://www.astho.org/Profile/Volume-Three

health official is appointed by the governor. Governors and state legislatures also are involved in the budget-approval process for almost all state health agencies. This means that the health agency is beholden to these elected officials who, in turn, respond to voters and lobbyists.

A national survey of state health agencies indicates that approximately half of their budgets are spent on clinical programs and the Special Supplemental Nutrition Program for Women Infants Children (WIC), including nutrition education.[44] Approximately 10% of their budget is spent on infectious-disease prevention and control while another 10% is spent on forensic examination and providing infrastructure funds to local public health agencies.[45] Each of the following also garners 5% of the budget: chronic disease prevention; programs to ensure the quality of equipment and health services, such as through professional licensure and certification; and environmental health, food service, and lodging inspections.[46] The remainder of expenditures is directed at hazard preparedness, administration, laboratory needs, vital statistics, health data, and injury prevention.

In addition to state health agencies, there are approximately 2,800 local health departments.[47] Some are local or regional units of the state health agency, others are agencies within the local government, and still others are governed by both state and local authorities.[48] Local health departments may be more directly involved with food law than the state health agencies. The most common programs and services provided directly by local health departments include communicable/infectious disease surveillance, child and adult immunizations, tuberculosis screening and treatment, environmental health surveillance, food service establishment inspections, food safety education, population-based nutrition services, school and day care center inspections, and WIC.[49] Most local health departments also provide population-based prevention services focused on nutrition, tobacco use, and food safety education. They are also the primary entities that regulate, inspect, and license food service establishments.

---

[44] ASTHO Profile of State Public Health, Volume Three. 2014. Pages 83 and 86. http://www.astho.org/Profile/Volume-Three

[45] ASTHO Profile of State Public Health, Volume Three. 2014. Pages 83 and 86. http://www.astho.org/Profile/Volume-Three

[46] ASTHO Profile of State Public Health, Volume Three. 2014. Pages 83 and 86. http://www.astho.org/Profile/Volume-Three

[47] National Association of City and County Health Officials. The National Profile of Local Health Departments. http://nacchoprofilestudy.org/wp-content/uploads/2014/02/2013_National_Profile021014.pdf

[48] National Association of City and County Health Officials. The National Profile of Local Health Departments. http://nacchoprofilestudy.org/wp-content/uploads/2014/02/2013_National_Profile021014.pdf

[49] National Association of City and County Health Officials. The National Profile of Local Health Departments. http://nacchoprofilestudy.org/wp-content/uploads/2014/02/2013_National_Profile021014.pdf

Local health departments are involved in policy and advocacy activities related to obesity, chronic disease, and food safety. From 2011 to 2012, these activities included school or child care policies to reduce the availability of unhealthy foods, increasing retail availability of fruits and vegetables, nutrition labeling, and limiting fast food outlets.[50]

In most states, the executive branch also houses the state attorney general. The state attorneys general are in a unique position with a great deal of power because their authority intersects law and public policy.[51] Every state, territory, and the District of Columbia has an attorney general. The majority are elected in popular elections, but others are appointed by the governor or other government entities within the state. Attorneys general represent both the state and the public's interests and have historically played a leading role in addressing public health issues. For example, the state attorneys general were the initiators of the tobacco litigation that led to the Master Settlement Agreement. Their powers include bringing litigation against entities that harm the state or its citizens, writing amicus briefs ("friend of the court" briefs to offer guidance on how a court should rule on an issue integral to the state), writing advisory opinions to the public or the government, engaging in consumer education, and in some states, rulemaking. Attorneys general can work independently or together across state lines in multistate actions, and they also can work with federal agencies.

Attorneys general bring actions pursuant to their *parens patriae* authority (literally "parent of the country"—a vestige of our English roots). The parens patriae authority of state attorneys general is used to vindicate "quasi-sovereign interests" of their state. According to the U.S. Supreme Court, there are generally two types of quasi-sovereign interests: "First, a State has a quasi-sovereign interest in the health and well-being—both physical and economic—of its residents in general. Second, a State has a quasi-sovereign interest in not being discriminatorily denied its rightful status within the federal system."[52] Historically, this power was utilized as a method for states to prevent or correct harm caused to property, air, or water rights by another state,[53] but courts later accepted states' standing to sue private parties to seek vindication of similar rights. Parens patriae was the legal theory used during the tobacco litigation, where 46 state attorneys general sued the tobacco companies for reimbursement of the medical costs, including for Medicaid, incurred for treating consumers with smoking-related illnesses. Thus, they were seeking to vindicate the states' interests in "the health and

---

[50] National Association of City and County Health Officials. The National Profile of Local Health Departments. http://nacchoprofilestudy.org/wp-content/uploads/2014/02/2013_National_Profile021014.pdf

[51] J. L. Pomeranz , K. D. Brownell. Advancing public health obesity policy through state attorneys general. *American Journal of Public Health*. 2011;101(3):425–431.

[52] *Alfred L. Snap & Son, Inc v Puerto Rico*, 458 U.S. 592, 607 (1982).

[53] *Hawaii v. Standard Oil Co. of California.*, 405 U.S. 251, 258 (1972).

well-being—both physical and economic—of its residents."[54] Parens patriae is an evolving doctrine; debates continue as to whether a similar theory can be used in the context of food.[55]

In the context of food and other products with potential public health ramifications, the attorney general more frequently initiates an informal inquiry or brings formal litigation against a company pursuant to his or her consumer protection authority. Each state and the District of Columbia have statutes colloquially referred to as UDAP statutes, which to varying degrees are patterned after the Federal Trade Commission Act. The statutes' name stems from the Federal Trade Commission Act's prohibition on "unfair or deceptive acts or practices" or UDAP.[56] Although private plaintiffs can bring actions under their state's UDAP statutes, the attorneys general have more authority to do so and often have more success when they do.[57] This type of litigation is discussed further in Chapter 8. Attorneys general also can make pre-litigation inquiries of companies and, like the FTC, can require companies to turn over their substantiation documents. For example, in 2009, the Connecticut attorney general investigated the food industry's Smart Choices Program, which labeled processed foods as healthy despite questionable nutrition profiles.[58] The FDA later sent a letter to the program; shortly thereafter the program voluntarily shut itself down. Given the FDA's limited resources and authority to address food labeling issues, the action by the Attorney General was likely pivotal in the Smart Choices Program's decision to cease operations.

Finally, the attorneys general have a powerful voice among the population and can engage in consumer education or advocate for policies using their bully pulpit. For example, in 2010, the Vermont Attorney General created an initiative and established working groups to identify and develop potential actions to reduce obesity and address the retail-food and physical-activity environment in the state.[59] He also testified in the state legislature on instituting measures agreed upon by the working groups. In sum, state attorneys general have vast potential to influence food law to benefit the public's health.

State legislatures generally are structured like the federal Congress, although not all state legislatures meet regularly. For example, a regular session of the Alabama state legislature meets approximately 30 legislative days within the

---

[54] *Alfred L. Snap & Son, Inc v Puerto Rico,* 458 U.S. 592, 607 (1982).

[55] J. L. Pomeranz. Litigation to Address Misleading Food Label Claims and the Role of the State Attorneys General, 26 *Regent University Law Review.* 2014; 421: 450–454.

[56] Federal Trade Commission Act, 15 U.S.C. § 45(a)(1) (2012).

[57] J. L. Pomeranz. Litigation to Address Misleading Food Label Claims and the Role of the State Attorneys General. *Regent University Law Review.* 2014; 421.

[58] J. L. Pomeranz, K. D. Brownell. Advancing public health obesity policy through state attorneys general. *American Journal of Public Health.* 2011;101(3):425–431.

[59] J. L. Pomeranz, K. D. Brownell. Advancing public health obesity policy through state attorneys general. *American Journal of Public Health.* 2011;101(3):425–431.

framework of a 105-calendar day period.[60] State legislatures pass laws directed at their states and citizens. Local governments may have a city or town council, which typically only has one chamber and passes local legislation.

The state court system is generally organized like the federal courts, although each state is different. Cases begin in a trial court, of which there are many within a state. Most states have an intermediate court that is a court of appeals. Every state has one highest court. There are also county courts that deal with specific matters such as parking tickets.

Questions and Exercises for Classroom Discussion

What are some of the pros and cons of enacting law through the legislative process versus agency rulemaking?

Students should familiarize themselves with the government's website: www.regulations.gov. Browse through some of the regulations on food or health. If an agency proposed a regulation pertinent to the course during the semester, students should draft responses and submit them on regulations.gov. Conversely, students should respond to a previous regulation for class.

Ideas for policy come from many different avenues, including genuine needs of the community, grassroots movements, government officials' personal experiences, major events or crises, local events, hometown issues, lobbyists, donors, information and feedback from constituents who vote, and issues that result in good publicity. How can the various government entities respond to these influences and which government entities might be best suited to address them?

Students should look up the state attorney general in their home state and learn about his or her priorities and whether he or she has addressed public health in general or food specifically. How has the attorney general acted to further public health in a manner not necessarily available to other government entities discussed in this chapter?

---

[60] Welcome To The Official Website Of The Alabama Legislature. http://www.legislature.state.al.us/

2

United States Constitution and Public Health Food Policy

Introduction

In the United States, the federal Constitution is the basis for all law and establishes the government's duties, as well as limitations on the government's power. No law created by a federal or state entity can violate the Constitution. Therefore, when government acts to protect public health, it must remain within constitutional boundaries. The Constitution is made up of two related parts. The main text, which consists of a preamble explaining the purpose of the Constitution, and seven Articles, was ratified in 1789. The rest of the Constitution consists of Amendments to the Constitution that have been passed over the centuries following ratification. The first ten amendments are called the Bill of Rights, and they were ratified together in 1791. The purpose of the Bill of Rights is to protect the rights of the people, and as such, it is directed at the government, setting limits on what the government can do with respect to the people. There is thus a constant tension between individual rights and the government's exercise of its authority to protect public health. The Constitution also sets forth the division of responsibilities between the federal and state governments. This results in disagreements between the federal and state governments on their respective rights and responsibilities in the federalist framework. This chapter provides foundational information for all public health law within the context of food.

The Constitution provides Congress with a list of enumerated powers and reserves all other powers for the states.[1] Of these powers, the federal government has four legal mechanisms to impact public health: regulate interstate commerce, tax, spend, and promulgate information. States have some concurrent and some

[1] U.S. Constitution Amendment X.

unique public health powers. The constitutionally based powers will be described in this chapter and Chapter 9 will focus exclusively on state and local public health authority over food. Constitutional principles will arise throughout the book and are the backbone of food law in the context of public health.

Preemption

The U.S. Constitution contains what is referred to as the Supremacy Clause, which provides: "This Constitution, and the laws of the United States . . . shall be the supreme law of the land . . . laws of any State to the contrary notwithstanding."[2] This means that the federal government's laws are supreme and that no state law can conflict with federal law. Also remember that no federal law enacted by Congress or a federal agency can violate the Constitution. So this means the U.S. Constitution is supreme, followed by federal laws, followed by state laws, and then local laws.

Part and parcel of this hierarchical framework is the concept of preemption. Preemption occurs when a higher level of government restricts or trumps the authority of a lower level of government to address a specific issue. The term preemption usually refers to "ceiling" preemption, meaning that the higher level of government sets a ceiling on what lower levels of government can do. The word preemption will be used in this sense throughout the book. Higher levels of government, however, are not required to limit lower levels in this manner. Instead, the higher level of government can enact minimum requirements, also referred to as floor preemption, that all jurisdictions must follow while still allowing states to enact stronger laws to protect their citizens. Definitions related to preemption can be found in Table 2.1.

The concept of preemption is very important to all public health law. States have the same power to preempt local governments and use preemption to varying degrees. When the federal or state government preempts states or locales from acting to protect health, it contravenes basic principles of the federalist framework and can also hurt public health progress. A particularly revered Supreme Court Justice, Justice Brandeis, explained: "It is one of the happy incidents of the federal system that a single courageous State may, if its citizens choose, serve as a laboratory; and try novel social and economic experiments without risk to the rest of the country."[3] Writing in 1932, he portended novel food policy experiments, such as those enacted under New York City Mayor Bloomberg's administration from 2002 to 2013. Many of the city's food policies were later adopted by other cities and states around the country and also led to changes at the federal level. Had New York City been preempted from trying out these novel approaches, we

---

[2] U.S. Constitution Article VI, Clause 2.

[3] *New State Ice Co. v. Liebmann*, 285 U.S. 262, 311 (1932) (Brandeis dissenting).

TABLE 2.1
Preemption Definitions

Ceiling Preemption	When a higher level of government takes away the power of lower jurisdictions to laws on a specific topic.
Floor Preemption	When a higher level of government enacts *minimum* health and safety standards, allowing the lower jurisdictions to adopt stronger laws.
Express Preemption	Occurs when a law contains a clause explicitly preempting the lower jurisdictions from enacting a law on the topic. Preemption clauses may use the word "preempt," "consistent with," "uniform," "identical," or "occupy the field" to signify preemption.
Implied Preemption	Occurs when a court finds that legislators intended a law to be preemptive even in the absence of a clause explicitly stating so.
Conflict Preemption	When there is a conflict between a higher level of government's law and a lower level of government's law, the higher level always prevails.
Savings Clause	A clause in a law that *preserves* the authority of lower jurisdictions to act on the issue to avoid implied preemption.

Source: Pertschuk, M, Pomeranz, JL, Aoki, JR, Larkin, MA, Paloma, M. Assessing the impact of federal and state preemption in public health: a framework for decision makers. *Journal of Public Health Management Practices*. 2013;19(3):213–219.

might not have prohibitions on trans fat in our food supply or menu-labeling laws today.

Preemption often occurs at the impetus of the industry being regulated. Industry members lobby policymakers in higher levels of government to urge them to withdraw the power of lower levels of government to act on a particular issue. Most public health advocates and policymakers seeking to support public health have had to face preemptive challenges. The industry argues that it does not want to deal with a "patchwork" of regulations at the state or local level, so it urges the federal or state government to pass one law, often with weaker standards than enacted at the lower level, and include a clause expressly preempting stronger actions. For example, when two cities in California, Santa Clara and San Francisco, enacted two different menu-labeling laws, the California Restaurant Association successfully lobbied the state legislature to pass a state menu-labeling law that preempted local laws. When the California law passed, it nullified the previously enacted Santa Clara and San Francisco laws.

Sometimes an industry seeks to avoid all regulation on a topic by lobbying for a national or statewide law preempting any lower government action. The industry urges pro-business policymakers to preempt public health laws, arguing that the law would undermine profits or make doing business in the jurisdiction more difficult. For example, after the city of Cleveland, Ohio passed a trans fat ban, the Ohio state legislature passed a broad law preempting the ability of local governments to regulate food service establishments. Recall from Chapter 1 that local governments are generally the primary regulators of food service establishments. This is thus an example of a case where state uniformity was not necessary and the legislature was seeking to support business interests over public health concerns in the state. See the case study in Box 2.1 for more details on the outcome of this law.

BOX 2.1

Case Study: Cleveland v. Ohio, Trans Fat Ban

In April of 2011, the city of Cleveland, Ohio adopted an ordinance titled, "Foods Containing Industrially-Produced Trans Fat Restricted," which prohibited the use of industrially produced trans fats in food sold at food service establishments. Subsequently, the Ohio state legislature adopted a law that expressly conflicted with the Cleveland ordinance by broadly disallowing municipalities from regulating food service operations by using a method that would ban food based on nutrition information. Cleveland sued the state of Ohio and argued, among other things, that the state law violated the state constitution's grant of Home Rule authority to local governments. Specifically, the Ohio Constitution's Home Rule Amendment gives municipalities the "authority to exercise all powers of local self-government and to adopt and enforce within their limits such local police, sanitary and other similar regulations, as are not in conflict with general laws."[a]

The Ohio Court of Appeals had to determine the constitutionality of the Ohio law according to the Ohio Constitution. Among other determinations, the court noted the process by which the law was passed was questionable, stating: "We also have concerns regarding the process behind how the amendments were passed. In response to the city of Cleveland's trans-fats Ordinance, the Ohio Restaurant Association ("ORA") sent an email to the Ohio Department of Agriculture with an attached legislative proposal. The email stated that the Ordinance was 'exactly what we want to preempt with the attached amendment.' The email also stated that the amendment was 'a high priority for Wendy's, McDonalds and YUM! [YUM! Brands, Inc. operates and licenses Taco Bell, KFC, and Pizza Hut].' According to the email, a senator had already been given a copy of ORA's proposed legislation and would offer it in the Senate Finance Committee. Thus, the amendments were drafted on behalf of a special interest group with the specific purpose of snuffing out the Ordinance."[b] Moreover, the Court found that the amendment was "tucked away" in the state's appropriations bill and thus was "not vetted by the usual committee process."[c] The court found that the state law unconstitutionally limited the municipality's Home Rule powers.

Cleveland was fortunate to be in a Home Rule state. In contrast, in 2013, Mississippi passed a law broadly preempting local jurisdictions from regulating restaurants in several ways, including banning trans fats, or limiting portion sizes or salt content.[d] Mississippi, however, is a Dillon's Rule state,[e] so local jurisdictions did not have the same recourse as Cleveland if they disagreed. Therefore, unless the federal government passes a law mandating such requirements, or the state changes course and does the same, no city or town in Mississippi may regulate restaurants in the manner proscribed by the preemptive law. (See Chapter 5 on the federal Food and Drug Administration's 2015 action to remove trans fats from food; the federal government has not proposed a law to limit portion size or sodium content.)

Source: *Cleveland v. State of Ohio*, 989 NE.2d 1072 (Oh. Ct. App. 2013).

[a]Ohio Constitution, Section 3, Article XVIII.

[b]*Cleveland v. State of Ohio*, 989 NE.2d 1072, 1085 (Oh. Ct. App. 2013).

[c]*Cleveland v. State of Ohio*, 989 NE.2d 1072, 1085 (Oh. Ct. App. 2013).

[d]K. Severson. 'Anti-Bloomberg Bill' in Mississippi Bars Local Restrictions on Food and Drink. *New York Times*. March 13, 2013.

[e]National League of Cities. Local Government Authority. http://www.nlc.org/build-skills-and-networks/resources/cities-101/city-powers/local-government-authority

Sometimes a single national rule makes sense and thus preemption may be more acceptable to public health advocates. This occurs when there is a need for national uniformity or when it would be difficult or impossible for an industry to comply with various different laws across the country. The penultimate example pertains to airline regulations. It would be impractical for an airplane flying across the country to comply with different laws as it passed over each state. In the food context, it is generally agreed that national labeling requirements for packaged food make sense so food companies doing business nationally do not have to conform to 50 different state requirements for food labels (or even more divergent local requirements), which would make conducting business throughout the country difficult. Conversely, in the case of regulating local businesses, such as food service establishments, statewide or national uniformity is not necessary. As will be discussed in Chapter 9, most regulation that impacts local interests in public health, safety, and welfare occurs at the state and local level. Consider restaurants: they are subject to inspection by state or local authorities for compliance with health codes, building codes, and labor codes, and these vary by jurisdiction.

Often the best thing for public health is for the federal or state government to enact minimum floor requirements that lower levels of government must follow, but which simultaneously permit the latter to go further to protect public health. The Institute of Medicine recommends this strategy, explaining that federal and state policy makers "should set minimum standards . . . allowing states and localities to further protect the health and safety of their inhabitants," and "should avoid language that hinders public health action."[4] This type of scheme is utilized in the federal National School Lunch Program (NSLP), for example. In order to ensure that the nation's children have access to healthful food at school, the federal government enacted nutrition standards for all schools participating in the NSLP; however, state and local governments can enact stronger requirements to protect the children in their jurisdictions.

In addition to permitting elected officials to respond to the needs of their constituents, floor requirements allow jurisdictions to respond to evolving science and novel problems. When a government entity preempts local control, this effectively halts progress. For example, in the menu-labeling context, the federal law requires that covered restaurants must disclose calories on their menus and preempts nonidentical state and local laws. So if scientific research reveals that the calorie labeling is not as effective as previously hoped and the disclosure of portion size information, for example, would be more effective instead; or, if a local community's population is plagued by diabetes so perhaps sugar labeling would be helpful; or, if another community has a high prevalence of hypertension and would benefit from

---

[4] Institute of Medicine. *For the Public's Health: Revitalizing Law and Policy to Meet New Challenges*. Washington, DC: The National Academies Press; 2011.

sodium information, state and local governments are preempted from enacting these laws because they would conflict with the federal law.

Commerce Clause

The Commerce Clause of the U.S. Constitution provides Congress with the power to regulate commerce "among the several states."[5] This is an express grant of power to Congress, which it often uses to justify exercising legislative power over a diverse range of public health activities.[6] For example, Congress used this power to place a prohibition on altering of any part of a food, drug, medical device, tobacco product, or cosmetic label after shipment in interstate commerce.[7]

The United States Supreme Court has interpreted the Commerce Clause as also placing a prohibition on states' ability to pass legislation that discriminates against or excessively burdens interstate commerce. This is called the Dormant Commerce Clause, and a state violates this doctrine if it passes a law that benefits the state or citizens within the state at the expense of out-of-state interests. For example, in 1933, New York State enacted a Milk Control Act setting the minimum price for milk sales and barring the resale of milk purchased from out-of-state producers (namely Vermont) for less than New York prices. The Supreme Court struck down the Act as an improper attempt to set a barrier to commerce between states.[8] More recently, the state of Michigan enacted a law that permitted in-state wineries to sell wine directly to consumers in that state over the Internet but hindered out-of-state wineries from doing the same; this was also struck down as violating the Commerce Clause.[9] Finally, even absent any obvious discrimination against out-of-state interests, such as what is presented in these cases, courts will look to determine whether any incidental burden imposed on interstate commerce is "clearly excessive in relation to the putative local benefits."[10] This involves weighing competing interests. A nondiscriminatory regulation that serves a substantial state purpose will not be considered invalid simply because it causes some business to shift to an out-of-state industry.[11] To determine whether a state's purpose is substantial in the context of food law, it is necessary to understand state government authorities, described below and further in Chapter 9.

---

[5] U.S. Constitution Article 1, Section 8, Clause 3.

[6] L. Rutkow, J. S. Vernick. The U.S. Constitution's Commerce Clause, the Supreme Court, and Public Health. *Public Health Report.* 2011;126(5):750–753.

[7] 21 USC § 331(k).

[8] *Baldwin v. G. A. F. Seelig, Inc.*, 294 U.S. 511(1935).

[9] *Granholm v. Heald,* 544 U.S. 460 (2005).

[10] *Minnesota v. Clover Leaf Creamery Co.*, 449 U.S. 456 (1981).

[11] *Minnesota v. Clover Leaf Creamery Co.*, 449 U.S. 456 (1981).

Power to Tax and Spend

The U.S. Constitution provides Congress with the related powers to levy taxes and spend money for the general welfare of the nation.[12] States have concurrent powers to tax and spend. The federal government collects various types of taxes, such as those on businesses, personal income, and consumer goods. Although there is no general federal sales tax, the federal government imposes excise taxes on products with public health consequences such as tobacco, firearms, and alcohol. An excise tax is "a duty or impost levied upon the manufacture, sale, or consumption of commodities."[13] This results in an increase in the base price of the product, unlike a sales tax, which is added on upon checkout. One of the benefits of excise taxes is that the government can earmark the funds, meaning it can dedicate the revenue stream to a particular purpose. The dual purpose of a tax on products with potential health ramifications can be to raise revenue and decrease consumption. Just after the U.S. Constitution was ratified, Congress passed the nation's first excise tax on whisky for both of these purposes. State and local governments, by imposing sales taxes, are the primary taxing authority over food and beverages. For example, in 2014, 13 states assessed sales tax on all food at general sales tax rates, while other states only imposed sales taxes on specific foods such as soft drinks and candy.[14]

The federal government's power to spend has meaningful ramifications for the nation. The federal government can provide money directly for public health programs. For example, through the American Recovery and Reinvestment Act of 2009, Congress allotted $650 million to the Department of Health and Human Services (HHS) to support evidence-based prevention and wellness strategies. The cornerstone of the initiative is the Communities Putting Prevention to Work Community Program, administered by the Centers for Disease Control and Prevention, under which HHS awarded grants to communities around the country to engage in evidence-based strategies to support physical activity and nutrition, and prevent obesity and tobacco use.[15]

The federal government also can condition funding to states upon states' agreement to do something that they would not otherwise do. One hallmark case on this topic involved the federal government's interest in having a national minimum alcohol consumption age of 21 years. Many states had enacted laws permitting people younger than 21 years to purchase alcohol, so Congress offered the states a financial incentive of federal highway funding if they agreed to raise their minimum drinking age to 21 years. South Dakota sued the federal government, but the Supreme Court upheld the conditional funding scheme, noting

---

[12] U.S. Constitution Article 1, Section 8, Clause 1.

[13] David Becker, Ed. *U.S. Master Excise Tax Guide* (6th ed.). Chicago, IL: CCH; 2008.

[14] Bridging the Gap. 2014 State-by-State Soda Tax Rates. April 2014. http://www.bridgingthegapresearch.org/_asset/s2b5pb/BTG_soda_tax_fact_sheet_April2014.pdf

[15] 77 *Federal Register* 30535 (May 23, 2012).

that Congress may attach conditions to the receipt of federal funds to accomplish federal policy objectives.[16] The conditional funding agreement must meet four criteria: Congress must be seeking to advance the general welfare of the country, it must give states a clear and legitimate choice to take or refuse the funds, the scheme must be related to the federal interest in national projects or programs, and it must not violate the U.S. Constitution.[17]

The Bill of Rights

The first 10 amendments to the U.S. Constitution are called the Bill of Rights, which are rights secured by the people. The Bill of Rights is directed at the federal government and applies to state governments through the Fourteenth Amendment. Most of these amendments are not relevant to food law, given that they relate to criminal law, courtroom proceedings, protection against unreasonable government actions, and the right to bear arms. The exception is the First Amendment, which protects the freedom of speech, among other freedoms such as religion, and is directly related to food marketing, labeling, and lobbying. It is important to note that there is no right to health recognized anywhere in the Constitution or by the United States as a government entity.

First Amendment

The First Amendment of the U.S. Constitution states that the government shall make no law "abridging the freedom of speech."[18] The Supreme Court has explained that the original purpose of this clause "was to protect the free discussion of governmental affairs," which reflects the Constitution's "profound national commitment to the principle that debate on public issues should be uninhibited, robust, and wide-open."[19] Thus, protection of political speech underlies the core First Amendment value, but this also translates into the protection of religious speech and artistic expression. The Court has determined that other aspects of speech qualify as "core speech," including books, plays, movies, lying about one's military honors, and violent videogames.[20] For example, in a 2011 case where California tried to ban the sale of violent videogames to children, the Supreme Court compared them to the violence in the classic children's fairy tale book, *Grimm's Fairy Tales*, and struck down the law.[21]

---

[16] *South Dakota v. Dole*, 483 U.S. 203 (1987).
[17] *South Dakota v. Dole*, 483 U.S. 203 (1987).
[18] U.S. Constitution Amendment I.
[19] *Buckley v. Valeo*, 424 U.S. 1, 14 (1976).
[20] *United States v. Alvarez*, 132 S. Ct. 2537 (2012).
[21] *Brown v. Entertainment Merchants. Association*, 131 S. Ct. 2729 (2011).

Recall that the First Amendment is a right granted to the people as against the government. Therefore, any government restriction on this core First Amendment expression is subject to "strict scrutiny" by courts examining the government's action. This is the most stringent level of judicial review and governmental suppressions of core First Amendment speech are rarely upheld. This applies equally to people, nonprofit organizations, and businesses.[22] In this context, just as the U.S. government cannot restrict free expression, it cannot compel it either. So government compulsions of core speech are similarly struck down.[23] This means, for example, that just as the government cannot stop you from protesting against a political figure, it cannot force you to affirm your political affiliation.

The First Amendment right is not limitless. For example, the Supreme Court has ruled that the First Amendment does not protect defamation[24] (intentional false communication that harms someone's reputation) or words to incite a fight.[25] The government also may enact restrictions on the time, place, or manner of core speech. This means that in certain circumstances, the government can require speech to be limited in a very specific manner; for example, the government can require parades to take place on a certain street at a certain time of the day so as not to disrupt the community. Otherwise, free expression is a tightly guarded value in the United States.

In 1976, the Supreme Court confirmed that another type of speech deserves First Amendment protection, albeit to a lesser degree. In the case of *Virginia State Board of Pharmacy v. Virginia Citizens Consumer Council*, the Supreme Court determined that commercial speech—in this case the advertisement of prescription drug prices—is subject to First Amendment protections.[26] Commercial speech has been defined as the proposal of a commercial transaction, and is generally understood to encompass advertising,[27] labeling, [28] and other types of commercial solicitations, such as brochures[29] and even Tupperware parties.[30] If the government restricts commercial speech, courts subject the government's action to intermediate scrutiny, which is less stringent than that afforded to core speech, but more than afforded to factual disclosure requirements, which are discussed next. The intermediate level of review does not permit government to restrict commercial speech haphazardly. The government, however, may regulate commercial speech that is false, deceptive, or misleading. For example, the Federal Trade Commission determined that the Kellogg Company's claim that its cereal supported a child's immune system was false and ordered the company to refrain from

---

[22] *Citizens United v. FEC*, 558 U.S. 310 (2010).
[23] *Riley v. National Federation of the Blind of North Carolina*, 487 U.S. 781, 797 (1988).
[24] *Gertz v. Robert Welch, Inc.*, 418 U.S. 323 (1974).
[25] *United States v. Stevens*, 130 S. Ct. 1577 (2010).
[26] *Virginia State Board of Pharmacy v. Virginia Citizens Consumer Council*, 425 U.S. 748 (1976).
[27] *Lorillard Tobacco Co. v. Reilly*, 533 US 525 (2001).
[28] *Rubin v. Coors Brewing Co.*, 514 U.S. 476 (1995).
[29] *Bolger*, 463 US 60 (1983); see also, *Cincinnati v. Discovery Network*, 507 U.S. 410, 422 (1993).
[30] *Board of Trustees, State University of New York v. Fox*, 492 U.S. 469, 473–474.

making misleading claims about the health benefits of its food that are not backed by scientific evidence.[31] Commercial speech and food marketing will be discussed further in Chapter 7.

Through the years since 1976, the Court has granted increasingly more protection to commercial speech, which makes restricting food marketing difficult for the government. It is important to note that other countries do not protect commercial speech to the extent that it is protected in the United States. Therefore, in other countries, for example, in the United Kingdom and the Canadian Province of Quebec, food marketing directed at children is limited by the government. Conversely, in the United States, many industries regulated by public health authorities argue that commercial speech should be protected to the same extent as political speech. Thus far the courts have not obliged, but increasing protections leave this question open.

The final aspect of the First Amendment relevant to food law is commercial factual disclosure requirements. The government is permitted to compel commercial entities to disclose factual information about the products for sale in the marketplace. This allowance forms the basis for all of the required information on processed food packages and labels, including the Nutrition Fact Panel, allergen information, the ingredient list, and the net quantity of the product. This is also the basis for menu-labeling laws that require the disclosure of calorie content of restaurant food. Food labeling will be discussed further in Chapter 6. Commercial factual disclosure requirements are subject to the least exacting form of judicial scrutiny, namely, "reasonable basis" review.[32] This means that if the government has a reasonable basis for the factual disclosure requirement, courts generally uphold the law. Supreme Court precedent is not clear as to whether the government's interest in enacting commercial factual disclosure requirements must be related to preventing consumer deception or if the government may enact them for informational or educational purposes only. Disclosures enacted for safety reasons, such as allergen warning labels, are not in dispute. Nonetheless, the required disclosures on food packaging and menus are accepted as a valid use of the government's authority to protect the public's health.

Tenth Amendment

The Tenth Amendment to the U.S. Constitution provides that all powers not delegated to the federal government or prohibited to the states, are reserved for the states or for the people, respectively.[33] An example of a power delegated to Congress and prohibited to the states is the power to regulate interstate commerce.

---

[31] FTC Investigation of Ad Claims that Rice Krispies Benefits Children's Immunity Leads to Stronger Order Against Kellogg. June 3, 2010. http://www.ftc.gov/news-events/press-releases/2010/06/ftc-investigation-ad-claims-rice-krispies-benefits-childrens

[32] *Zauderer v. Office of Disciplinary Counsel*, 471 U.S. 626 (1985).

[33] U.S. Constitution Amendment X.

Conversely, states have a concurrent power to tax and spend. States also have two unique powers to address matters related to public health. The first, discussed in Chapter 1, is the legal concept of *parens patriae*, a power used by state attorneys general to vindicate the state's interest in the health and well-being of the state and its populace. The second power is the legal concept called the "police power," under which states may govern matters related to health and especially local food environments.

The police power of the states originates differently than the powers expressly granted to the federal government by the Constitution. The Supreme Court explains that the police power is "a power which the State did not surrender when becoming a member of the Union under the Constitution."[34] It is a power based on the understanding that states are self-governing entities within the federalist system of the U.S. government.[35]

Pursuant to their police power, state governments possess the authority to enact laws and regulations to protect, preserve, and promote the health, safety, morals, and general welfare of their population.[36] They also may restrict private interests to protect these same values. The police power affords the government the discretion to determine the method to regulate injurious and unhealthy practices to protect the common good.[37] Therefore, except as restricted by the U.S. Constitution, states may use the police power to benefit population interests that on balance trump personal interests as long as they do not do so in an arbitrary or unreasonable manner.[38] This means that if the regulation does not restrict rights granted in the Constitution, courts will defer to the government when it is seeking to promote public health. Thus, public health ordinances are subject to a "reasonable basis" inquiry by courts.[39] This is sometimes called "rational basis" review and is a highly deferential standard. Common examples include ordinances related to sanitation, safety, and zoning. All states delegate the police power to their political subdivisions, cities, counties, and towns, to varying degrees. Therefore, the authorities of local governments are diverse nationally.

State governments are considered to have the primary authority over public health. In a seminal Supreme Court case, *Jacobson v. Massachusetts*, the Court upheld Massachusetts's right to require compulsory vaccination.[40] In its decision, the Court explicitly stated that the police power of a state embraces all such reasonable regulations established directly by the state to protect the public health

---

[34] *Jacobson v. Massachusetts*, 197 U.S. 11 (1905).

[35] L.O. Gostin. *Public Health Law: Power, Duty, Restraint* (2nd ed.). Los Angeles: University of California Press. 2008, p. 118.

[36] L.O. Gostin. *Public Health Law: Power, Duty, Restraint.* (2nd ed.). Los Angeles: University of California Press. 2008,pp. 92–93.

[37] *Jacobson v. Massachusetts*, 197 U.S. 11 (1905).

[38] *Schmidinger v. Chicago*, 226 U.S. 578 (1913).

[39] *Jacobson v. Massachusetts*, 197 U.S. 11 (1905).

[40] *Jacobson v. Massachusetts*, 197 U.S. 11 (1905).

and public safety.[41] The police power has been recognized as the basis for a great many state food laws and state government attempts to shape the local food environment. As discussed in detail in Chapter 9, states engage in many different types of activities pursuant to the police power. For example, they grant rights and restrictions on the use of land, called zoning, which determines where food retail establishments may be located within a community. State and local governments may attach conditions to a person's ability to obtain and maintain a license to run a food retail location. They may also ban products that have public health consequences.

In light of the recognition that states are the primary regulators of public health, public health advocates' concerns about preemption should be even more understandable. States can respond to the needs of their communities and local officials are directly accountable to their constituents. Based on this understanding, President Obama issued an executive order directing the federal executive departments and agencies not to interfere with state prerogatives unless there is a sufficient reason to do so. [42] The President recognized that much policy innovation occurs at the state level and explained his rationale as follows: "Throughout our history, State and local governments have frequently protected health, safety, and the environment more aggressively than has the national Government. An understanding of the important role of State governments in our Federal system is reflected in longstanding practices by executive departments and agencies, which have shown respect for the traditional prerogatives of the States."[43] But recall that state and federal legislatures, rather than agencies, are more commonly the bodies that enact preemptive laws. Thus, the tension between state and federal control is one that will continually arise as governments attempt to protect a diverse array of interests.

Fourteenth Amendment

As mentioned, the Bill of Rights applies to state governments through the Fourteenth Amendment. The Fourteenth Amendment also contains the Equal Protection Clause, which provides that: "No state shall ... deny to any person within its jurisdiction the equal protection of the laws."[44] This clause is mainly directed at protecting specific groups of people from unequal

---

[41] *Jacobson v. Massachusetts*, 197 U.S. 11 (1905), at 25.

[42] The White House. Memorandum for the Heads of Executive Departments and Agencies. Subject: Preemption. May 20, 2009. Available: http://www.whitehouse.gov/the_press_office/Presidential-Memorandum-Regarding-Preemption

[43] The White House. Memorandum for the Heads of Executive Departments and Agencies. Subject: Preemption. May 20, 2009. Available: http://www.whitehouse.gov/the_press_office/Presidential-Memorandum-Regarding-Preemption

[44] U.S. Constitution. Amendment XIV.

treatment and ensuring that the government does not deprive people of their fundamental rights (e.g., the right to vote). If a law burdens a fundamental right or creates a "suspect classification" by singling out people based on a protected characteristic such as race, the law will be subject to strict or intermediate scrutiny depending on the type of equal protection violation. This does not mean, however, that the government must treat everyone exactly the same. Rather, the government must treat like cases alike and may treat unlike cases differently.[45] For example, the government may quarantine all persons suspected of contracting a disease, but not quarantine other persons, or provide benefits to all persons at a specified poverty level, but not to those with higher incomes.

If a law does not violate these principles, it will be subject to rational basis review. For example, the Minnesota legislature enacted a law banning the retail sale of milk in plastic nonreturnable, nonrefillable containers, but permitted the sale of milk in paperboard cartons.[46] The purpose of the law was to address environmental and solid waste disposal problems that the legislature found stemmed from the plastic, as opposed to the cardboard, containers. Businesses impacted by the law sued the state to prevent enforcement of the restriction and the case made its way to the U.S. Supreme Court. The Court analyzed whether the state's proffered reasons "supporting the classification between plastic and nonplastic nonreturnables is rationally related to the articulated statutory purposes" to determine whether the law violated the Equal Protection Clause.[47] The Court found that the state's rationale was rationally related to the classifications and sustained the law. Thus, the state government must have a valid purpose to enact a law.

Questions for Classroom Discussion

When the restaurant association sued New York City to prevent enforcement of the nation's first menu-labeling law, it argued that the ordinance was preempted by the federal Food Drug and Cosmetic Act and that it violated the First Amendment of the U.S. Constitution. Explain these arguments.

Explain why and when the federal government might be a better entity than state governments to regulate in the name of public health.

Explain why and when state governments might be the better entities than the federal government to regulate in the name of public health.

---

[45] L. O. Gostin. *Public Health Law: Power, Duty, Restraint* (2nd ed.). Los Angeles: University of California Press. 2008, p. 137.

[46] *Minnesota v. Clover Leaf Creamery Co.*, 449 U.S. 456 (1981).

[47] *Minnesota v. Clover Leaf Creamery Co.*, 449 U.S. 456 (1981), at 465.

Why are factual disclosure requirements on food products necessary to protect the public's health and safety? Could you argue that they also prevent deception?

Sugary beverage manufacturers often argue that it is unfair to single out sugary beverages for public health regulation. Do you think they have a viable claim that this violates the Equal Protection Clause of the U.S. Constitution?

3

Federal Nutrition Guidelines

Introduction

The federal government, through Congress and the United States Department of Agriculture (USDA), has a long history of providing nutrition and dietary guidelines for its food and nutrition programs, as well as providing them in an advisory capacity for the population as a whole. This chapter provides background information for Chapter 4's discussion of the federal government's food and nutrition programs, many of which rely on the USDA's nutrition guidelines and advice. Specifically, this chapter discusses the USDA's Dietary Guidelines for Americans and nutrition guidelines relevant to school food programs. Both are developed at the federal level by the USDA. The school food programs are administered in most states by state education agencies through agreements with school food authorities.

The USDA has several agencies within it that work to meet its many mission areas.[1] The division of Food, Nutrition and Consumer Services comprises two agencies: the Center for Nutrition Policy and Promotion (CNPP) and the Food and Nutrition Service (FNS). CNPP is responsible for developing and promoting the USDA's Dietary Guidelines.[2] FNS is in charge of the USDA's food assistance programs, including the school food programs. Each of these will be discussed in turn.

Dietary Guidelines for Americans

The USDA released its first dietary recommendations of its own volition in 1894. These were directed at males and suggested a diet of protein, carbohydrate,

---

[1] United States Department of Agriculture Mission Areas. http://www.usda.gov/wps/portal/usda/usdahome?navid=USDA_MISSION_AREAS

[2] United States Department of Agriculture. Center for Nutrition Policy and Promotion. http://www.cnpp.usda.gov/

fat, and "mineral matter" because specific minerals and vitamins had not yet been discovered.[3] The department also created the translational guides to assist Americans in incorporating the advice into their eating patterns. The USDA's first food guides were released in 1916, directed at children, and 1917, directed at the general public. These divided food into five groups: milk and meat, cereals, vegetables and fruits, fats and fatty foods, and sugars and sugary foods.[4] These earliest recommendations and guides focused on addressing nutritional deficiencies in the country.[5]

The USDA's subsequent recommendations and guides were released during the Great Depression and during the World Wars and reflected the limited resources and decreased food availability facing Americans.[6] The USDA released the Basic Seven food guide in 1943 and the Basic Four in 1956, listing only milk, meat, fruits and vegetables, and grain products.[7] In the 1970s, research began to emerge that diet was linked to the development of chronic disease. In 1979, the USDA issued a food guide adding to the Basic Four a fifth group of foods to consume in moderation: fats, sweets, and alcohol to prevent chronic disease. The USDA published the first Dietary Guidelines for Americans in 1980 and issued the first Food Pyramid in 1992 after four years of development.[8] This Food Pyramid remained the USDA's food guide until 2005. The original pyramid can be found in Figure 3.1.

The 1980, 1985, and 1990 editions of the Dietary Guidelines for Americans were issued voluntarily. Thereafter, Congress passed the National Nutrition Monitoring and Related Research Act in 1990,[9] requiring the Secretaries of USDA and Health and Human Services (HHS) to jointly issue Dietary Guidelines for Americans at least every five years.[10] The 1995 edition of Dietary Guidelines for Americans became the first such guidelines issued pursuant to statute. The goal is

---

[3] E. Frazão. America's Eating Habits: Changes and Consequences. Agriculture Information Bulletin No. (AIB-750) p. 494. May 1999. Dietary Recommendations and How They Have Changed Over Time. http://www.ers.usda.gov/media/91022/aib750b_1_.pdf

[4] E. Frazão. America's Eating Habits: Changes and Consequences. Agriculture Information Bulletin No. (AIB-750) p. 494. May 1999. Dietary Recommendations and How They Have Changed Over Time. http://www.ers.usda.gov/media/91022/aib750b_1_.pdf

[5] M. Nestle. In Defense of the USDA Food Guide Pyramid. In *Taking Sides*. Marion Nestle and L. Beth Dixon, Eds. New York, NY: McGraw-Hill/Dushkin, 2004.

[6] E. Frazão. America's Eating Habits: Changes and Consequences. Agriculture Information Bulletin No. (AIB-750) p. 494. May 1999. Dietary Recommendations and How They Have Changed Over Time http://www.ers.usda.gov/media/91022/aib750b_1_.pdf

[7] E. Frazão. America's Eating Habits: Changes and Consequences. Agriculture Information Bulletin No. (AIB-750) p. 494. May 1999. Dietary Recommendations and How They Have Changed Over Time http://www.ers.usda.gov/media/91022/aib750b_1_.pdf

[8] M. Nestle In Defense of the USDA Food Guide Pyramid. In *Taking Sides*. Marion Nestle, L. Beth Dixon, Eds. New York, NY: McGraw-Hill/Dushkin. 2004.

[9] 7 USC §§ 5301 et seq. (1990).

[10] Elizabeth Frazão. America's Eating Habits: Changes and Consequences. Agriculture Information Bulletin No. (AIB-750) p. 494. May 1999. Dietary Recommendations and How They Have Changed Over Time http://www.ers.usda.gov/media/91022/aib750b_1_.pdf

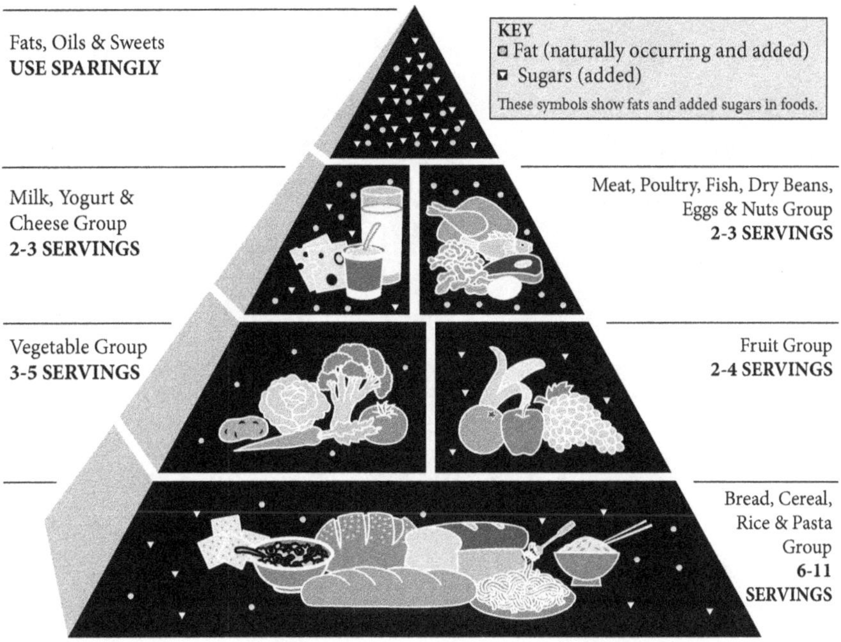

FIGURE 3.1 Original United States Department of Agriculture Food Pyramid.

to provide sound advice that promotes good health and a healthy weight and helps prevent disease for Americans ages 2 years and older. The 1995 guidelines introduced the concept of physical activity for the first time, but it was not depicted visually in the food guide until MyPyramid in 2005. MyPyramid was widely criticized for being confusing and requiring access to the Internet—something much less common at that time than today, especially among those of lower economic means—to understand how to use the recommendations. MyPlate accompanied the 2010 Dietary Guidelines, released in 2011, and was intended to be self-explanatory and easier to use. These two recent guides can be seen in Figure 3.2 and Figure 3.3. Although most Americans have not read the Dietary Guidelines for Americans, these food guides are widely circulated and displayed in locations such as schools and hospitals.

The 2010 Dietary Guidelines made specific recommendations on which foods and nutrients to increase or to reduce and introduced the concept of SoFAS, Solid Fats, and Added Sugars. The guidelines noted that Americans generally consume an excess amount of sodium, solid fats (major sources of saturated fats and trans fats), cholesterol, added sugars, refined grains, and in some cases, alcohol, and all these should be reduced. Further, it recommended the consumption of specific foods for nutrient adequacy, disease prevention, and overall good health: vegetables, fruits, whole grains, fat-free or low-fat milk and milk products, seafood, lean meat and poultry, eggs, beans and peas, soy products, nuts and seeds, and oils. The 2010 guidelines also noted the nutrients of public health concern included potassium, dietary fiber, calcium, and vitamin D.

FIGURE 3.2 United States Department of Agriculture's MyPyramid.

The 2015 Dietary Guidelines

The 2015 Dietary Guidelines Advisory Committee convened in June 2013 to provide independent, science-based advice and recommendations for the development of the Dietary Guidelines for Americans, 2015. The committee was made up of an interdisciplinary group of experts well known in fields such as nutrition, epidemiology, behavioral science, policy, and food science. Its overarching goal was to address food and nutrition issues in order to inform public health action to promote population health and to reduce the significant burden of avoidable disease in the U.S. population as a whole or in specific population subgroups.[11] The committee was charged with:

- Examining the 2010 Dietary Guidelines for Americans and determining where new scientific evidence is available to inform revisions or to suggest new guidance is necessary.
- Systematically reviewing and analyzing the evidence published since the last Dietary Guideline deliberations.
- Developing food-based recommendations that are of public health importance for Americans ages 2 years and older.

---

[11] 2015 Dietary Guidelines Advisory Committee. 2015 Dietary Guidelines Advisory Committee Topic Selection Criteria and Approaches for Examining the Evidence. http://www.health.gov/dietaryguidelines/2015-binder/2015/topicSelectionCriteria.aspx

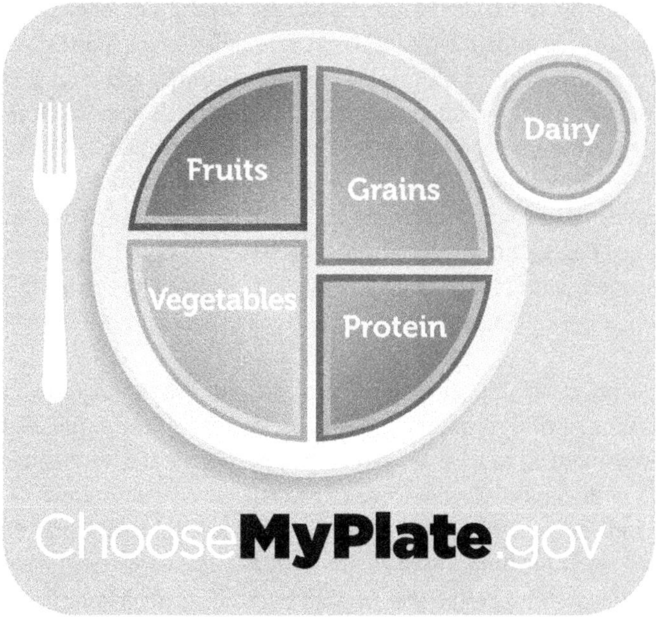

FIGURE 3.3 United States Department of Agriculture's My Plate.

- Preparing, authoring, and submitting to the Secretary of Health and Human Services and the Secretary of Agriculture a report of technical recommendations, with rationales, to inform the development of the 2015 Dietary Guidelines for Americans. (This does not include translating the recommendations into policy or communication documents.)
- Disbanding upon the submittal of the recommendations, called the "Report of the Dietary Guidelines Advisory Committee on the Dietary Guidelines for Americans, 2015."
- Completing all work within the required two-year time frame. [12]

The Advisory Committee submitted the "Scientific Report of the 2015 Dietary Guidelines Advisory Committee" to the Secretaries of HHS and USDA in February 2015.[13] The purpose of the report is to inform the federal government of current scientific evidence on topics related to diet, nutrition, and health. HHS and USDA will determine how and to what extent they will use the information in the Advisory Report to develop the Dietary Guidelines for Americans, which are scheduled to be released later in 2015.

---

[12] Charge to the 2015 Dietary Guidelines Advisory Committee. http://www.health.gov/dietaryguidelines/2015-binder/2015/chargeCommittee.aspx

[13] Scientific Report of the 2015 Dietary Guidelines Advisory Committee. http://www.health.gov/dietaryguidelines/2015-scientific-report/

The report made many recommendations; several key ones are described here. The report recommended that the U.S. population consume diets that are "rich in vegetables, fruit, whole grains, seafood, legumes, and nuts; moderate in low- and non-fat dairy products and alcohol (among adults); lower in red and processed meat; and low in sugar-sweetened foods and beverages and refined grains."[14] The Committee created a list of policies and programs at the local, state, and national levels to support diets lower in added sugars and sugar-sweetened beverages. See Box 3.1 for this list. The Committee also noted concerns related to the consumption of highly caffeinated beverages (e.g., energy drinks) but found that moderate coffee consumption can be incorporated into a healthy dietary pattern.

The report called for stronger federal policies related to food insecurity, including among immigrant populations specifically.[15] It recommended that the federal government align food assistance programs such as SNAP and WIC with the Dietary Guidelines for Americans to provide purchasing standards to create "new demands for healthy foods, such as vegetables and fruits, and discourage the purchase and consumption of foods, such as sugar-sweetened beverages."[16] The Committee also suggested that further work needs to be done to restructure the built environment to facilitate healthy eating and physical activity, especially for high-risk populations. The Committee focused on four settings: community food access, child care, schools, and worksites, in its analysis.

The Advisory Committee delved into the topic of sustainable diets, which emerged as the most controversial of its recommendations. The report noted the significant impact of food production, processing, consumption, and disposal on the environment, and, therefore, included recommendations on the need for dietary guidance to consider the wider issue of sustainability. The Committee's position was that promoting a sustainable diet will promote human health and the sustainability of natural resources to ensure current and long-term food security. The major findings regarding sustainable diets were that a diet higher in plant-based foods and lower in calories and animal-based foods is more health promoting and associated with less environmental impact than the current American diet. It also noted the need for sustainable seafood sources.

The Dietary Guidelines have not approached the topic of sustainability or the environment in the past. In an interview with the *Wall Street Journal,*

---

[14] Scientific Report of the 2015 Dietary Guidelines Advisory Committee. http://www.health.gov/dietaryguidelines/2015-scientific-report/PDFs/Scientific-Report-of-the-2015-Dietary-Guidelines-Advisory-Committee.pdf

[15] Scientific Report of the 2015 Dietary Guidelines Advisory Committee. http://www.health.gov/dietaryguidelines/2015-scientific-report/PDFs/Scientific-Report-of-the-2015-Dietary-Guidelines-Advisory-Committee.pdf

[16] Scientific Report of the 2015 Dietary Guidelines Advisory Committee. http://www.health.gov/dietaryguidelines/2015-scientific-report/PDFs/Scientific-Report-of-the-2015-Dietary-Guidelines-Advisory-Committee.pdf

BOX 3.1

Dietary Guidelines Advisory Committee recommendations for policies and programs to support diets lower in added sugar and sugar-sweetened beverages

- Free, readily accessible, safe water should be available in public settings, as well as child care facilities, schools, worksites and other community places and promoted in all settings where beverages are offered.
- The Nutrition Facts Panel should include added sugars (in grams and teaspoons) and include a percent daily value of added sugars in foods and beverages.
- A standardized, easily understood front-of-package label on all food and beverage products should be administered, which would include added sugars.
- Economic and pricing approaches, using incentives and disincentives should be explored to promote the purchase of healthier foods and beverages. For example, higher sugar-sweetened beverage taxes may encourage consumers to reduce sugar-sweetened beverage consumption. Using the revenues from the higher sugar-sweetened beverage taxes for nutrition health promotion efforts or to subsidize fruits and vegetables could have public health benefits.
- Efforts to reduce added sugars in foods and sugar-sweetened beverages in school meals and through the new smart snacks in schools should continue and also be expanded to other settings, including early child care (through the Child and Adult Care Food Program), parks, recreation centers, sports leagues, after school programs, work sites, and other community settings.
- Policies that limit exposure and marketing of foods and beverages high in added sugars to young children, youth and adolescents are needed.
- Health promotion efforts and policies are needed to reduce sugar-sweetened beverages in settings, such as postsecondary institutions and worksites to target young adults (ages 20–29 years).
- Policy changes within the federal Supplemental Nutrition Assistance Program (SNAP), similar to policies in place for the Special Supplemental Nutrition Program for Women, Infants, and Children (WIC), should be considered to encourage purchase of healthier options, including foods and beverages low in added sugars. Pilot studies using incentives and restrictions should be tested and evaluated.
- Public education campaigns are needed to increase the public's awareness of the health effects of added sugars and help consumers reduce added sugar intake and reduce intake of sugar-sweetened beverages through policy, food environment, and education initiatives.

Source: Scientific Report of the 2015 Dietary Guidelines Advisory Committee http://www.health.gov/dietaryguidelines/2015-scientific-report/PDFs/Scientific-Report-of-the-2015-Dietary-Guidelines-Advisory-Committee.pdf

Secretary of Agriculture Tom Vilsack spoke against addressing sustainability in the Dietary Guidelines, noting that he believed the law requires the USDA to formulate dietary and nutrition guidelines only.[17] The meat industry, especially cattle ranchers and beef producers, also pushed back against the sustainability recommendations, which it found problematic, especially when coupled with the

[17] Tennille Tracy. Vilsack: Dietary Guidelines Are About Health, Not Environment. March 11, 2015. http://blogs.wsj.com/washwire/2015/03/11/vilsack-dietary-guidelines-are-about-health-not-environment/

report's recommendation to eat a diet lower in red and processed meat, as noted above.[18,19]

See Box 3.2 for the perspective of a member of the Scientific Advisory Committee on the committee's process and key aspects of the report, including the sustainability issue.

Finally, the Advisory Committee set consumption goals for sodium, saturated fat, and added sugars for the general population to be: less than 2,300 mg dietary sodium per day (or age-appropriate Dietary Reference Intake amount), less than 10% of total calories from saturated fat per day, and a maximum of 10% of total calories from added sugars per day. The sugar recommendation is particularly noteworthy.

The USDA historically provided qualitative recommendations on sugar consumption, such as "use sugars only in moderation" in the 1990 Dietary Guidelines, and "choose a diet moderate in sugars" in the 1995 guidelines. The 2010 guidelines suggested that the public "reduce the intake of calories from solid fats and added sugars" and "limit the consumption of foods that contain refined grains, especially refined grain foods that contain solid fats, added sugars, and sodium."[20] The appendix to the 2010 Dietary Guidelines included a bit more of a quantitative recommendation: that solid fats and added sugars together should be no more than 13% of the total calories of an average person requiring a 2,000-calorie diet.[21]

It is noteworthy that influential nongovernment organizations have made recommendations for sugar consumption. The American Heart Association recommended limiting daily intake of added sugar to approximately 4.5% to 6.5% of total calories, which for an average man equals 150 calories a day and 100 calories a day for an average woman.[22] The World Health Organization's 2002 recommendations state that sugars should make up less than 10% of total energy intake per day and its draft 2014 recommendations reiterate this advice but further suggest "that a reduction to below 5% of total energy intake per day would have additional benefits. Five per cent of total energy intake is equivalent to around 25 grams (around 6 teaspoons) of sugar per day for an adult of normal Body Mass Index."[23]

---

[18] Amanda Blair. 2015 Scientific Report of the Dietary Guidelines Advisory Committee: A Meat Industry Perspective. April 15, 2015 http://www.agweb.com/article/2015-scientific-report-of-the-dietary-guidelines-advisory-committee-a-meat-industry-perspective-NAA-university-news-release/

[19] Tennille Tracy. Vilsack: Dietary Guidelines Are About Health, Not Environment. March 11, 2015 http://blogs.wsj.com/washwire/2015/03/11/vilsack-dietary-guidelines-are-about-health-not-environment/

[20] United States Department of Agriculture. Dietary Guidelines for Americans, 2010. Chapter 3.

[21] United States Department of Agriculture. Dietary Guidelines for Americans, 2010. Appendix 7. .

[22] R. K. Johnson, L. J. Appel, M. Brands, et al. Dietary Sugars Intake and Cardiovascular Health: A Scientific Statement from the American Heart Association. *Circulation.* 2009;120(11):1011–1020.

[23] World Health Organization. WHO opens public consultation on draft sugars guideline. March 5, 2014. http://www.who.int/mediacentre/news/notes/2014/consultation-sugar-guideline/en/

BOX 3.2

Discussion with 2015 Dietary Guidelines Advisory Committee member: Dr. Frank Hu of the Harvard T.H. Chan School of Public Health

Dr. Hu described the Dietary Guidelines Advisory Committee (DGAC) process as very open, transparent, and systematic. The committee communicated on a regular basis and also invited public comments. Members of the community, including food industry representatives, presented their positions in public meetings and through written comments. The committee reviewed and discussed these views during their deliberations. The DGAC systematically reviewed and synthesized the vast amount of evidence on all related topics to create their report, which serves as the scientific basis for the development of the policy document, Dietary Guidelines for Americans, 2015.

On the topic of sustainability, Dr. Hu explained that the issue did not come out of nowhere but rather it arose directly in response to their effort to address the issue of food insecurity. One of the tasks given to the DGAC was to address food insecurity, as it is a risk factor for obesity and related chronic diseases. Dr. Hu explained that in order to address food security, the committee had to think about strategies to ensure safe and healthy food for current and future generations. The committee conducted a systematic literature review to compare different dietary patterns on the environment and on health outcomes. They found that current U.S. dietary patterns that include high amounts of meat had a greater environmental impact than dietary patterns that include more plant-based foods. Dr. Hu explained that it would be almost impossible to separate environmental outcomes from health outcomes because health is affected by the environment, and food production and consumption have a huge impact on the environment. Therefore, because sustainability is directly linked to food security, this topic was within the scope of their work.

The 2015 DGAC was able to provide a strong recommendation on reducing added-sugar intake because the science on this has advanced considerably over the past several years. The committee reviewed available evidence from prospective cohort studies, randomized controlled trials, and meta-analyses and found compelling evidence that a diet high in added sugar and sugar-sweetened beverages is an important risk factor for obesity, diabetes, and cardiovascular disease. Based on the current evidence, the committee recommends limiting added sugars to a maximum of 10% of total caloric intake. The 10% upper limit recommendation aligns with the World Health Organization's original recommendation. This recommendation should be helpful for policy changes, such as the FDA's proposed changes to the Nutrition Facts Panel to include an added-sugar disclosure; removing sugar-sweetened beverages from schools and other public venues; and increasing a sugar-sweetened beverage tax.

Dr. Hu said the committee disbanded after the DGAC report was submitted to the Secretaries of the United States Department of Agriculture and the Department of Health and Human Services, as required by law. The committee members are hopeful that their evidence-based recommendations will be adopted by the Dietary Guidelines for Americans, 2015, which will be released by the end of 2015. The beef and soda industries are pushing back on some of the key recommendations, including those related to sustainability and sugar-sweetened beverage taxes. Dr. Hu explained that it would be more than just disappointing if the federal government bows to these interests; it would be very bad for public health if the committee's key recommendations are excluded due to political pressure. It remains to be seen whether politics will override science in the official dietary guidelines.

The 2015 Dietary Guidelines for Americans are expected in 2015 and any changes to the food guide would be issued thereafter. Advocates from across the country wrote a letter to the Dietary Guidelines Advisory Committee, calling for water to be included on MyPlate.[24,25] This would be in line with the Advisory Committee's call for policies to increase water in public settings. It will be interesting to compare the Advisory Committee's report with the final guidelines and the food guide for 2015.

Of note, the 2014 Farm Bill required that the Dietary Guidelines include specific dietary recommendations for children under the age of 2 years, by no later than the 2020 edition.[26] In 2012, the USDA and HHS initiated the process of developing guidance for the birth-to-24-month age group.[27] The agencies plan to finalize this guidance and provide it to the 2020 Dietary Guidelines Advisory Committee so the committee can incorporate this age group into the 2020 Dietary Guidelines Advisory Committee Report, which will provide the scientific basis for the 2020 Dietary Guidelines for Americans.

School-based Nutrition Guidelines

The federal National School Lunch Program was developed over the course of decades, but cities and states already had begun experimenting with their own programs by the early 1900s.[28] Federal assistance started in the 1930s in response to the Great Depression and was provided primarily through surplus commodity products to schools. In 1946, Congress passed the Richard B. Russell National School Lunch Act, which appropriated funds to states for school food. In order to receive funds from the state agencies, schools had to agree to certain requirements, such as operating on a nonprofit basis, meeting minimum nutritional requirements, and serving meals at reduced or no cost to those in financial need. The Special Milk Program began in 1954 and was later incorporated into the Child Nutrition Act of 1966, which also established the national School Breakfast Program (SBP), first as a pilot program and then as a permanent program.

The National School Lunch Program (NSLP) is an entitlement program, which means that the federal government guarantees the benefit to a particular group or segment of the population by allocating funding to cover all potential

---

[24] National Public Radio. The Salt. What Might Be Missing From MyPlate? Water. January 12, 2015 http://www.npr.org/blogs/thesalt/2015/01/12/376172800/what-might-be-missing-from-myplate-water

[25] Letter to Dietary Guidelines Advisory Committee, September 10, 2014: http://ucanr.edu/blogs/food/blogfiles/26976.pdf

[26] Agricultural Act of 2014, Section 4204.

[27] Materials Relating to Scientific Discussions. http://www.health.gov/dietaryguidelines/2015-binder/2015/birthTo24Months.aspx

[28] http://www.fns.usda.gov/sites/default/files/NSLP-Program%20History.pdf

recipients. The program relies on a federal–state partnership, so the state must opt-in to provide the benefits; all states provide NSLP benefits. Most states have a state board of education that is responsible for adopting statewide standards.[29] Other states rely on a chief school officer (e.g., commissioner) or on a different department to take on this role. States generally delegate power to local school boards to varying degrees; these establish policies and regulations to govern their local schools in accordance with state and federal law.[30]

Over half of the nation's grade school students participate in the NSLP, with a large portion of them receiving free or reduced meals. Receiving free or reduced meals is primarily a function of the income of the recipient's family, but when school districts have a very large percentage of low-income students, they provide free or reduced meals to the whole student population. During times of economic downturn, the total number of children participating in the NSLP may not change, but the share of participants receiving free and reduced-price meals does increase.[31] See Box 3.3 for more information on free and reduced-priced meals.

The Healthy, Hunger-Free Kids Act of 2010 (HHFKA) amended the National School Lunch Program, the Special Milk Program for Children, the School Breakfast Program, the Summer Food Service Program, the Child and Adult Care Food Program, State Administrative Expense Funds, the Special Supplemental Nutrition Program for Women, Infants and Children (WIC), and the WIC Farmers' Market Nutrition Program.[32] The HHFKA required the USDA to issue regulations updating the meal patterns and nutrition standards for school lunches and breakfasts based on the recommendations of the Food and Nutrition Board of the National Research Council of the National Academies of Science, which is part of the Institute of Medicine.[33] On January 13, 2011, the USDA published a proposed rule in the Federal Register to update the meal patterns and nutrition standards for the NSLP and the SBP and align them with the 2005 Dietary Guidelines.[34] The 2010 Dietary Guidelines were released later that month.[35] In March 2011, the USDA issued a Notice in the Federal Register

---

[29] National Association of State Boards of Education. State Education Governance, 2014: State-by-State Matrix. http://www.nasbe.org/wp-content/uploads/Governance-matrix-July-2014-with-cover.pdf

[30] National School Boards Association. FAQ. http://www.nsba.org/about-us/frequently-asked-questions

[31] http://www.usda.gov/wps/portal/usda/usdahome?contentid=2012/09/0307.xml

[32] United States Department of Agriculture. Food and Nutrition Service. Cooperation in USDA Studies and Evaluations, and Full Use of Federal Funds in Nutrition Assistance Programs Nondiscretionary Provisions of the Healthy, Hunger-Free Kids Act of 2010, Public Law 111-296. Final Rule. *Federal Register.* June 29, 2011;76(125):37979–37983. http://www.ncbi.nlm.nih.gov/pubmed/21721318

[33] 77 Federal Register 4088 (January 26, 2012).

[34] 77 Federal Register 4088 (January 26, 2012).

[35] 77 Federal Register 4088 (January 26, 2012).

BOX 3.3

Free and Reduced Meals

The "Federal Poverty Level" (FPL) sets poverty thresholds that are used for administrative purposes to determine financial eligibility for certain federal programs, including the National School Lunch Program, the School Breakfast Program, and the Special Milk Program. The government relies on one set of FPL thresholds for the 48 contiguous states, Washington, DC, and the U.S. territories, while Hawaii and Alaska each has its own FPL guidelines, and thereby its own income eligibility for these programs.[a]

The NSLP is the largest of the school-based meal programs. Any child at a NSLP-participating school may purchase a meal through the program. Children from families with incomes at or below 130% of the federal poverty level are eligible for free meals.[b] Children from families with incomes between 130% and 185% of the federal poverty level are eligible for reduced-price meals. Reduced-price lunches cannot be more than 40 cents for qualifying students. A school may certify that all of its students are eligible for free lunches if a substantial percentage of the student body (historically 80%) is eligible for free or reduced-price lunches.[c] Children from families with incomes over 185% of the federal poverty level pay the full price for the lunch, but their meals are still subsidized, just to a lesser extent. Local school-food authorities set the price for full-price meals within the confines of the requirement that they must operate meal services on a nonprofit basis.

Children spend more time in school than anywhere else outside of the home and consume between 19% and 50% of their total daily calories at school.[d] In 2014, 71.5% of lunches served were for free or reduced-price meals.[e] Thus, the provision of healthier food during the school day has the potential to significantly and positively impact low-income children's diets.

For most schools during the 2014–2015 school year, the United States Department of Agriculture (USDA) reimbursed the school $2.93 for free lunches, $2.53 for reduced-price lunches, and .28 for full-price lunches.[f] The Congressional Budget Office (CBO) is a federal agency administered by Congress to develop, coordinate, and enforce Congressional budgetary priorities[g] in a nonpartisan manner.[h] The CBO regularly issues reports on options to reduce the federal deficit. The purpose of the report is to examine federal spending; the CBO does not calculate the impact of its suggestions impact on state budgets or individuals. In its 2013[i] and 2014[j] reports, the CBO calculated the financial implications on the federal budget if Congress eliminated the subsidies for meals served to students from households with income greater than 185% of the FPL. The CBO estimated that this would reduce federal spending by approximately $10 billion through 2024,[k] and that the impact on these children's families would be "minimal."[l] This reduction, however, likely would increase the budget squeeze that schools feel in operating the NSLP.[m] It remains to be seen whether Congress pursues this policy option.

[a]*Federal Register*. Vol. 79, No. 43. March 5, 2014 /Notices 12467–12469.

[b]United States Department of Agriculture. National School Lunch Program Fact Sheet. September 2013. http://www.fns.usda.gov/sites/default/files/NSLPFactSheet.pdf

[c]United States Department of Agriculture. Economic Research Service. Report No. 61. 2008. The National School Lunch Program: Background, Trends, and Issues. http://www.ers.usda.gov/media/205594/err61_1_.pdf.

[d]Mary Story, Marilyn S. Nanney, and Marlene B. Schwartz. Schools and Obesity Prevention: Creating School Environments and Policies to Promote Healthy Eating and Physical Activity. *Milbank Quarterly*. March 2009; 87(1): 71–100.

[e]United States Department of Agriculture. Child Nutrition Tables. National School Lunch—Participation and Meals Served. http://www.fns.usda.gov/sites/default/files/pd/slsummar.pdf

[f]United States Department of Agriculture. Child Nutrition Tables. National School Lunch—Participation and Meals Served. http://www.fns.usda.gov/sites/default/files/pd/slsummar.pdf

[g]Congressional Budget Office. History. https://www.cbo.gov/about/founding

[h]Congressional Budget Office. Overview. http://www.cbo.gov/about/overview

[i]Congressional Budget Office. Options for Reducing the Deficit: 2014 to 2023. Eliminate Subsidies for Certain Meals in the National School Lunch and School Breakfast Programs. November 13, 2013. https://www.cbo.gov/budget-options/2013/44747

[j]Congressional Budget Office. Options for Reducing the Deficit: 2015 to 2024. Eliminate Subsidies for Certain Meals in the National School Lunch and School Breakfast Programs. November 20, 2014. https://www.cbo.gov/budget-options/2014/49516

[k]Congressional Budget Office. Options for Reducing the Deficit: 2015 to 2024. Eliminate Subsidies for Certain Meals in the National School Lunch and School Breakfast Programs. November 20, 2014. https://www.cbo.gov/budget-options/2014/49516

[l]Congressional Budget Office. Options for Reducing the Deficit: 2014 to 2023. Eliminate Subsidies for Certain Meals in the National School Lunch and School Breakfast Programs. November 13, 2013. https://www.cbo.gov/budget-options/2013/44747

[m]United States Department of Agriculture. Economic Research Service.Report No. 61. 2008. The National School Lunch Program: Background, Trends, and Issues. http://www.ers.usda.gov/media/205594/err61_1_.pdf.

---

seeking public comment on the need to modify the proposed rule to reflect the 2010 Dietary Guidelines recommendations.[36] After significant public comment, the USDA issued the final regulation on January 26, 2012. The USDA considered and responded to the comments and based much of the new rules on the recommendations from the Institute of Medicine.

In order for schools to receive reimbursement for their food programs, they must abide by USDA regulations. The HHFKA provides an additional 6 cents to schools for each NSLP lunch that meets the updated requirements. The new rule requires schools to increase the availability of fruits, vegetables, whole grains, and fat-free and low-fat fluid milk and to reduce sodium, saturated fat, and trans fat in meals, while meeting children's caloric requirements.[37] For the first time, school nutrition standards took into account the benefit of providing a variety of fruits and vegetables to children while also addressing problematic food components. The revised lunch and breakfast meal patterns can be found in Table 3.1 and Table 3.2

An interesting change under the HHFKA was the adoption of an "offer versus serve" rule, intended to cut down on food waste and give students options by allowing them to decline certain foods offered and still permit the schools to be reimbursed for the lunch or breakfast.[38] This is a required change for high school lunch programs. State educational agencies have the option of implementing "offer versus serve" at the middle and elementary school levels for lunch and any education level for breakfast.

---

[36] 77 Federal Register 4088 (January 26, 2012).

[37] 77 Federal Register 4088 (January 26, 2012).

[38] United States Department of Agriculture. Food and Nutrition Service. Offer Versus Serve: Guidance for the National School Lunch Program and the School Breakfast Program. School Year 2014–2015.

TABLE 3.1

United States Department of Agriculture Lunch Meal Pattern

	Lunch Meal Pattern		
	Grades: K–5	Grades 6–8	Grades: 9–12
Meal Pattern	Amount of Food Per Week (Minimum Per Day)		
Fruits (cups)	2.5 (0.5)	2.5 (0.5)	5(1)
Vegetables (cups)	3.75 (0.75)	3.75 (0.75)	5(1)
Dark green	0.5	0.5`	0.5
Red/Orange	0.75	0.75	1.25
Beans & peas (legumes)	0.5	0.5	0.5
Starchy	0.5	0.5	0.5
Other	0.5	0.5	0.75
Additional Vegetable to Reach Total	1	1	1.5
Grains (oz eq)	8–9 (1)	8–10 (1)	10–12 (2)
Meats/Meat Alternatives (oz eq)	8–10 (1)	9–10 (1)	10–12 (2)
Fluid milk (cups)	5 (1)	5 (1)	5 (1)
Other Specification: Daily Amount Based on the Average for a 5-Day Week			
Minimum–maximum calories (kcal)	550–650	600–700	750–850
Saturated fat (% of total calories)	< 10	< 10	< 10
Sodium fat (% of total calories)	< 10	< 10	< 10
Sodium (mg)	≤ 640	≤ 710	≤ 740
Trans fat	Nutrition label or manufacturer specifications must indicate zero grams of *trans* fat per serving.		

Source: USDA. New Meal Pattern Requirements and Nutrition Standards: USDA's National School Lunch and School Breakfast Programs http://www.fns.usda.gov/sites/default/files/LAC_03-06-12_0.pdf.

A food component is one of the food groups that comprise a reimbursable meal.[39] For lunches, there are five food components: meats/meat alternate, grains, fruits, vegetables, and fluid milk. Schools must offer all five food components in the minimum required quantities. Under "offer versus serve," a student must take at least three components in the required quantities and one selection must be either the fruit or vegetable component. For the breakfast meal, three food components constitute a reimbursable meal: fruits or vegetable substitution, grains or optional meat/meat alternate substitution, and fluid milk. Schools must offer all three food components in the minimum required quantities and students must select three food items, with one coming from the fruit or vegetable category.

Competitive foods are all the food and beverages available for sale to students on the school campus during the school day that are not part of the reimbursable programs authorized by the National School Lunch Act and the Child

[39] United States Department of Agriculture. Food and Nutrition Service. Offer Versus Serve: Guidance for the National School Lunch Program and the School Breakfast Program. School Year 2014–2015.

TABLE 3.2
United States Department of Agriculture Breakfast Meal Pattern

	Breakfast Meal Pattern		
	Grades K-5	Grades 6-8	Grades 9-12
Meal Pattern	Amount of Food Per Week (Minimum Per Day)		
Fruits (cups)	5 (1)	5 (1)	5 (1)
Vegetables (cups)	0	0	0
Dark green	0	0	0
Red/Orange	0	0	0
Beans and peas (legumes)	0	0	
Starchy	0	0	0
Other	0	0	0
Additional Vegetable to Reach Total	0	0	0
Grains (oz eq)	7–10 (1)	8–10 (1)	9-10 (1)
Meats/Meat Alternatives (oz eq)	0	0	0
Fluid milk (cups)	5 (1)	5 (1)	5 (1)
Other Specifications: Daily Amount Based on the Average for a 5-Day Week			
Minimum—maximum calories (kcal)	350–500	400–550	450–600
Saturated fat (% of total calories)	< 10	< 10	< 10
Sodium (mg)	≤ 430	≤ 470	≤ 500
Trans fat	Nutrition label or manufacturer specifications must indicate zero grams of *trans* fat per serving.		

Source: USDA. New Meal Pattern Requirements and Nutrition Standards: USDA's National School Lunch and School Breakfast Programs http://www.fns.usda.govisitesidefault/files/LAC 03-06-12 0.pdf.

Nutrition Act. These foods can be found in vending machines, school stores, and ala carte lines. The HHFKA authorized the USDA to update the competitive food standards, which it did. These new standards, called "Smart Snacks in Schools," set limits on calories, salt, sugar, and fat, and promote snack foods that have whole grains, low-fat dairy, fruits, vegetables, or protein.[40] The federal law does not preempt state or local education agencies from implementing stricter nutrition standards and only provides minimum requirements for schools. The new standards increase the healthfulness of competitive foods sold in schools, as shown by the USDA's Infographic in Figure 3.4.

Certain groups, including the National School Boards Association, argued that the new NSLP guidelines are burdensome to school districts and that school districts have lost money, found increased plate waste, and garnered complaints from students and parents.[41] These groups supported the passage of a House Bill that, among other items, would require the Secretary of Agriculture to establish

[40] Centers for Disease Control and Prevention. Adolescent and School Health Competitive Foods in Schools. http://www.cdc.gov/healthyyouth/nutrition/standards.htm

[41] Childhood Nutrition Reauthorization: Key Provisions & Status Of Implementation. August 2014. http://www.nsba.org/sites/default/files/reports/NSBA-Issue-Brief-on-School-Nutrition.pdf

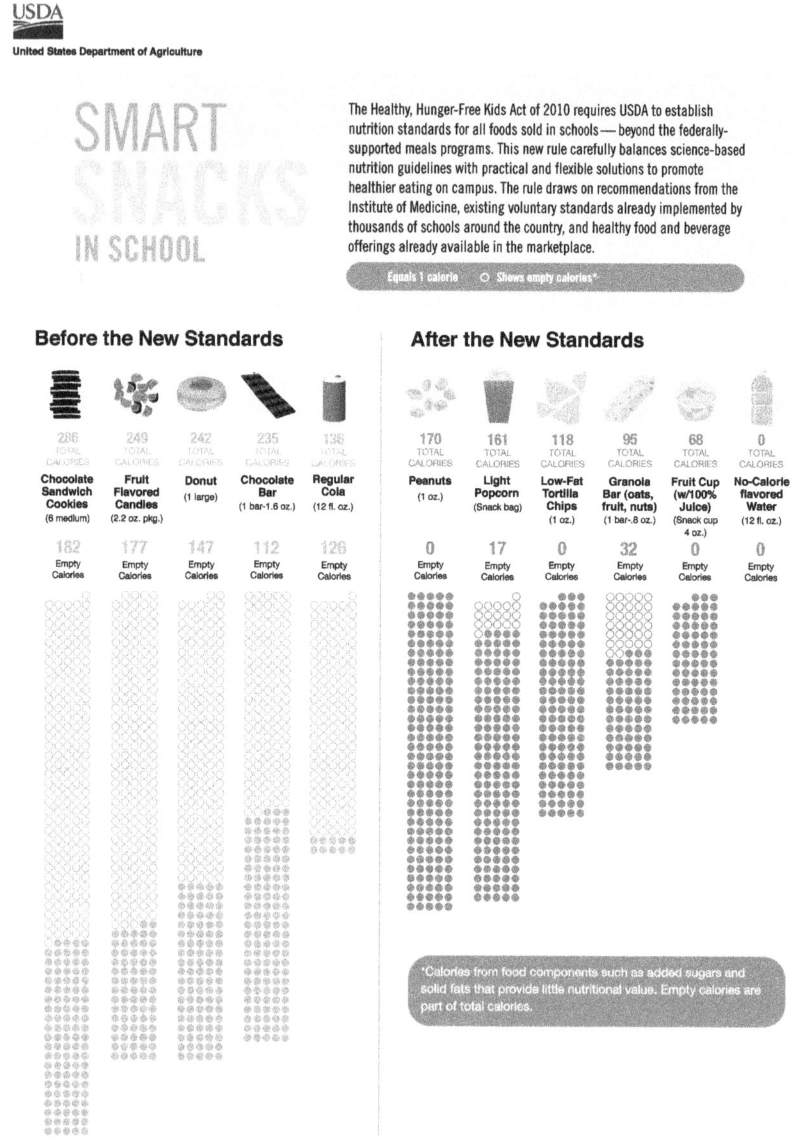

FIGURE 3.4 United States Department of Agriculture Infographic Competitive Foods.[a]

[a]USDA. *Healthier School Day Tools for Schools:* Focusing on Smart Snacks http://www.fns.usda.gov/sites/default/files/allfoods_infographic.pdf

a process for states to grant a waiver from compliance with the new school-food standards to schools that verify that they are operating at a net loss from the food service program for a period of at least 6 months.[42] The Obama Administration strongly opposed passage of this bill.[43] It did not pass and it is unclear the extent

[42] HR 4800 Agriculture, Rural Development, Food and Drug Administration, and Related Agencies Appropriations Act, 2015; Sec. 739 (2014).

[43] Office of Management and Budget. Statement Of Administration Policy. June 10, 2014.

schools are actually operating at a net loss. Moreover, a study published in 2015 found positive outcomes from the revised school meal standards, including increased consumption of fruit and reduced plate waste from entrees and vegetables.[44]

A related bill did become law, which permits states to grant an exemption from the whole-grain requirement (for both the lunch and breakfast programs) through the school year 2015–2016, if school food authorities demonstrate hardship, including financial hardship, "in procuring specific whole grain products which are acceptable to the students and compliant with the whole grain-rich requirements." If a school is granted a waiver, it must comply with the grain component or standard that was in effect prior to the 2014–2015 school year.[45]

In 2014, 30.3 million school children participated in the National School Lunch Program.[46] The number of lunches served nationally dropped a bit from 2013 and previously from 2012 to 2013, but the percentage of children receiving free or reduced-price meals has increased steadily over the years, to 71.5% in 2014. The School Breakfast Program did not see a similar decrease in participation rates.[47] In 2014, 13.51 million children participated in the breakfast program, with 84.8% of them receiving free or reduced-price meals.

Future Regulations

The Child and Adult Care Food Program (CACFP) has the broadest scope of all the USDA food and nutrition programs and serves people at all stages of the lifespan, from infants to the elderly. The Healthy, Hunger-Free Kids Act of 2010 required that the USDA update nutrition standards for CACFP. The Institute of Medicine (IOM) issued a report, "Child and Adult Care Food Program: Aligning Dietary Guidance for All" in 2011, providing guidance for nutrition requirements for various age groups in the program. In January 2015, the USDA FNS issued a draft rule with proposed science-based nutrition standards for meals provided through CACFP, based on the IOM report and aligned with the meal patterns of the 2010 Dietary Guidelines for Americans.[48] Once finalized, these

---

[44] M. B. Schwartz, K. E. Henderson, M. Read, N. Danna, J. R. Ickovics. New school meal regulations increase fruit consumption and do not increase total plate waste. *Childhood Obesity.* 2015;11(3):242–247.

[45] HR 83 Consolidated and Further Continuing Appropriations Act, 2015 (12/16/14). Public Law No. 113–235

[46] United States Department of Agriculture. Child Nutrition Tables. National School Lunch—Participation and Meals Served. http://www.fns.usda.gov/sites/default/files/pd/slsummar.pdf

[47] United States Department of Agriculture. Child Nutrition Tables. School Breakfast—Participation and Meals Served http://www.fns.usda.gov/sites/default/files/pd/sbsummar.pdf

[48] Child and Adult Care Food Program: Meal Pattern Revisions Related to the Healthy, Hunger-Free Kids Act of 2010. January 9, 2015. http://www.fns.usda.gov/sites/default/files/CACFP_Meal_Pattern_Rule_010915.pdf

new standards will be the first update to the program's nutrition requirements since its creation in 1968.[49]

Questions for Classroom Discussion

Should the federal government be in the business of providing nutrition and dietary guidelines to Americans in general or to federal program recipients in particular? If not the government, who should take on this role, if anyone?

Look up the 2015 Dietary Guidelines for Americans. Compare these to the Scientific Report of the 2015 Dietary Guidelines Advisory Committee. What recommendations were adopted and which ones were discarded? Do you agree or disagree with these decisions? Why or why not? What are some of the improvements from the 2015 Dietary Guidelines for Americans over the 2010 version? Where do you see room for further improvement?

The USDA explained that the original rational for providing reimbursements for lunches was to align with the general purpose of many of its food and nutrition assistance programs: to increase demand for agricultural commodities.[50] The focus of the program has since shifted to more of a safety net for low-income children who obtain a large proportion of their daily calories at school. Children used to go home during the school day and many still bring their own lunches. What should the government's role be in providing meals at school? Should the federal government stop subsidizing meals served to students from households with income greater than 185% of the FPL in accordance with the policy option analyzed by the CBO?

As of 2014, 18 states had students on their state boards of education in either an advisory capacity or with voting rights.[51] What should students' role be in deciding school food standards, if any?

---

[49] United States Department of Agriculture. Press Release. USDA Proposes New Science-Based Meal Patterns for Child and Adult Care Food Program. January 9, 2015. http://www.fns.usda.gov/pressrelease/2015/fns-0001-15

[50] United States Department of Agriculture. Economic Research Service (ERS). Report No. 61. 2008. The National School Lunch Program: Background, Trends, and Issues. http://www.ers.usda.gov/media/205594/err61_1_.pdf.

[51] National Association of State Boards of Education. State Boards of Education. http://www.nasbe.org/about-us/state-boards-of-education/

4

Federal Food and Nutrition Programs

Introduction

The federal government creates and directs the nation's agriculture policy and supports food and nutrition programs to assist vulnerable populations. Congress passes legislation underlying the relevant policies and programs and directs the United States Department of Agriculture (USDA) to administer them. President Lincoln created the USDA in 1862, calling it the "People's Department," because at that time half of all Americans lived on farms.[1] The USDA administers several crucial pieces of legislation, including, for example, the Farm Bill, which provides a safety net to farmers, and the Supplemental Nutrition Assistance Program, which provides a safety net to individuals at risk for food insecurity. The Farm Bill and USDA's food and nutrition programs will be reviewed below.

The Farm Bill

The term "Farm Bill" is a generic phrase used to describe federal legislation that forms the basis of much of the nation's agricultural policy. The Farm Bill has been a controversial piece of legislation since its inception. The first version of the Farm Bill was the Agricultural Adjustment Act of 1933, which was enacted to address a "national economic emergency."[2] During the Great Depression, the price of agricultural commodities (wheat, cotton, field corn, hogs, rice, and milk products) were so low that farmers were in financial distress. The Act provided farmers payments in return for reducing acreage or production of commodity products. It raised revenue for this purpose through the imposition of

---

[1] http://www.usda.gov/wps/portal/usda/usdahome?navid=USDA150

[2] *United States v. Butler*, 297 U.S. 1 (1936).

a tax.[3] A cotton milling corporation that was assessed this tax sued the federal government to challenge the taxation method. In *United States v. Butler*, the United States Supreme Court found that the Act was unconstitutional. However, Congress passed the Agricultural Adjustment Act of 1938 to address the same type of financial issues using quotas and penalties. It was upheld by the Supreme Court in 1939.[4]

Several Farm Bills followed. The next radical change occurred in the 1970s when the Secretary of Agriculture, Earl Butz, led agriculture policy in a new direction. He famously said, "Get big or get out," creating a payment and exportation system that favored large farms and led to the industrialization of American agriculture.[5] Industrial farms grew and smaller family farmers sold their farms and left the business.

Farms became increasingly more productive. This stemmed from innovations driven by public and private research funding and a move away from human and animal labor and toward machinery and intermediate inputs including energy, agricultural chemicals, and purchased services.[6] For example, harvesting machines replaced human labor, tractors replaced animal labor, and fertilizers and pesticides that increased crop yield were developed.

Congress reauthorizes the Farm Bill every five or so years; however, this does not always progress smoothly due to competing interests. Even if one Farm Bill expires, it is not always clear exactly when the next Farm Bill will be reauthorized. For example, the 2008 Farm Bill expired in 2012, but Congress was mired in lengthy debates about the future of certain provisions so it extended most provisions in the 2008 law for one year—to September 30, 2013.[7] This extension functionally extended those provisions through the end of the fiscal year 2013.[8] In January 2014, Congress came to an agreement about the 2014 Farm Bill and on February 7, 2014, the President signed the Agricultural Act of 2014. The provisions of the 2014 Farm Bill expire at the end of 2018, rendering an expectation that a 2019 Farm Bill may be next. In total, there have been 17 iterations of the Farm Bill between 1933 and 2014.

The primary controversies over the modern Farm Bills involve the titles devoted to nutrition assistance and commodity subsidization. Nutrition assistance programs make up the majority of all funding in the recent Farm Bills. In the 2008 Farm Bill, 67% of financial outlays were allocated to nutrition programs,

---

[3] *United States v. Butler*, 297 U.S. 1 (1936).

[4] *Mulford v. Smith*, 307 U.S. 38 (1939).

[5] Daniel Imhoff. *Food Fight: The Citizens Guide to the Next Food and Farm Bill*. Healdsburg, CA: A Watershed Media Book, 2012.

[6] http://www.ers.usda.gov/amber-waves/2014-januaryfebruary/agricultural-productivity-growth-in-the-united-states-1948-2011.aspx#.U7G3uECuCio

[7] http://www.nfu.org/blog/?p=620

[8] Jim Monke, Randy Alison Aussenberg, and Megan Stubbs. Expiration and Extension of the 2008 Farm Bill. *CRS*. December 16, 2013.

primarily the Supplemental Nutrition Assistance Program (SNAP). Many of the debates over reauthorization involved different perspectives on how much should be spent on SNAP and whether the program should be more akin to monetary distribution or actually provide nutritional assistance. Although certain groups in the legislature threatened major cuts to SNAP spending, this did not come to fruition in 2014, and the foundation of the program was not significantly altered by the Agricultural Act of 2014.

In the 2008 Farm Bill, crop subsidies made up the second largest financial investment at 14% of all funding.[9] From 2003 to 2009, commodity crop payments were made primarily for corn (41%), cotton (26%), wheat (11%), rice (7%), and soybeans (7%).[10] Corn is used for a variety of purposes, falling into three major categories: animal feed, fuel in the form of ethanol, and food for humans.[11] The USDA Economic Research Service reports that less than 10% of the U.S. field corn crop is used for direct domestic human consumption, approximately 40% is used directly as animal feed for livestock and poultry, and the remainder is used for animal feed, exports, ethanol production, seed, and industrial uses.[12]

One product made from corn for human consumption is high fructose corn syrup, which is a sweetener derived from the wet milling of corn. (Other products made from the wet milling of corn include glucose, dextrose, corn starch, and ethanol.)[13] Corn starch is converted into high fructose corn syrup in a three-step controlled enzymatic process.[14] During the 2000s, food manufacturers replaced more expensively priced sugar with high fructose corn syrup. The vast majority of high fructose corn syrup is used by the beverage industry, followed by processed food manufacturers, cereal and bakery producers, and others such as the dairy industry. Less than 5% of the total U.S. corn crop is used to produce high fructose corn syrup.[15]

The subsidization of corn, wheat, and soy is frequently blamed for the very low cost of foods produced with these commodity products and the livestock raised on corn feed.[16] For example, a fast food hamburger is relatively inexpensive and comprised of corn-fed cattle beef; a bun formulated with wheat, soy, and high fructose corn syrup; and ketchup with high fructose corn syrup as a primary ingredient.[17] The soda that might accompany the hamburger contains high fructose corn syrup as its second ingredient after water.

---

[9] http://www.snaptohealth.org/farm-bill-usda/u-s-farm-bill-faq/

[10] Daniel Imhoff. *Food Fight: The Citizens Guide to the Next Food and Farm Bill*. Healdsburg, CA: A Watershed Media Book, 2012.

[11] http://www.ers.usda.gov/topics/crops/corn/background.aspx#.U7GcRUCuCio

[12] http://www.ers.usda.gov/topics/farm-economy/bioenergy/findings.aspx#.U7Gf-oCuCio

[13] http://www.ers.usda.gov/topics/crops/corn/background.aspx#.U7GcRUCuCio

[14] Peter S. Murano. *Understanding Food Science and Technology*. Belmont, CA: Thomson Wadsworth, 2003, p. 145.

[15] http://www.ers.usda.gov/topics/crops/corn/background.aspx#.U7GcRUCuCio

[16] Daniel Imhoff. Food Fight: The Citizens Guide to the Next Food and Farm Bill. Healdsburg, CA: A Watershed Media Book, 2012.

[17] http://nutrition.mcdonalds.com/getnutrition/ingredientslist.pdf

The USDA Economic Research Service (ERS) found that agricultural contributions to food account for only a small percentage of the total food cost. This is especially true for products that require more processing and packaging, because so much of the retail price reflects marketing costs, which include packaging, processing, advertising, transportation, and other related costs. The ERS estimated in 2008 that 15.8 cents of each dollar spent on food related to the farm value of the food, while the remainder related to the marketing costs.[18] It studied products made with corn, including corn flakes cereal and soda with high fructose corn syrup, and found that a 49% increase in corn prices would be expected to raise the price of a box of corn flakes by about 0.5% and the price of a 2-liter soda by about 1%.[19]

The ERS found that less-processed foods, such as eggs and fresh produce, would increase in retail price along with increases in farm prices.[20] Other research has found that if all farm subsidies were removed, the price of fruit and vegetables would decrease.[21] Given that dietary guidance recommends eating more fruits and vegetables, a decrease in produce prices would be considered a positive outcome. The Farm Bill has never invested in fruits and vegetables, which are considered "specialty crops," to the same extent as commodity crops in terms of raw program dollars or in terms of priority. Specialty crop funding was one of the programs left out of the 2008 Farm Bill extension. Further, spending on specialty crop research has not kept up with the growth in the value of specialty crop production.[22] The good news is that the 2014 Farm Bill contained increased funding and attention paid to specialty crop issues.

Agricultural Act of 2014

Through the main provisions of the Agricultural Act of 2014, Congress reshaped the structure of farm commodity support by eliminating direct payments, expanded crop insurance coverage, consolidated conservation programs, reauthorized and revised nutrition assistance, and extended authority to appropriate funds for many of the USDA's discretionary programs through fiscal year 2018.[23]

---

[18] Patrick Canning. *A Revised and Expanded Food Dollar Series: A Better Understanding of Our Food Costs.* Economic Research Report No. (ERR-114). Washington, DC: USDA Economic Research Service, February 2011. http://www.ers.usda.gov/publications/err-economic-research-report/err114.aspx

[19] http://webarchives.cdlib.org/sw1vh5dg3r/http://ers.usda.gov/AmberWaves/February08/Features/CornPrices.htm

[20] http://webarchives.cdlib.org/sw1vh5dg3r/http://ers.usda.gov/AmberWaves/February08/Features/CornPrices.htm

[21] J. M. Alston, D. A. Sumner, S. A. Vosti. Farm Subsidies and Obesity in the United States: National Evidence and International Comparisons. *Food Policy*, 2008;33:. .470–479.

[22] Julian M. Alston, Philip G. Pardey. Public Funding for Research into Specialty Crops. *HortScience*. 2008; 43(5):1461–1470.

[23] Ralph M. Chite. The 2014 Farm Bill (P.L. 113–79): Summary and Side-by-Side. Congressional Research Service. February 12, 2014. http://nationalaglawcenter.org/wp-content/uploads/2014/02/R43076.pdf

The former direct payments were transitioned to a risk-management approach to provide support for farmers during a time of need and address market volatility. In addition, the new law strengthened crop insurance for weather disasters.[24] There are 12 titles to the 2014 Farm Bill: Commodity, Conservation, Trade, Nutrition, Credit, Rural Development, Research, Forestry, Energy, Horticulture, Crop Insurance, and Miscellaneous; each one will be reviewed briefly. The projected spending on all 12 titles for 2014 through 2018 are as follows: 80% allocated to Nutrition, 8% allocated for Crop Insurance, 6% allocated for Conservation, 5% allocated for Commodity, and 1% for the remaining programs.[25]

Title I, Commodity, established price loss coverage and agriculture risk coverage. It also provides loans and disaster assistance and continues dairy program supports (except for the discontinued Dairy Product Price Support Program). This section continued the sugar program unchanged. Under this program the USDA is directed to maintain market prices above loan rates by limiting the amount of sugar produced from sugar beets and sugarcane that is sold on the U.S. market, while simultaneously restricting imports under a quota, among other requirements. The outcome of this program is that U.S. sugar prices remain higher than world prices and higher than they would be within the United States without the sugar program.[26] This is one of the primary drivers behind companies switching to high fructose corn syrup as a sweetener.

The most important change under the Commodity title is that Congress repealed direct payments to producers and landowners that were based on historical production of covered commodity crops. Covered commodities include wheat, corn, grain sorghum, barley, oats, upland cotton, long grain rice, medium and short grain rice, pulse crops, soybeans, and other oilseeds.[27] Pulse crops include dry peas, lentils, small chickpeas, and large chickpeas.[28] "Other oil seeds" include sunflower seed, rapeseed, canola, safflower, flaxseed, mustard seed, crambe, sesame seed, and any oilseed designated by the Secretary of Agriculture.[29] The elimination of direct payments was considered a success of the 2014 Farm Bill, because predecessor Bills had provided these payments regardless of farmers' needs.[30]

Under the Agricultural Act of 2014, farmers were required to choose between two new programs that will remain in place through the 2018 crop year: Price Loss Coverage and Agricultural Risk Coverage. If famers do not make a selection,

---

[24] U.S. Senate Committee on Agriculture, Nutrition & Forestry. http://www.ag.senate.gov/newsroom/press/release/farm-bill-ends-direct-payment-subsidies

[25] http://www.ers.usda.gov/agricultural-act-of-2014-highlights-and-implications.aspx#.U7GMkECuCio

[26] http://www.ers.usda.gov/topics/crops/sugar-sweeteners/background.aspx#.U7GcRECuCio

[27] 7 USCS § 8702(4), (9).

[28] 7 USCS § 8702(14).

[29] 7 USCS § 8702(10).

[30] U.S. Senate Committee on Agriculture, Nutrition & Forestry. http://www.ag.senate.gov/newsroom/press/release/farm-bill-ends-direct-payment-subsidies

they shall be deemed to have elected price loss coverage for all covered commodities through the 2018 crop year.[31] Under price loss coverage, payments are provided to producers of covered commodities on a commodity-by-commodity basis when market prices fall below a pre-established reference price.[32] Agricultural risk coverage requires the selection of county or individual coverage; county coverage can be selected for certain crops (and producers may use price loss coverage for the others), while an individual coverage selection must apply to all crops. Agricultural risk coverage is determined for each crop year if the actual crop revenue (for a county or for an individual producer) is less than the agriculture risk coverage guarantee determined for that crop year.[33] There are several formulas involved in calculating payments that take into consideration national market prices and other financial realities.

Title II, Conservation, retained and consolidated the agricultural conservation programs, such as the Environmental Quality Incentives Program (EQIP) and the Conservation Stewardship Program, to encourage conservation and address regional issues.[34],[35] Animal Feeding Operations (AFOs), which are operations where animals are kept and raised in confined situations—and where feed, manure, urine, dead animals, and production processes may all be found within close proximity to one another—are permitted to apply for funds under the EQIP.[36] They reportedly receive a great deal of funding from this program.[37]

Title III, Trade, maintained investments in international market development and reauthorized international food aid programs.[38] The largest of these programs is Food for Peace, a program operated by the United States Agency for International Development (USAID), which is a government agency that works to end poverty and assist democratic societies.[39] Food for Peace provides emergency food and development assistance to those affected by conflict and natural disasters to address food insecurity.[40]

---

[31] 113 P.L. 79, Sec. 1115(c).

[32] http://www.ers.usda.gov/agricultural-act-of-2014-highlights-and-implications/crop-commodity-programs.aspx#.U7FY30CuCio

[33] 113 P.L. 79, Sec. 1117.

[34] Ralph M. Chite. The 2014 Farm Bill (P.L. 113–79): Summary and Side-by-Side. Congressional Research Service. February 12, 2014. http://nationalaglawcenter.org/wp-content/uploads/2014/02/R43076.pdf

[35] United States Department of Agriculture. 2014 Farm Bill Highlights. www.usda.gov/documents/usda-2014-farm-bill-highlights.pdf

[36] United States Department of Agriculture. Environmental Quality Incentives Program. http://www.nrcs.usda.gov/wps/portal/nrcs/main/ct/programs/financial/eqip/

[37] National Sustainable Agriculture Coalition. NSAC's Blog. 2014 Farm Bill Drill Down: Conservation—Working Lands Programs. February 10, 2014. http://sustainableagriculture.net/blog/2014-farm-bill-working-lands/

[38] Ralph M. Chite. The 2014 Farm Bill (P.L. 113–79): Summary and Side-by-Side. Congressional Research Service. February 12, 2014. http://nationalaglawcenter.org/wp-content/uploads/2014/02/R43076.pdf

[39] http://www.usaid.gov/who-we-are

[40] http://www.usaid.gov/who-we-are/organization/bureaus/bureau-democracy-conflict-and-humanitarian-assistance/office-food

Title IV, Nutrition, is by far the largest portion of the Farm Bill and provides nutrition assistance through several programs including the Supplemental Nutrition Assistance Program (SNAP), the Emergency Food Assistance Program, Commodity Supplemental Food Program, and the Senior Farmers' Market Nutrition Program, among others. Through this Title, Congress required the USDA to administer a pilot project where at least five states that participate in the Fresh Fruit and Vegetable Program, which provides fresh fruit and vegetables to low-income children at school, offer frozen, canned, and dried fruits and vegetables. Congress additionally authorized the USDA to enter into reprocessing agreements with private companies that process commodity foods for donation and distribution to the USDA's nutrition programs.[41]

There were several substantive changes to SNAP in the 2014 Farm Bill. The one that received the most attention was a readjustment in the way benefits were calculated in some states. Fifteen states and the District of Columbia tied SNAP benefits to a streamlined system for determining utility payments that resulted in an increased amount of SNAP benefits for certain households.[42] The Agricultural Act of 2014 ceased this process, resulting in reduced benefits for about 850,000 households (or 4 percent of beneficiaries[43]) by approximately $90 per household per month.[44] Another change included the passage of the "Food Insecurity Nutrition Incentive," which provides "incentive grants" for projects that incentivize SNAP participants to buy fruits and vegetables. This title also required the USDA and state agencies to enter into cooperative agreements to carry out pilot programs that could develop and test methods to increase employment and training programs and services to raise the number of working SNAP recipients. The goal of these efforts is to increase the income of the registrants in order to reduce the reliance on SNAP.[45]

Congress also adjusted requirements for SNAP retailers in the Nutrition Title. Among other changes, Congress required SNAP retailers to pay for their own Electronic Benefit Transfer equipment, with the exception of farmers' markets and nonprofit vendors. This went into effect immediately upon passage of the Farm Bill. Another change for retailers was an increase in the minimum staple food inventory necessary to qualify as a SNAP retailer, discussed further below in the section on SNAP.

---

[41] Ralph M. Chite. The 2014 Farm Bill (P.L. 113–79): Summary and Side-by-Side. Congressional Research Service. February 12, 2014. http://nationalaglawcenter.org/wp-content/uploads/2014/02/R43076.pdf.

[42] NCSL. "Heat and Eat" and SNAP Changes in the 2014 Farm Bill 4/16/2014 http://www.ncsl.org/research/human-services/-heat-and-eat-and-snap-changes-in-the-2014-farm-bill.aspx

[43] Niraj Chokshi. Why the food stamp cuts in the farm bill affect only a third of states. Washington Post. February 5, 2014.

[44] CBO. Letter to Honorable Frank D. Lucas. September 16, 2013

[45] 113 P.L. 79, Sec. 4022

The Credit and Rural Development titles (Titles V and VI, respectively) guide the USDA in its credit and rural development activities, with the latter including funding for various programs intended to assist rural populations by supporting rural business development and growth, as well as water infrastructure.[46] Another statute permanently establishes the USDA as a backup lender for farmers and ranchers.[47] Pursuant to the Research title, Title VII, the USDA conducts agricultural research and provides support for cooperative research, extension, and education programs in the states.[48] The Forestry title, Title VIII, provides the USDA with the authority to address forestry restoration and care for the national forestry system; other statutes provide permanent authority for other forestry assistance programs.[49] Under the Energy title, Title IX, Congress extended funds for the USDA to research, develop, and produce biofuels, including fuel derived from renewable biomass other than corn kernel starch (i.e., ethanol, which was formerly the primary focus for biofuels) and renewable energy sources (e.g., wind, solar).[50]

The Horticulture title, Title X, expanded programs and funding assistance supporting farming operations in the certified organic and specialty crop sectors.[51] Organic farming uses methods to preserve the environment and avoid certain materials. For example, in order to earn the USDA organic seal, food producers must not use irradiation, sewage sludge, synthetic fertilizers, prohibited pesticides, and genetically modified organisms.[52] The Farm Bill provides annual funding to reimburse organic farmers for the cost of organic certification if their products are certified to be sold or labeled as "organic" or "100% organic."[53] This title also increases support for pest and disease management.

Specialty crops are defined as "fruits, vegetables, tree nuts, dried fruits, horticulture, and nursery crops (including floriculture)."[54] The Horticulture title

---

[46] United States Department of Agriculture. 2014 Farm Bill Highlights. www.usda.gov/documents/usda-2014-farm-bill-highlights.pdf

[47] Ralph M. Chite. The 2014 Farm Bill (P.L. 113–79): Summary and Side-by-Side. Congressional Research Service. February 12, 2014. http://nationalaglawcenter.org/wp-content/uploads/2014/02/R43076.pdf.

[48] Ralph M. Chite. The 2014 Farm Bill (P.L. 113–79): Summary and Side-by-Side. Congressional Research Service. February 12, 2014. http://nationalaglawcenter.org/wp-content/uploads/2014/02/R43076.pdf.

[49] Ralph M. Chite. The 2014 Farm Bill (P.L. 113–79): Summary and Side-by-Side. Congressional Research Service. February 12, 2014. http://nationalaglawcenter.org/wp-content/uploads/2014/02/R43076.pdf.

[50] Ralph M. Chite. The 2014 Farm Bill (P.L. 113–79): Summary and Side-by-Side. Congressional Research Service. February 12, 2014. http://nationalaglawcenter.org/wp-content/uploads/2014/02/R43076.pdf.

[51] Ralph M. Chite. The 2014 Farm Bill (P.L. 113–79): Summary and Side-by-Side. Congressional Research Service. February 12, 2014. http://nationalaglawcenter.org/wp-content/uploads/2014/02/R43076.pdf.

[52] United States Department of Agriculture National Organic Program. http://www.ams.usda.gov/AMSv1.0/NOPOrganicStandards

[53] 113 P.L. 79, Sec. 10004

[54] United States Department of Agriculture. Specialty Crop Block Grant Program. http://www.ams.usda.gov/AMSv1.0/SCBGP

established Specialty Crop Block Grants,[55] which authorized the USDA to provide historic support to state and territorial departments of agriculture for projects designed to benefit specialty crop farmers. The USDA suggested these grants could be used for research and development, education, expanded access to specialty crops in underserved communities, or developing school and community gardens and farm-to-school programs, among other pertinent measures.[56] The Horticulture title also supports producer-to-consumer market opportunities and local food promotion programs by providing funding for domestic farmers' markets, roadside stands, community supported agriculture programs, agritourism activities, and local and regional food business enterprises.[57]

Title XI, Crop Insurance, provides coverage for losses related to natural disasters. It functions in addition to other permanent insurance authorized through another statute. This title increased and expanded crop insurance to specialty crops, livestock, sorghum, alfalfa and peanuts. It also requires the USDA to conduct research on such insurance and farm revenues.[58]

The final title, Title XII, is called Miscellaneous.[59] This title contains a multitude of diverse parts.[60] For example, there is a section on livestock, livestock safety, and strengthening and enhancing the production and marketing of sheep. Title XII also directs the USDA to award a grant to a university to establish a policy research center to be known as the "Socially Disadvantaged Farmers and Ranchers Policy Research Center." It also directs the USDA to make competitive grants to states, tribal governments, and research institutions to promote the domestic maple syrup industry. In this Title, Congress directed the USDA to work with the Food and Drug Administration to determine whether a federal standard identity for honey is necessary; this requirement has an interesting history that is discussed in Box 4.1. Title XII also requires the USDA to conduct an economic analysis of the final rule published by the Department of Agriculture requiring "Mandatory Country of Origin Labeling of Beef, Pork, Lamb, Chicken, Goat Meat, Wild and Farm-raised Fish and Shellfish, Perishable Agricultural Commodities, Peanuts, Pecans, Ginseng and Macadamia Nuts."

---

[55] 113 P.L. 79, Sec. 10010

[56] United States Department of Agriculture. USDA Announces Specialty Crop Block Grant Program—Historic Farm Bill Support Available through State Departments of Agriculture. Press Release. April 17, 2014. http://www.usda.gov/wps/portal/usda/usdahome?contentidonly=true&contentid=2014/04/0064.xml

[57] Ralph M. Chite. The 2014 Farm Bill (P.L. 113–79): Summary and Side-by-Side. Congressional Research Service. February 12, 2014. http://nationalaglawcenter.org/wp-content/uploads/2014/02/R43076.pdf.

[58] Ralph M. Chite. The 2014 Farm Bill (P.L. 113–79): Summary and Side-by-Side. Congressional Research Service. February 12, 2014. http://nationalaglawcenter.org/wp-content/uploads/2014/02/R43076.pdf.

[59] Ralph M. Chite. The 2014 Farm Bill (P.L. 113–79): Summary and Side-by-Side. Congressional Research Service. February 12, 2014. http://nationalaglawcenter.org/wp-content/uploads/2014/02/R43076.pdf.

[60] 113 P.L. 79, Section 12101

BOX 4.1

Citizens' Petition Makes it into the Farm Bill

The Food and Drug Administration (FDA) is responsible for developing a standard of identity for commodities such as honey. On March 3, 2006, trade organizations that represent businesses engaged in the production, import, export, packaging, and marketing of honey submitted a citizens' petition to the FDA requesting that the agency adopt a standard definition for honey. Honey is one of three products infamous for being adulterated.[a] (The other two are olive oil and juice.) The petitioners suggested that their proposed standard would "promote honesty and fair dealing" in the best interest of both the consumer and the honey industry.

In August 2006, the FDA responded by stating that it lacked the resources to respond substantively to the petition.[b] In October 2011, the FDA formally denied the petition, stating that it did not find the suggested standard of honey appropriate for adoption.[c,d]

The Agricultural Act of 2014 specifically states that the Secretary of Agriculture "shall submit to the Commissioner of Food and Drugs a report describing how an appropriate Federal standard for the identity of honey would be in the interest of consumers, the honey industry, and United States agriculture."[e] In the Miscellaneous Title, Title XII, Congress directed the Secretary to "take into consideration the March 2006, Standard of Identity citizens' petition filed with the Food and Drug Administration" in the preparation of the Honey Report.

In an action unrelated to the Farm Bill, the FDA issued draft guidance in April 2014 explaining the agency's current thinking on the topic of honey labeling and a standard of identify for honey.[f] The FDA explained that current regulations addressing misbranding and adulteration address the concerns espoused in the citizens' petition with respect to honey and it provided guidance on its current regulations for the honey industry. The USDA did not collaborate with the FDA on this guidance document.[g]

Section 10012 of the Agricultural Act of 2014 required the Agricultural Marketing Service (AMS) branch of the USDA to issue a report for the Secretary to send to the FDA Commissioner on the standard of identity for honey. In August 2014, AMS issued a Notice in the Federal Register requesting comments on how a federal standard for the identity of honey would benefit consumers, the honey industry, and United States agriculture and specifically consider the 2006 citizen's petition.[h] The comment period was extended into October 2014[i] and the agency is reviewing the comments.

[a]Catherine Zuckerman. Food Fraud: Labels on What We Eat Often Mislead. *National Geographic*. July 12, 2013. http://news.nationalgeographic.com/news/2013/07/130712-food-fraud-science-economic-adulteration-seafood-honey-juice/

[b]http://www.regulations.gov/contentStreamer?objectId=09000064816ac176&disposition=attachment&contentType=pdf

[c]http://www.regulations.gov/contentStreamer?objectId=09000064816ac177&disposition=attachment&contentType=pdf

[d]http://www.fda.gov/food/guidanceregulation/guidancedocumentsregulatoryinformation/labelingnutrition/ucm389501.htm#_ftn1

[e]113 P.L. 79, Sec. 10012. REPORT ON HONEY.

[f]Food and Drug Administration. Draft Guidance for Industry: Proper Labeling of Honey and Honey Products. April 2014. http://www.fda.gov/food/guidanceregulation/guidancedocumentsregulatoryinformation/labelingnutrition/ucm389501.htm

[g]Personal communication between the author and the USDA, July 1, 2014.

[h]*Federal Register.* Notices. 2014;79(161): 49279–49280.

[i]http://www.regulations.gov/#!docketDetail;D=AMS-FV-14-0025

The USDA considers this a consumer information requirement, rather than a food safety or traceability necessity, and it is discussed further in Chapter 6, Food Labeling.[61]

USDA Food and Nutrition Programs

The USDA's Food and Nutrition Service (FNS) administers comprehensive federal nutrition assistance programs. FNS's mission is "to increase food security and reduce hunger by providing children and low-income people access to food, a healthful diet and nutrition education in a way that supports American agriculture and inspires public confidence."[62] Table 4.1 provides a description of all of the USDA food and nutrition programs and services administered by FNS, in addition to one where the USDA collaborates with another agency to fulfill the program's mission. The largest of all nutrition assistance programs in the country is the Supplemental Nutrition Assistance Program. This, along with the Special Supplemental Nutrition Program for Women, Infants, and Children will be described in greater detail below, along with a discussion of commodities and the American Indian population.

Interestingly, the Department of Defense (DOD) also has a Fruit and Vegetable Program under which the DOD supplies fresh fruit and vegetables directly to schools. Schools are permitted to allocate a portion of their federal entitlement funds toward this program and can serve the fruits and vegetables during normal meal service.[63] Congress required the USDA to encourage institutions to purchase locally grown produce "to the maximum extent practicable and appropriate" for the NSLP and permits schools to note a geographic preference for the procurement of fruits and vegetables from relevant programs including the DOD program.[64] Due to the success of the DOD's distribution of fresh produce to schools, the Food Distribution Program on Indian Reservations also began purchasing fruit and vegetables through it in 2010.[65] The responsible school, state or local agency, or Indian tribal organization places its order directly with the DOD.

---

[61] http://www.fsis.usda.gov/wps/portal/fsis/topics/food-safety-education/get-answers/food-safety-fact-sheets/food-labeling/country-of-origin-labeling-for-meat-and-chicken/country-of-origin-labeling-for-meat-and-chicken

[62] United States Department of Agriculture. Food and Nutrition Service. About http://www.fns.usda.gov/about-fns

[63] United States Department of Defense. Fresh Fruit and Vegetable Program http://www.fns.usda.gov/fdd/dod-fresh-fruit-and-vegetable-program

[64] 42 USCS § 1758.

[65] United States Department of Defense. Fresh Fruit and Vegetable Program http://www.fns.usda.gov/sites/default/files/DOD_FreshFruitandVegetableProgram2011.pdf

TABLE 4.1

United States Department of Agriculture Food and Nutrition Service Programs and Services

Program Category	Program Name	Description
Food Distribution Programs	Commodity Supplemental Food Program (CSFP)	USDA purchases commodity foods and distributes them, along with administrative funds, to state agencies and Indian tribal organizations to provide food to low-income pregnant and breastfeeding women, new mothers up to one year postpartum, infants, children up to age six years, and elderly people at least 60 years of age. (Unlike WIC, this program provides food directly; eligible persons cannot participate in both programs.)[a]
	Food Distribution Program on Indian Reservations (FDPIR)	USDA purchases commodity foods and distributes them to state agencies and Indian tribal organizations, which distribute food to low-income Native Americans residing on Indian reservations, in designated areas near reservations, or in Oklahoma Tribal Jurisdictions.
	The Emergency Food Assistance Program (TEFAP)	USDA purchases commodity foods and distributes them, along with administrative funds, to state distributing agencies. These provide the food to local agencies such as food banks, which distribute the food to soup kitchens and food pantries that directly serve the public.[b]
	Nutrition Services Incentive Program (NSIP)	Although originally administered by the USDA, NSIP appropriation was transferred to the Administration on Aging in 2003. NSIP provides funding to state agencies and eligible Indian tribal organizations to be used to purchase commodity food products from the USDA for older individuals.[c] USDA donates additional food, called "bonus foods," to NSIP when feasible.[d]
Child Nutrition Programs	Child and Adult Care Food Program (CACFP)	USDA provides cash reimbursement, and donates agricultural foods or cash-in-lieu of donated foods to institutions that serve infants, preschool children, and children younger than 12 years in child care centers and homes, older children in at-risk afterschool programs and emergency homeless shelters, and disabled and older adults in adult day care centers. CACFP support may include breakfast, lunch, dinner, and snacks.[e]
	Fresh Fruit and Vegetable Program (FFVP)	USDA provides state education agencies money to reimburse low-income elementary schools nationwide for providing students with free fresh fruits and vegetables. The produce must be provided during hours outside of the National School Lunch Program and School Breakfast Program.[f] All 50 states, the District of Columbia, Guam, Puerto Rico and the Virgin Islands participate in FFVP.[g]

TABLE 4.1

Continued

Program Category	Program Name	Description
	National School Lunch Program (NSLP)	USDA provides state education agencies cash subsidies and donated commodities to reimburse school districts and independent schools that take part in the lunch program. Participating schools must serve lunches that meet federal requirements and offer free or reduced price lunches to income-eligible children. School food authorities can also be reimbursed for snacks served to children through age 18 years in afterschool educational or enrichment programs.[h]
	School Breakfast Program (SBP)	USDA provides state education agencies cash subsidies to reimburse school districts and independent schools that take part in the breakfast program. Participating schools must serve breakfasts that meet federal requirements and offer free or reduced price lunches to income-eligible children.[i]
	Special Milk Program (SMP)	USDA provides state education agencies money to reimburse participating schools, child care institutions, and eligible camps for each half pint of pasteurized fat-free or 1% milk they serve. Participating entities agree to use the federal reimbursement to reduce the selling price of milk to all children.
	Summer Food Service Program (SFSP)	USDA provides money to state agencies to reimburse providers who serve free healthy meals to children and teens (younger than 19 years) in low-income areas during the summer months.[j] These meals are often combined with summer camps or activities. The goal of SFSP is to fill the gap for children who rely on the NSLP and SBP during the school year.
Supplemental Nutrition Assistance	Supplemental Nutrition Assistance Program (SNAP)	USDA works with state agencies to provide a monthly financial allotment based on the Thrifty Food Plan that recipients can use to purchase almost any food. SNAP was formerly the Food Stamp Program, but now benefits are distributed on EBT cards, rather than through paper stamps. The USDA and state agencies additionally provide SNAP-Education based on the Dietary Guidelines for Americans.
Women, Infants, and Children Programs	Special Supplemental Nutrition Program for Women, Infants, and Children (WIC)	USDA provides grants to states for supplemental foods, health care referrals, and nutrition education for low-income pregnant, breastfeeding, and non-breastfeeding postpartum women, and to infants and children up to age five years who are found to be at nutritional risk. The WIC package includes an established set of foods selected to be beneficial to participants, such as fruit, vegetables, yogurt, milk, and whole grains.[k]

(continued)

TABLE 4.1
Continued

Program Category	Program Name	Description
	WIC Farmers' Market Nutrition Program (FMNP)	USDA provides cash grants to state agencies that administer the program and determine eligibility of both the WIC participants and market providers. In addition to their regular WIC benefits, FMNP WIC participants are issued FMNP coupons that can be used to buy eligible foods from farmers, farmers' markets, or roadside stands that have been approved by the state agency to accept FMNP coupons. The coupons are redeemed for reimbursement by the state agency.[l]
Senior Farmers' Market Nutrition	Senior Farmers' Market Nutrition Program (SFMNP)	USDA awards grants to states, territories, and federally recognized Indian tribal governments to provide low-income seniors who are at least 60 years old with coupons that can be exchanged for eligible foods at farmers' markets, roadside stands, and community supported agriculture programs.[m]

Source: USDA Food and Nutrition Service Programs and Services. http://www.fns.usda.gov/programs-and-services

Notes: [a]United States Department of Agriculture. Commodity Supplemental Food Program. Fact Sheet. http://www.fns.usda.gov/sites/default/files/pfs-csfp.pdf

[b]The Emergency Food Assistance Program. Fact Sheet. July 2013. http://www.fns.usda.gov/sites/default/files/pfs-tefap.pdf

[c]Department of Health and Human Service Administration on Aging. Nutrition Services Incentive Program.

[d]United States Department of Agriculture. Nutrition Services Incentive Program. Fact Sheet. http://www.fns.usda.gov/sites/default/files/pfs-nsip.pdf

[e]http://www.fns.usda.gov/cacfp/why-cacfp-important

[f]Fresh Fruit and Vegetable Program. Fact Sheet. September 2013. http://www.fns.usda.gov/sites/default/files/FFVPFactSheet.pdf

[g]http://www.fns.usda.gov/ffvp/program-history

[h]National School Lunch Program. Fact Sheet. http://www.fns.usda.gov/sites/default/files/NSLPFactSheet.pdf

[i]National School Breakfast Program. Fast Sheet. http://www.fns.usda.gov/sites/default/files/SBPfactsheet.pdf

[j]Summer Food Service Program. Fact Sheet. http://www.fns.usda.gov/es/summer-food-service-program-fact-sheet

[k]http://www.fns.usda.gov/pressrelease/2014/003114

[l]http://www.fns.usda.gov/fmnp/overview

[m]http://www.fns.usda.gov/sfmnp/overview

Comparing SNAP and WIC

The Supplemental Nutrition Assistance Program (SNAP) is the largest of all the USDA food and nutrition programs. Although much smaller, the Special Supplemental Nutrition Program for Women, Infants, and Children (WIC) is often compared to SNAP in political debates and is recognized as a successful program. SNAP is reauthorized pursuant to the Farm Bill, while the Healthy,

Hunger-Free Kids Act of 2010 reauthorized funding and set new policy for WIC, among other programs.[66]

SNAP

SNAP is an entitlement program. This means that the government guarantees a certain benefit to a particular group or segment of the population by allocating funding to cover all potential recipients. Funding is not subject to annual review. SNAP benefits are conditioned on the financial income of the recipient. During times of economic downturn, SNAP is considered the nation's primary safety net and is referred to as "the nation's first line of defense against hunger."[67] The program depends on federal–state partnerships and is administered by state agencies.

SNAP was formerly known as the Food Stamps Program. In addition to creating low agricultural prices, the Great Depression created food insecurity and reduced purchasing power in the general population. The first Farm Bill was enacted to address this problem. Farmers produced crop surpluses, but the problem of hunger persisted. From 1939 to 1943, Congress ran a program that distributed food stamps at a cost to participants. For every $1 worth of orange stamps that participants purchased, they received 50 cents worth of blue stamps. Orange stamps could be used to purchase any food and blue stamps could be used to buy agricultural surpluses.[68] The government ended the program when the economic situation of the country started to improve, but many in Congress sought to enact a permanent program.

In 1961, President Kennedy passed an Executive Order forming a Food Stamp Pilot Program, and Congress passed permanent legislation with the Food Stamp Act of 1964.[69] The stated goals were to strengthen the agricultural economy and provide improved levels of nutrition among low-income households.[70] Participants were still required to purchase food stamps. This legislation also created federal–state partnerships to administer the program. In the 1970s, the government established uniform national eligibility standards and work requirements but expanded the program to reach more people. In 1977, Congress eliminated the requirement to purchase benefits. In the 1980s, however, the government increased restrictions on the receipt of SNAP benefits[71] and

---

[66] United States Department of Agriculture. Food and Nutrition Service. Cooperation in USDA Studies and Evaluations, and Full Use of Federal Funds in Nutrition Assistance Programs Nondiscretionary Provisions of the Healthy, Hunger-Free Kids Act of 2010, Public Law 111–296. Final Rule. *Federal Register.* 2011;June 29;76(125):37979–37983. http://www.ncbi.nlm.nih.gov/pubmed/21721318

[67] http://www.usda.gov/wps/portal/usda/usdahome?contentid=2012/09/0307.xml

[68] http://www.fns.usda.gov/snap/short-history-snap

[69] http://www.fns.usda.gov/snap/short-history-snap

[70] http://www.fns.usda.gov/snap/short-history-snap

[71] http://www.fns.usda.gov/snap/short-history-snap

participation decreased.[72] In 1988, a law was enacted to permit pilot programs for Electronic Benefits Transfer (EBT) cards, which are similar to debit cards. As of 2004, all 50 states, the District of Columbia and U.S. territories accepted EBT cards.

Under the 2008 Farm Bill, Congress made EBT cards the sole method to redeem benefits, prohibiting the issuance of food stamps as of June 2009.[73] Under this farm bill, the Food Stamp Program was renamed the Supplemental Nutrition Assistance Program (SNAP). Congress directed the USDA FNS to carry out pilot projects to identify methods that could reduce overweight and obesity and improve the dietary and health status of SNAP-eligible households.

Participation increased sharply during the economic recession in 2010 and reached its peak in 2013, when there were 47,636,000 participants in the SNAP program.[74] This is more than double the participation rate in 2004. The rate dropped to 46.5 million in 2014. The total cost of the program in 2013 was close to $80 billion.[75] Approximately 16% of SNAP benefits are provided to households with disabled persons, 9% go to households with senior citizens, and 49% of SNAP participants are children, with almost two-thirds of SNAP children living in single-parent households.[76]

The basis of SNAP allotments is the USDA's food plan model called the "Thrifty Food Plan." It was revised in 2006 based on the 2005 Dietary Guidelines for Americans as well as the 2005 MyPyramid Food Guidance System.[77] The goal of the Thrifty Food Plan is to provide a representative healthful and minimal cost meal plan to help SNAP beneficiaries achieve a nutritious diet with limited resources. [78] The Plan assumes that all food purchased is consumed at home. Note that the USDA created three other food plans that are used for purposes other than SNAP: the Low-Cost, Moderate-Cost, and Liberal Food Plan; implementing these for SNAP would require an increase in SNAP benefit dollars.

The maximum monthly allotment for SNAP in 2014–2015 was $194 for one person and $649 for a household of four people.[79] The allotments increase with

---

[72] SNAP National Level Annual Summary: Participation and Costs, 1969–2013 http://www.fns.usda.gov/sites/default/files/pd/SNAPsummary.pdf

[73] USDA Food Stamp Provisions of the Farm Bill. http://www.fns.usda.gov/sites/default/files/arra/070308.pdf from website: SNAP 2008 Farm Bill http://www.fns.usda.gov/snap/2008-farm-bill

[74] SNAP National Level Annual Summary: Participation and Costs, 1969–2013. http://www.fns.usda.gov/sites/default/files/pd/SNAPsummary.pdf Available for UPDATE http://www.fns.usda.gov/pd/supplemental-nutrition-assistance-program-snap

[75] SNAP National Level Annual Summary: Participation and Costs, 1969–2013. http://www.fns.usda.gov/sites/default/files/pd/SNAPsummary.pdf Available for UPDATE http://www.fns.usda.gov/pd/supplemental-nutrition-assistance-program-snap

[76] SNAP to Health. FAQ. http://www.snaptohealth.org/snap/snap-frequently-asked-questions/

[77] A. Carlson, M. Lino, W-Y. Juan, K. Hanson, P. P. Basiotis. *Thrifty Food Plan, 2006*. (CNPP-19). U.S. Department of Agriculture, Center for Nutrition Policy and Promotion, 2007.

[78] A. Carlson, M. Lino, W-Y. Juan, K. Hanson, P. P. Basiotis. *Thrifty Food Plan, 2006*. (CNPP-19). U.S. Department of Agriculture, Center for Nutrition Policy and Promotion, 2007.

[79] http://www.fns.usda.gov/snap/how-much-could-i-receive

each additional person. In 2013, the average monthly benefit for individuals throughout the country was $133.07,[80] and $480 for a four-person household.[81]

The definition of "eligible food" includes (1) any food or food product intended for human consumption except alcoholic beverages, tobacco, and hot foods and hot food products prepared for immediate consumption; (2) seeds and plants to grow foods for personal consumption; (3) meals prepared and delivered by an authorized meal delivery service, served by an authorized communal dining facility, or served by a group-living arrangement facility to eligible persons, including persons who are 60 years of age or older or who receive supplemental security income benefits or disability or blindness payments; (4) meals prepared and served to narcotic addicts or alcoholics and their live-in children by a drug or alcoholic treatment and rehabilitation center; (6) meals prepared and served by a shelter for battered women and children; (7) meals prepared for and served by an authorized public or private nonprofit establishment, approved by an appropriate state or local agency, serving homeless SNAP eligible persons (e.g., soup kitchen, temporary shelter); (8) meals prepared by a restaurant that contracts with an appropriate state agency to serve meals to eligible persons at concessional (low or reduced) prices; and (9) in the case of certain eligible households living in areas of Alaska where access to food stores is extremely difficult and the households rely on hunting and fishing for subsistence, equipment for the purpose of procuring food for eligible households, including nets, lines, hooks, fishing rods, harpoons, knives, and other equipment necessary for subsistence hunting and fishing.[82,83]

As mentioned, the Agricultural Act of 2014 changed retailer qualifications. In order for a food retailer to be approved to accept SNAP benefits, it must offer for sale, on a continuous basis, a variety of at least seven foods (an increase from three) in each of the four categories of staple foods, including perishable foods in at least three (an increase from two) of the categories, or more than 50% of the retailer's total sales must derive from staple foods.[84] This 50% allowance was in place prior to the 2014 Farm Bill and remained unchanged. The four categories of staple foods are: meat, poultry, or fish; bread or cereals; vegetables or fruit; and dairy products.[85] The USDA is planning to propose a regulation to implement this change by the end of 2015, with the goal of finalizing it in 2016. Notably, this condition does not require that SNAP participants purchase any of these staple foods, rather they simply must be made available.

The restaurant meal program, referenced in (8) above, is an optional program for state and local agencies to contract with a restaurant to prepare and

---

[80] http://www.fns.usda.gov/sites/default/files/pd/18SNAPavg$PP.pdf For UPDATE: http://www.fns.usda.gov/pd/supplemental-nutrition-assistance-program-snap

[81] http://www.cbpp.org/cms/index.cfm?fa=view&id=2226

[82] 7 CFR 271.2

[83] 7 USCS § 2012

[84] 7 USCS § 2012.

[85] 7 USCS § 2012.

serve or deliver low-cost meals to homeless persons, elderly persons and social security recipients, and in the case of meal delivery services, to elderly persons or handicapped persons and their spouses.[86] Only a small handful of states run a SNAP restaurant program.[87]

A third location where SNAP benefits may be accepted is at farmers' markets. The USDA describes a farmers' market as a multistall market at which farmer–producers sell agricultural products directly to the public at a central or fixed location.[88] Farmers' markets typically sell fresh produce but may also sell meat, dairy products, or grain-based products. Participating farmers' markets must accept EBT cards.[89] The government is permitted, however, to waive the cost of the electronic benefit transfer point-of-sale equipment, supplies, and services for farmers' markets, unlike for approved for-profit retailers and restaurants, which must pay 100% of the costs.[90] Every state and the District of Columbia have farmers' markets that accept SNAP benefits. Some cities and states have programs that provide SNAP recipients who spend money at a farmers' market extra dollars to purchase fruit and vegetables there.[91,92]

SNAP Debate

Most SNAP recipients purchase food from authorized SNAP retailers. In this scenario, beneficiaries can purchase any food or food product intended for human consumption except alcoholic beverages and hot foods prepared for immediate consumption.[93] This does not include food-type products labeled as dietary supplements, such as energy drinks, but does include energy drinks labeled as beverages. Several policymakers have suggested that SNAP benefits should be better aligned with food that has positive nutritional benefits, while those who oppose restructuring benefits argue that SNAP recipients should be able to make their own food choices. The debate centers around the latent conflict between a federally funded program intended to provide nutrition assistance and the lax requirements for foods that qualify for purchase. Although

[86] 7 CFR 278.1.

[87] Marion Nestle. Using SNAP Benefits for Fast Food Restaurants Is a State Decision. September 14, 2011. http://www.theatlantic.com/health/archive/2011/09/using-snap-benefits-for-fast-food-restaurants-is-a-state-decision/245085/

[88] http://www.fns.usda.gov/ebt/what-farmers-market

[89] http://www.fns.usda.gov/sites/default/files/snap/SNAP-FM-0514.xlsx Available from: Learn About SNAP Benefits at Farmers' Markets. http://www.fns.usda.gov/ebt/learn-about-snap-benefits-farmers-markets

[90] 113 P.L. 79, Sec. 4002.

[91] C. R. Young, J. L. Aquilante, S. Solomon, L. Colby, M. A. Kawinzi, N. Uy, et al. Improving Fruit and Vegetable Consumption Among Low-Income Customers at Farmers Markets: Philly Food Bucks, Philadelphia, Pennsylvania, 2011. *Preventing Chronic Disease*. 2013;10:120356.

[92] GrowNYC. Health Bucks. http://www.grownyc.org/greenmarket/ebt/healthbucks

[93] 7 CFR 271.2

SNAP is run through a federal–state partnership, states cannot veer from the federal program requirements. Congress is the only entity that can make substantive changes to the program; however, the USDA is permitted to conduct pilot projects.

In 2004, Minnesota requested a waiver from the USDA to allow the state to prohibit the use of food stamps for the purchase of most types of candy and soft drinks. The USDA denied this request, stating that it would stigmatize food stamp recipients.[94] In 2010, New York City and New York State requested authorization from the USDA to conduct a two-year demonstration program to remove sugar-sweetened beverages from the list of allowable SNAP purchases in the city.[95] New York City argued that SNAP was created to further the health and nutritional quality of low-income households, but sugary beverages are a unique contributor to obesity and diabetes, and the burden of these diseases was very high among income-eligible residents of the city.[96] The city argued that the "federal government spends hundreds of millions of dollars to prevent obesity and diabetes. It shouldn't simultaneously subsidize the largest single contributor to those conditions." [97] Generally, public health groups support this viewpoint,[98] and likewise support research that would provide data to inform such policy decisions.[99]

The Food Research and Action Center (FRAC) is a food insecurity advocacy organization that represents the viewpoint of many antihunger groups nationwide. It responded to the suggestion that food choice be more restricted under SNAP by arguing (1) that such a move would unfairly single-out low-income people by restricting their food choices; (2) no clear standards exist to define foods as healthy or unhealthy; (3) it is unfair to implement restrictions when many recipients lack reasonable access to eligible foods at affordable prices; and (4) revised requirements would increase program complexity and cost.[100] Both

---

[94] John Skorburg. Feds Deny Minnesota Request for Ban on Junk Food Purchases with Food Stamps. August 1, 2004. http://news.heartland.org/newspaper-article/2004/08/01/feds-deny-minnesota-request-ban-junk-food-purchases-food-stamps

[95] New York City. Removing SNAP Subsidy for Sugar-Sweetened Beverages. October 2010. http://www.nyc.gov/html/doh/downloads/pdf/cdp/cdp-snap-faq.pdf

[96] New York City. Removing SNAP Subsidy for Sugar-Sweetened Beverages. October 2010. http://www.nyc.gov/html/doh/downloads/pdf/cdp/cdp-snap-faq.pdf

[97] New York City. Removing SNAP Subsidy for Sugar-Sweetened Beverages. October 2010. http://www.nyc.gov/html/doh/downloads/pdf/cdp/cdp-snap-faq.pdf

[98] David S. Ludwig, Susan J. Blumenthal, Walter C. Willett. Opportunities to Reduce Childhood Hunger and Obesity Restructuring the Supplemental Nutrition Assistance Program (the Food Stamp Program). *JAMA*. 2012;308(24):2567–2568.

[99] K. D. Brownell, D. S. Ludwig. The Supplemental Nutrition Assistance Program, Soda, and USDA Policy Who Benefits? *JAMA*. 2011;306(12):1370–1371.

[100] Food Research and Action Center. A Review of Strategies to Bolster SNAP's Role in Improving Nutrition as well as Food Security. January 2013. frac.org/wp-content/uploads/2011/06/SNAPstrategies.pdf

FRAC and the USDA have argued that limiting product choice among SNAP recipients could be stigmatizing.[101,102]

It is worth noting that the processed food industry also benefits from SNAP recipients' ability to use benefits to purchase manufactured food products.[103] Food companies and trade organizations have lobbied against program reforms. In response to the New York City request, a representative from the American Beverage Association objected, arguing that the government should not tell people what they can drink and that singling out sugary beverages is "discriminatory and unfair."[104]

The USDA denied New York City's request for a waiver in August 2011.[105] The USDA rested its decision on the following concerns: the scale and scope of the proposal was too large and complex, there would be operational challenges to enacting the demonstration project that would need to be resolved, there could be retailer confusion over which products qualify, there could be stigma for SNAP participants at the point of sale, and the proposed evaluation design did not ensure an effect on obesity and health.[106] States continue to debate this issue.[107,108,109] Legislators across the country have proposed a range of bills that would permit their state to seek a waiver from the USDA, seek to conduct a pilot program, or pass a resolution urging Congress to remove certain foods from SNAP eligibility.[110] Some of the bills specify which foods the legislators believe should be removed from SNAP coverage; this list often includes sugar-sweetened beverages and candy.[111,112,113]

Certain groups seek to cut the amount of SNAP benefits in order to reduce government spending.[114] Both public health and food insecurity groups oppose

---

[101] Food Research and Action Center. A Review of Strategies to Bolster SNAP's Role in Improving Nutrition as well as Food Security. January 2013. frac.org/wp-content/uploads/2011/06/SNAPstrategies.pdf

[102] United States Department of Agriculture. Food and Nutrition Service. Supplemental Nutrition Assistance Program (SNAP) Implications of Restricting the use of Food Stamp Benefits—A Summary. Available at: http://www.fns.usda.gov/sites/default/files/arra/FSPFoodRestrictions.pdf

[103] M. Simon. Food Stamps: Follow the Money Are Corporations Profiting from Hungry Americans? Eat Drink Politics, June 2012.

[104] K. D. Brownell, D. S. Ludwig. The Supplemental Nutrition Assistance Program, Soda, and USDA Policy Who Benefits? *JAMA*. 2011;306(12):1370–1371.

[105] www.foodpolitics.com/wp-content/uploads/SNAP-Waiver-Request-Decision.pdf

[106] www.foodpolitics.com/wp-content/uploads/SNAP-Waiver-Request-Decision.pdf

[107] IL HB 5626 (2014) SNAP waiver requested to specify certain ineligible foods.

[108] IN HB 1105 (2014) Pilot Program for SNAP Benefit Restrictions.

[109] MO HB 1283 (2014) Prohibiting SNAP Benefits for Purchase of Energy Drinks.

[110] J. L. Pomeranz, J. F. Chriqui. The supplemental nutrition assistance program: Analysis of program administration and food law definitions. *American Journal of Preventive Medicine*. (published online ahead of print June 16, 2015).

[111] IL SB 1742 (2013).

[112] SC HB 4651 (2014).

[113] WV SB 262 (2014).

[114] Ron Nixon. House Republicans Pass Deep Cuts in Food Stamps. September 19, 2013. http://www.nytimes.com/2013/09/20/us/politics/house-passes-bill-cutting-40-billion-from-food-stamps.html

this position, and some argue that the amount of benefits should be increased in order to provide recipients with enough funding to provide food throughout the month.[115] Research by the USDA's Economic Research Service suggests that an increase in benefits is associated with a greater percentage of redemptions at superstores where prices tend to be lower, but which may be farther away or require greater travel costs.[116] The authors theorize that the increase in resources are used to accommodate transportation costs.

Access to SNAP approved retailers is an issue for some people. Box 4.2 discusses an alternative program for American Indians living on or near Indian reservations and Oklahoma Tribal Jurisdictions who lack access to SNAP approved retailers. Box 4.2 also provides a history of issues related to the United States government supplying commodity foods to American Indians.

WIC

The Supplemental Nutrition Program for Women, Infants, and Children (WIC) was first piloted in 1972 and then made permanent in 1974.[117] At its inception in 1974, approximately 88,000 people received WIC benefits.[118] Participation rose gradually over the years with the highest usage occurring in 2010 with 9,175,000 recipients.[119] By 2013, participation dropped to 8,663,000.

WIC is administered by the USDA to provide grants to state agencies, which administer the benefits through authorized WIC retailers.[120] Unlike SNAP, WIC is considered a discretionary program and not an entitlement program.[121] Congress does not set aside funds to allow every eligible individual to participate in the program but rather appropriates a specific amount of funds each year for the program. When the program is funded enough to cover all applicants, it functions like an entitlement program, but if not, the program operators must

---

[115] Food Research and Action Center. A Review of Strategies to Bolster SNAP's Role in Improving Nutrition as well as Food Security. January 2013. frac.org/wp-content/uploads/2011/06/SNAPstrategies.pdf

[116] Margaret Andrews, Rhea Bhatta, Michele Ver Ploeg. An alternative to developing stores in food deserts: Can changes in SNAP benefits make a difference? *Applied Economic Perspectives and Policy*. 2013;35(1):150–170.

[117] United States Department of Agriculture. About WIC. http://www.fns.usda.gov/wic/about-wic-wics-mission

[118] WIC Program. National Level Annual Summary: FY 1974–2013. http://www.fns.usda.gov/sites/default/files//pd/wisummary.pdf Available for Updating: http://www.fns.usda.gov/pd/wic-program

[119] WIC Program. National Level Annual Summary: FY 1974–2013. http://www.fns.usda.gov/sites/default/files//pd/wisummary.pdf Available for Updating: http://www.fns.usda.gov/pd/wic-program.

[120] United States Department of Agriculture. About WIC. http://www.fns.usda.gov/wic/about-wic-wic-glance

[121] David A. Super. The Political Economy of Entitlement. 104 *Columbia Law Review*. 2004;633.

BOX 4.2

History of American Indian Commodity Issues

There are 566 federally recognized American Indian and Alaska Native tribes and villages in the United States.[a] The U.S. Constitution recognizes tribes as a distinct entity, allowing Congress to "regulate commerce with foreign nations, and among the several states, and with the Indian tribes."[b] The United States Supreme Court has explained that, "Indian tribes are 'domestic dependent nations' that exercise 'inherent sovereign authority.'"[c]

The Food Distribution Program on Indian Reservations (FDPIR) began in 1977 as an alternative to the Supplemental Nutrition Assistance Program (SNAP) to assist American Indians who do not have easy access to SNAP offices or authorized food stores.[d] This applies to families and the elderly living on or near Indian reservations and Oklahoma Tribal Jurisdictions. (Oklahoma does not have reservations.) As of 2014, there were approximately 276 tribes receiving benefits under FDPIR through 112 Indian tribal organizations and five state agencies.[e] The USDA, however, had already begun purchasing and providing commodity foods to American Indians in the 1930s under what was called a USDA Donated Foods Program.[f]

In recent history, American Indians have among the highest rates of obesity and diabetes in the United States. These diseases were not found among American Indian communities prior to the 1930s. One group in particular, the Pimas, have among the highest rates in the world.[g,h] The Pimas traditionally lived along the Gila River in Arizona and used irrigation to raise crops of corn, squash, and two species of beans. They also fished, hunted local game, and gathered wild crops.[i,j] In the 1860s and 1870s, settlers began moving into the lands north of the Pima homeland and diverted water away for cattle ranches, farmland irrigation, and daily life in the arid climate.[k] The Gila river was reduced and the Pimas suffered; initially, they were starving.[l] The federal government, through the military, began distributing commodity foods of white flour, lard, and sugar to the Pimas.[m] These foods were very different from their traditional diet. The Pimas began to cook "fry bread," which is flat bread deep fried in lard, and which is now considered a traditional food of American Indians.[n] In the 1920s the government built what became known as the Coolidge Dam, which further depleted water supplies to the Pimas.[o]

In the 1930s the commodity list increased to include staple items of bacon, lard, cheese, and beans, and then more additions were made a couple of decades later to include canned meats, vegetables, fruit, dry cereals, and dried or evaporated milk.[p] The high prevalence of diabetes and obesity among the Pimas is partially attributed to the commodity program.

The FDPIR now has a list of about 70 food products among which recipients can choose.[q] FDPIR participants eligible to participate in SNAP may participate in both programs but not within the same month.[r] American Indians live below the poverty level at a greater rate than the rest of the U.S. population.[s] Access to food stores can be a problem in Native American communities. For example, in 2008, there was one small market on the Gila River Reservation and the full service supermarket was an hour outside of town.[t] This partially drives participation in FDPIR rather than SNAP for certain groups.

In the Agricultural Act of 2014, Congress required the USDA and the FDA to permit "the donation to and serving of traditional food" to licensed child care facilities, child nutrition programs, senior meal programs, and hospitals, clinics, and long-term care facilities that primarily serve American Indians.[u] The definition of "traditional food" includes wild game meat, fish, seafood, marine mammals, plants, and berries.[v] The stated purpose for providing access to traditional foods in these food service programs is "to encourage increased

BOX 4.2

Continued

consumption of traditional foods to decrease health disparities among Indians, particularly Alaska Natives and to provide alternative food options for food service programs."[w]

[a]United States Department of the Interior. Indian Affairs FAQ. http://www.bia.gov/FAQs/

[b]U.S. Constitution. Article 1, Section 8

[c]*Michigan v. Bay Mills Indian Community*, 134 S. Ct. 2024, 2030 (2014).

[d]Food Distribution Program on Indian Reservations. Fact Sheet. June 2014. http://www.fns.usda.gov/sites/default/files/pfs-fdpir.pdf

[e]Food Distribution Program on Indian Reservations. Fact Sheet. June 2014. http://www.fns.usda.gov/sites/default/files/pfs-fdpir.pdf

[f]*Commodity Distribution Procedures Handbook*. Oklahoma Department of Human Services. 2003.

[g]Mary Story, Marguerite Evans, Richard R. Fabsitz, Theresa E. Clay, Bonnie Holy Rock, and Brenda Broussard The Epidemic of Obesity in American Indian Communities and the Need for Childhood Obesity-Prevention Programs. *American Journal of Clinical Nutrition*. 1999;69(4):747S–754S.

[h]Jovana J. Brown. Enduring Legacies Native Cases. Evergreen State College. http://www.evergreen.edu/tribal/cases/

[i]Jovana J. Brown. Enduring Legacies Native Cases. Evergreen State College. http://www.evergreen.edu/tribal/cases/

[j]*UNNATURAL CAUSES is inequality making us sick*? Bad Sugar. Annotated Transcript.

[k]Jovana J. Brown. Enduring Legacies Native Cases. Evergreen State College. http://www.evergreen.edu/tribal/cases/

[l]*UNNATURAL CAUSES is inequality making us sick*? Bad Sugar. Annotated Transcript.

[m]*UNNATURAL CAUSES is inequality making us sick*? Bad Sugar. Annotated Transcript.

[n]*UNNATURAL CAUSES is inequality making us sick*? Bad Sugar. Annotated Transcript.

[o]*UNNATURAL CAUSES is inequality making us sick*? Bad Sugar. Annotated Transcript.

[p]*UNNATURAL CAUSES is inequality making us sick*? Bad Sugar. Annotated Transcript.

[q]Food Distribution Program on Indian Reservations. Fact Sheet. June 2014. http://www.fns.usda.gov/sites/default/files/pfs-fdpir.pdf

[r]Food Distribution Program on Indian Reservations. Fact Sheet. June 2014. http://www.fns.usda.gov/sites/default/files/pfs-fdpir.pdf

[s]Mary Story, Marguerite Evans, Richard R. Fabsitz, Theresa E. Clay, Bonnie Holy Rock, and Brenda Broussard The Epidemic of Obesity in American Indian Communities and the Need for Childhood Obesity-Prevention Programs. *American Journal of Clinical Nutrition*. 1999;69(4):747S–754S.

[t]*UNNATURAL CAUSES is inequality making us sick*? Bad Sugar. Annotated Transcript.

[u]113 P.L. 79, Sec. 4033 (2014).

[v]113 P.L. 79, Sec. 4033 (2014).

[w]113 P.L. 79, Sec. 4033 (2014).

figure out a system to prioritize funding. For discretionary programs such as WIC, the options range from reducing benefit levels, establishing wait lists, shutting down after the funds are exhausted, or prioritizing spending among potential recipients.[122]

[122] David A. Super. The Political Economy of Entitlement, 104 *Columbia Law Review*. 2004; 633.

Congress authorizes funding for the WIC program for education, medical referrals, and financial benefits for food to low-income, nutritionally at risk pregnant, breastfeeding, and postpartum women, as well as infants and children up to age five years. Because WIC is not an entitlement program, if the government does not have enough funding to provide WIC benefits for all those in need, the USDA directs state WIC agencies to provide benefits through the following priority levels: (1) Pregnant women, breastfeeding women and infants at nutritional risk as related to medical conditions that demonstrate the need for supplemental foods; (2) Infants of WIC participants who participated during pregnancy, up to six months of age, and infants up to six months of age born to women who were not WIC participants during pregnancy but whose medical records document that they were at nutritional risk during pregnancy; (3) Children at nutritional risk as demonstrated by documented medical conditions; (4) Pregnant women, breastfeeding women, and infants at nutritional risk because of an inadequate dietary pattern; (5) Children at nutritional risk because of an inadequate dietary pattern; and (6) Postpartum women at nutritional risk.[123] States have the option of expanding the program to a seventh category: Individuals certified for WIC solely due to homelessness or migrancy, or previously certified participants who might regress in nutritional status without continued provision of supplemental foods.[124]

WIC provides vouchers to recipients to obtain only the foods in a pre-established food package, called the WIC food package, from authorized WIC vendors. Some states have moved to EBT cards,[125] while other states are experimenting with a single EBT card that allows access to WIC and other program benefits such as SNAP on one card.[126] All states are required to transition to EBT cards for WIC by October 1, 2020.

Congress directs the USDA to "conduct a scientific review of the supplemental foods available under the program and amend the supplemental foods available, as necessary, to reflect nutrition science, public health concerns, and cultural eating patterns," as frequently "as necessary to reflect the most recent scientific knowledge, but not less than every 10 years."[127] In 2005, the Institute of Medicine issued a report, *WIC Food Packages: Time for a Change* suggesting the USDA revise the WIC food package to match dietary guidance for infants and young children and encourage a healthier diet. Based on the IOM report, the USDA issued interim rules to align food packages with more recent nutrition science, promote breastfeeding, increase food options for participants, and provide state agencies with flexibility.[128] WIC state agencies were required to implement

---

[123] 7 CFR 246.7.
[124] 7 CFR 246.7 .
[125] http://www.fns.usda.gov/wic/wic-ebt-activities
[126] http://www.fns.usda.gov/wic/wic-electronic-benefit-transfer-ebt-one-card-considerations
[127] 42 USCS § 1786.
[128] *Federal Register* 79(42), page 12274 (March 4, 2014).

the changes by October 2009 and succeeded in doing so. The USDA issued the final rule updating the nutritional requirements in March 2014.

Different foods are provided to each category of participant. WIC foods include infant cereal, iron-fortified adult cereal, fruit or vegetable juice, eggs, milk, cheese, peanut butter, dried and canned beans, peas and legumes, canned fish, soy-based beverages, tofu, fruits and vegetables, baby foods, yogurt, whole wheat bread, and other whole-grain options.[129] White potatoes are not permitted unless they are an ingredient (but not the primary ingredient) of otherwise approved baby food.[130] Some state agencies permit organic foods on their foods lists. WIC education promotes breastfeeding as the optimal source of nutrition for infants, but if a woman does not breastfeed, WIC provides iron-fortified infant formula. WIC may also cover special infant formulas and medical foods if prescribed by a physician to address a medical condition. Food must be provided free of charge.[131]

Federal law requires the state agency to develop and implement uniform criteria to authorize WIC-approved retailers.[132] The state must consider the business integrity of a vendor and may not authorize stores that engage in prohibited acts, such as providing reduced-cost lottery tickets to recipients. The state must also establish minimum requirements for the variety and quantity of foods that a vendor must stock, including a mandatory minimum of two different fruits, two different vegetables, one whole grain cereal authorized by the state agency, and infant formula purchased from sources permitted by the state agency.[133] A side benefit to the updated, more nutritious WIC food package is that it significantly improved the availability and variety of healthy foods in WIC-authorized retailers, which benefits all consumers in the community.[134]

The WIC Farmers' Market Nutrition Program (FMNP) operates through a federal–state partnership with states, federally recognized tribal organizations, and U.S. territories.[135] Unlike WIC, not all states participate in FMNP. In addition to regular WIC benefits, this program provides WIC participants with coupons that can be redeemed at farms, farmers' markets, or roadside stands that have been approved by the state agency for fresh fruits and vegetables. States can put further restrictions on the program, for example, by requiring the purchase of locally grown produce. As mentioned, white potatoes are not permitted under

---

[129] 79 Federal Register 12274 (March 4, 2014).

[130] 79 Federal Register 12274, 12284 (March 4, 2014).

[131] 7 CFR 246.12.

[132] 7 CFR 246.12.

[133] 7 CFR 246.12.

[134] T. Andreyeva, J. Luedicke, A. E. Middleton, M. W. Long, M. B. Schwartz. Positive Influence of the Revised Special Supplemental Nutrition Program for Women, Infants, and Children Food Packages on Access to Healthy Foods. *Journal of the Academy of Nutrition and Dietetics.* 2012;112(6):850–858.

[135] http://www.fns.usda.gov/fmnp/overview

the traditional WIC food package; likewise, they are the only fresh vegetable excluded from the FMNP.[136]

Questions for Classroom Discussion

CACFP

The Child and Adult Care Food Program (CACFP)'s nutrition guidelines apply to children in child care centers who are of lower socioeconomic status.[137] Is this capitalizing upon an opportunity to promote healthy eating for vulnerable populations or is it ignoring the nutrition needs of children from families of higher socioeconomic means? Should the dietary requirements for CACFP be extended to other licensed care providers? Why or why not?

SNAP

Congress's declaration of policy underlying SNAP is as follows:

> It is hereby declared to be the policy of Congress, in order to promote the general welfare, to safeguard the health and well-being of the Nation's population by raising levels of nutrition among low-income households. Congress hereby finds that the limited food purchasing power of low-income households contributes to hunger and malnutrition among members of such households. Congress further finds that increased utilization of food in establishing and maintaining adequate national levels of nutrition will promote the distribution in a beneficial manner of the Nation's agricultural abundance and will strengthen the Nation's agricultural economy, as well as result in more orderly marketing and distribution of foods. To alleviate such hunger and malnutrition, a supplemental nutrition assistance program is herein authorized which will permit low-income households to obtain a more nutritious diet through normal channels of trade by increasing food purchasing power for all eligible households who apply for participation.[138]

Does the federal government's allowance to purchase any food or beverage product except alcoholic beverages, tobacco, hot foods (unless specifically authorized) further this statement of purpose? Do you agree with changing the definition of eligible food under the SNAP program? If so, how would you address the issues raised by FRAC and the USDA? If not, how would you suggest improving the program for recipients to support health?

---

[136] http://www.nal.usda.gov/wicworks/Topics/FarmersMarketsFinalRuleFactSheet.pdf
[137] http://www.fns.usda.gov/cacfp/why-cacfp-important
[138] 7 USCS § 2011.

As part of the debate over restricting food purchase options discussed above, both the public health groups and the food insecurity groups state that the fact that SNAP recipients can use their own money to purchase sugary beverages supports their position. What type of arguments would they make to support their positions? What do you think about these perspectives?

WIC

Given political barriers and resource constraints, policymakers are often faced with difficult decisions when it comes to programs helping vulnerable populations. Because WIC is not an entitlement program, the government may not have enough WIC benefits for all those in need. As mentioned, the federal government directs state WIC agencies to provide benefits through a pre-established order of priority levels. What are some ethical issues that policy-makers face in making such a determination? How should policy-makers determine these needs? Do you agree with the order described above?

5

Food Safety

Introduction

The concept of food safety can take many forms. Perhaps the most commonly thought of notion related to unsafe food is the acute illness that follows from foodborne contamination threatening the health of all users of the product. Food might also be unsafe if it contains an undisclosed ingredient that is harmful to a portion of the population, such as a common allergen. Another type of unsafe food might occur when an ingredient is unsafe to consume over time, such as trans fat, or becomes unsafe at high levels, such as caffeine. Finally, certain production practices may result in food of questionable safety, subject to inquiry and debate by scientists, as occurred with the addition of growth hormones and antibiotics to food-animal feed. These and similar topics will be discussed in this chapter.

History of Food Safety in the United States

In the 1800s, adulterated and misbranded food and drugs were a relatively accepted part of the American landscape. Harvey Washington Wiley, Chief Chemist of the Bureau of Chemistry, which later became the Food and Drug Administration, worked for years to convince Congress and the American public that a federal law was necessary to prohibit the adulteration and misbranding of food and drugs.[1] During this time period, "reform-minded journalists,"[2] called the Muckrakers, helped expose the dangerous qualities of food and drugs

[1] John P. Swann. FDA's Origin. Food and Drug Administration History Office. http://www.fda.gov/AboutFDA/WhatWeDo/History/Origin/ucm124403.htm

[2] Amanda Foreman. A Brief History of Media Muckraking. *The Wall Street Journal*. July 25, 2014. http://www.wsj.com/articles/a-brief-history-of-media-muckraking-1406330669

available in the marketplace. The most famous exposé was Upton Sinclair's book, *The Jungle,* in which he sought to point out the atrocities of labor conditions for the "workingmen of America."[3] Ultimately, however, his vivid description of the meat packing industry shocked Americans regarding the true condition of meat sold for consumption—diseased, rat infested, and chemically treated—and is widely credited as helping to lead to the passage of the Food and Drug Act of 1906.[4]

The Pure Food and Drugs Act was passed by Congress on June 30, 1906, and signed into law by President Theodore Roosevelt. The Act was administered by the Bureau of Chemistry, which was housed in the Department of Agriculture at the time. The Pure Food and Drugs Act prohibited the manufacture, sale, or transportation of adulterated, misbranded, poisonous or deleterious foods, drugs, medicines, and liquors in interstate commerce.[5] In 1930, the Bureau of Chemistry became the Food and Drug Administration (FDA) and the agency sought to update the 1906 law. Congress resisted, but after more than one hundred people were killed from a poisonous ingredient added to a drug, Congress passed the Food, Drug, and Cosmetic Act in 1938.[6] The FDA was transferred to the Department of Health, Education, and Welfare in 1953, which became the Department of Health and Human Services in 1979.[7]

Today, the FDA has the regulatory authority to protect public health by overseeing the safety and labeling of food.[8] The FDA is responsible for enforcing the Food Drug and Cosmetic Act (FDCA), which prohibits the introduction of adulterated food into interstate commerce. The FDCA defines food as: (1) articles used for food or drink for man or other animals, (2) chewing gum, and (3) articles used for components of any such article.[9] The FDCA defines adulterated food as food that bears or contains any poisonous or deleterious substance that may render it injurious to health or food that bears or contains a poisonous or deleterious substance, pesticide chemical residue, food additive, or color additive that is unsafe.[10]

Although the FDA has primary jurisdiction over most foods, other agencies are involved in food safety. For example, although the FDA has jurisdiction over

---

[3] Upton Sinclair. Dedication. *The Jungle*. New York, NY: Airmont Publishing Company, Inc.; 1965.

[4] Roger I. Roots. A Muckraker's Aftermath: The Jungle of Meat-packing Regulation after a Century, *William Mitchell Law Review*. 2001;27(4): Article 1.

[5] Food and Drug Administration. Regulatory Information. Federal Food and Drugs Act of 1906. http://www.fda.gov/RegulatoryInformation/Legislation/ucm148690.htm

[6] FDA. About FDA. http://www.fda.gov/AboutFDA/WhatWeDo/History/FOrgsHistory/CFSAN/ucm083863.htm

[7] Food and Drug Administration. FDA Organizational Histories. http://www.fda.gov/AboutFDA/WhatWeDo/History/FOrgsHistory/default.htm.

[8] Food and Drug Administration. FDA Basics. What does FDA do? http://www.fda.gov/AboutFDA/Transparency/Basics/ucm194877.htm

[9] 21 USCS § 321(f).

[10] 21 USC § 342.

livestock intended for food, the United States Department of Agriculture (USDA) has jurisdiction over the slaughter and processing of the animals.[11] Similarly, the FDA has jurisdiction over bottled water and water used as an ingredient in food, but the Environmental Protection Agency (EPA) is responsible for the safety and purity of drinking water.[12] Fifteen federal agencies have responsibilities related to food safety as explained further in Table 5.1 below.

The EPA's role in food safety is primarily related to ensuring food is safe from harmful levels of pesticides, but it also addresses such issues as contaminated fish and harmful algae blooms, which can be toxic to humans and animals.[13] Pesticides are agents used to kill or control undesired insects, weeds, rodents, fungi, bacteria, and other organisms. The EPA approves all pesticides to be used on foods and sets tolerances, or maximum residue limits, on the amount of pesticide residue that can lawfully remain on a food.[14] The FDA, however, actually enforces the pesticide tolerances established by the EPA on all food under the FDA's domain,[15] and the USDA tests, samples, analyzes, and reports on pesticide residues under its Pesticide Data Program.[16]

In addition, state and local health departments are directly involved in food safety. The majority of local health departments engage in food safety education to food handlers, operators, and food service establishments for preventive purposes, and to the public during a recall or an outbreak.[17,18] The majority of local health departments are also in charge of regulating, inspecting, and/or licensing food service establishments.[19] Local health departments conduct food inspection in an array of other institutions under their authority, such as grocery stores, day-care facilities, hospitals, and schools. When a food is suspected to be contaminated, local health departments are often the first to receive the report and may initiate recalls.[20] Only a small percentage of local health departments have

---

[11] Neal Fortin. *Food Regulation: Law, Science, Policy, and Practice*. Hoboken, NJ: John Wiley & Sons, Inc.;2009, p. 39.

[12] Neal Fortin. *Food Regulation: Law, Science, Policy, and Practice*. Hoboken, NJ: John Wiley & Sons, Inc.;2009, pp. 39–40.

[13] Environmental Protection Agency. Agriculture. Food Safety. March 13, 2013. http://www.epa.gov/agriculture/tfsy.html#pesticideinfood

[14] Environmental Protection Agency. Pesticides: Topical & Chemical Fact Sheets. The EPA and Food Security. May 2012. http://www.epa.gov/pesticides/factsheets/securty.htm

[15] Environmental Protection Agency. Pesticides: Topical & Chemical Fact Sheets. The EPA and Food Security. May 2012. http://www.epa.gov/pesticides/factsheets/securty.htm

[16] United States Department of Agriculture. Quick Facts about the Pesticide Data Program (PDP). http://www.ams.usda.gov/AMSv1.0/getfile?dDocName=STELDEV3003252

[17] National Association of County and City Health Officials. Local Health Department Roles in Food Safety: Backgrounder. http://www.naccho.org/topics/environmental/foodsafety/upload/Local-Health-Department-Roles-in-Food-Safety-2-5.pdf

[18] National Association of County and City Health Officials. 2013 National Profile of Local Health Departments. (Downloaded from NACCHO website).

[19] National Association of County and City Health Officials. 2013 National Profile of Local Health Departments. (Downloaded from NACCHO website).

[20] National Association of County and City Health Officials. Local Health Department Roles in Food Safety: Backgrounder. http://www.naccho.org/topics/environmental/foodsafety/upload/Local-Health-Department-Roles-in-Food-Safety-2-5.pdf

TABLE 5.1

Federal Agency Food Safety Responsibilities

Department and/or Agency		Responsibility
U.S. Department of Agriculture	Food Safety and Inspection Service	Ensuring the nation's domestic and imported commercial supply of meat, poultry, and egg products is safe, wholesome, and correctly labeled and packaged, and for enforcing the Humane Methods of Slaughter Act of 1978, as amended; providing voluntary fee-for-service inspections for exotic animals; catfish inspection.
	Animal and Plant Health Inspection Service	Preventing the introduction or dissemination of (1) plant pests and (2) livestock pests or diseases.
	Grain Inspection, Packers and Stockyards Administration	Establishing quality standards, inspection procedures, and marketing of grain and other related products.
	Agricultural Marketing Service	Establishing quality and condition standards for, among other things, dairy, fruits, vegetables, and livestock.
	Agricultural Research Service	Providing the scientific research to help ensure that the food supply is safe and secure and that foods meet foreign and domestic regulatory requirements.
	Economic Research Service	Providing analyses of the economic issues affecting the safety of the U.S. food supply.
	National Agricultural Statistics Service	Providing statistical data, including agricultural chemical usage data, related to the safety of the food supply.
	National Institute of Food and Agriculture	Supporting food safety projects in the land-grant university system and other partner organizations that demonstrate an integrated approach to solving problems in applied food safety research, education, or extension.
Department of Health and Human Services	Food and Drug Administration	Ensuring that all domestic and imported foods, excluding meat, poultry, and processed egg products, are safe, wholesome, sanitary, and properly labeled.
	Centers for Disease Control and Prevention	Preventing the transmission, dissemination, and spread of foodborne illness to protect the public health.
Department of Commerce	National Marine Fisheries Service	Providing voluntary, fee-for-service examinations of seafood for safety and quality.
Environmental Protection Agency		Regulating the use of certain chemicals and substances that present an unreasonable risk of injury to health or the environment; issuing regulations to establish, modify, or revoke tolerances for pesticide chemical residues; setting national drinking water quality standards; and consulting with the Food and Drug Administration (FDA) before FDA promulgates regulations for quality standards for bottled water.

TABLE 5.1
Continued

Department and/or Agency		Responsibility
Department of the Treasury	Alcohol and Tobacco Tax and Trade Bureau	Regulating, enforcing, and issuing permits for the production, labeling, and distribution of alcoholic beverages.
Department of Homeland Security	Customs and Border Protection	Inspecting imports, including food products, plants, and live animals, for compliance with U.S. law and assisting all federal agencies in enforcing their regulations at the border.
Federal Trade Commission		Enforcing prohibitions against false, deceptive and unfair advertising for food products, among other things.

Source: GAO Report. GAO-15-180 Federal Food Safety Oversight. Additional Actions Needed to Improve. Table 1. http://www.gao.gov/assets/670/667656.pdf

food testing laboratory facilities, so in the majority of states the state department of health assumes this responsibility.

The Food Safety Modernization Act

In January 2011, President Obama signed the Food Safety Modernization Act (FSMA) with the goal of shifting the federal government's focus to preventing food safety issues, rather than relying primarily on responding to problems. The FSMA is directed at the Department of Health and Human Services (HHS). Most provisions apply to the FDA or require coordination among several federal agencies.[21] For example, the FDA, USDA, and Department of Homeland Security must submit to Congress on a biennial basis a joint food safety and food defense research plan.[22] The FSMA also requires the FDA to collaborate with state departments of health. Select collaborations among federal agencies are outlined in Table 5.2.

The FSMA contains many specific directions to the FDA; several interesting ones are noted here. Provisions of the FSMA require the FDA to engage in pilot projects to develop recommendations for improving the tracking and tracing of food and to work with the USDA to establish a product-tracing system that improves the capacity of the FDA to track and trace domestic or imported food effectively and rapidly.[23] The FDA is required to enact comprehensive, science-based preventive controls including establishing science-based, minimum standards for the safe production and harvesting of produce, overseeing food facilities' implementation of written preventive controls plans, and issuing regulations to protect against intentional food adulteration.[24]

---

[21] 21 USC 2202.

[22] 21 USC 2204.

[23] 21 USC 2223.

[24] Food and Drug Administration Background on Food Safety Modernization Act. FSMA FACTS. July 12, 2011.

TABLE 5.2

Selected Collaborative Mechanisms Involving the Food and Drug Administration and USDA's Food Safety and Inspection Service

Name	Description
Foodborne Diseases Active Surveillance Network (FoodNet)	A collaboration involving the Centers for Disease Control and Prevention (CDC), Food and Drug Administration (FDA), Food Safety and Inspections Service (FSIS), and 10 state health departments. It estimates the number of foodborne illnesses, monitors trends in incidence of specific foodborne illnesses over time, and attributes illnesses to specific foods and settings, among other things.
Healthy People 2020	A national health promotion and disease prevention initiative that includes 42 topic areas, including food safety. FDA and FSIS co-lead the food safety topic area, with an objective of, among other things, reducing rates of infection caused by foodborne pathogens.
Interagency Foodborne Outbreak Response Collaboration	A collaboration involving CDC, FDA, and FSIS to coordinate foodborne illness outbreak investigations.
Interagency Food Safety Analytics Collaboration	A collaboration involving CDC, FDA, and FSIS focusing on projects related to foodborne illness source attribution, the process of estimating the most common food sources responsible for specific foodborne illnesses.
Interagency Residue Control Group	A collaboration involving the Environmental Protection Agency, FDA, FSIS, and other agencies to discuss and resolve chemical residue issues.
Interagency Risk Assessment Consortium	A collaboration involving federal agencies with food safety responsibilities. It works to promote scientific research that will facilitate risk assessments to assist regulatory agencies in fulfilling their specific food-safety risk management mandates.
National Advisory Committee on Microbiological Criteria for Foods	A collaboration involving CDC, FDA, FSIS, and other federal agencies with food safety responsibilities. It develops methodologies for assessing microbiological hazards in foods, among other things.
National Antimicrobial Resistance Monitoring System	A collaboration involving CDC, FDA, FSIS, and state and local health departments that tracks whether foodborne and other bacteria are resistant to the antibiotics used to treat and prevent the spread of illness.
PulseNet	A collaborative surveillance network involving CDC, FDA, FSIS, and public health laboratories in each state. PulseNet uses molecular fingerprinting to connect cases of foodborne infection and detect outbreaks.

Source: GAO Report. GAO-15-180 Federal Food Safety Oversight. Additional Actions Needed to Improve. Table 3 http://www.gao.gov/assets/670/667656.pdf

The FSMA also requires the FDA to promulgate regulations to establish recordkeeping requirements for facilities that manufacture, process, pack, or hold foods designated as "high-risk foods."[25] The FDA issued a request for comments

[25] 21 USC 2223.

and scientific data and information in 2014 to determine which foods should be considered high-risk.[26] The FSMA specifies that the designation of high-risk foods must be based on the: (1) known safety risks of a particular food, including the history and severity of foodborne illness outbreaks attributed to such food, taking into consideration foodborne illness data collected by the Centers for Disease Control and Prevention; (2) likelihood that a particular food has a high potential risk for microbiological or chemical contamination or would support the growth of pathogenic microorganisms due to the nature of the food or the processes used to produce such food; (3) point in the manufacturing process of the food where contamination is most likely to occur; (4) likelihood of contamination and steps taken during the manufacturing process to reduce the possibility of contamination; (5) likelihood that consuming a particular food will result in a foodborne illness due to contamination of the food; and (6) likely or known severity, including health and economic impacts, of a foodborne illness attributed to a particular food.[27]

The FSMA also provided the FDA with new authority over imported food. Importers must verify that foreign food suppliers have preventive controls in place to ensure that the food they produce is safe.[28] Further, the FDA can deny entry of foods if the agency is not allowed to inspect the foreign facility (or enter the country in which it is located).[29]

Foodborne Illness Outbreaks

The FSMA overhauled the federal government's authority to address foodborne illness outbreaks. The Centers for Disease Control and Prevention (CDC) reports that 48 million cases of foodborne illness occur each year in the United States from people consuming contaminated food, resulting in thousands of hospitalizations and approximately 3,000 deaths.[30] Food may be contaminated during the production, processing, distribution, or preparation stages.[31] See Figure 5.1 for the foods associated with foodborne outbreak-associated illnesses from 2008 to 2012. The federal government defines "foodborne illness outbreak" as the occurrence of two or more cases of a similar illness resulting from the ingestion of a certain food.[32]

[26] Federal Register / Vol. 79, No. 23, pages 6596-6598 (February 4, 2014).

[27] Federal Register / Vol. 79, No. 23, pages 6596-6598 (February 4, 2014).

[28] Food and Drug Administration Background on Food Safety Modernization Act. FSMA FACTS. July 12, 2011.

[29] Food and Drug Administration Background on Food Safety Modernization Act. FSMA FACTS. July 12, 2011.

[30] Centers for Disease Control and Prevention. Foodborne Outbreak Tracking and Reporting. Fast Facts and FAQs. April 24, 2014. http://www.cdc.gov/foodsafety/fdoss/faq/index.html

[31] FoodSafety.gov. How Government Responds to Food Illness Outbreaks. http://www.foodsafety.gov/poisoning/responds/

[32] 21 USC 2224.

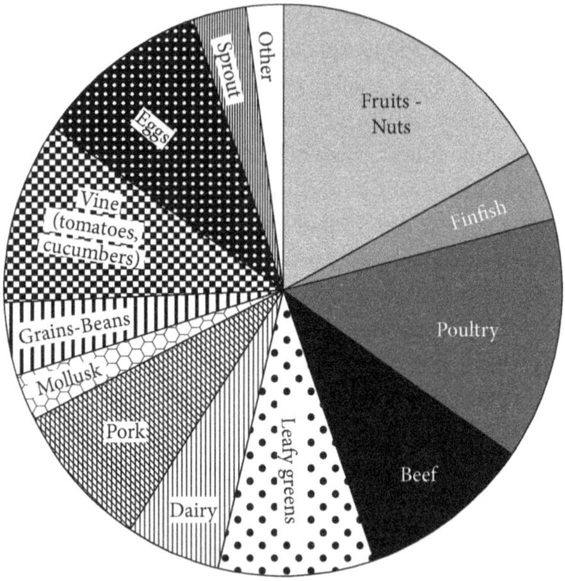

FIGURE 5.1 Total foodborne outbreak-associated illnesses, 2008–2012 = 81,757.

Source: CDC National Outbreak Reporting System, 2008–2012.[a]

[a]CDC. CDC and Food Safety. http://www.cdc.gov/foodborneburden/PDFs/CDC-and-Food-Safety.pdf

The most common method for government to respond to a foodborne disease outbreak is through identification and investigation by state, local, and territorial public health departments.[33] Generally an outbreak is first identified at the local level and the state health department offers assistance if it spreads across the state. If an outbreak overwhelms a state's capabilities and resources, the state may ask the CDC for assistance. In the case of multistate outbreaks, the CDC will collaborate with the FDA, the USDA's Food Safety and Inspection Service (FSIS), or the EPA, but the CDC generally leads the investigation. As required by the FSMA, the CDC also named the state health departments in Colorado, Florida, Minnesota, Oregon, and Tennessee as Integrated Food Safety Centers of Excellence to identify and implement best practices to assist the CDC in responding to foodborne disease outbreaks.[34]

The FSMA requires the FDA to inspect domestic food facilities on a regular basis, permits FDA to access the facilities' food safety plans and records, and requires the FDA to establish a program for food laboratory testing.[35] The FSMA

[33] Centers for Disease Control and Prevention. Foodborne Outbreaks. Guide to Confirming a Diagnosis in Foodborne Disease. November 13, 2013. http://www.cdc.gov/foodsafety/outbreaks/investigating-outbreaks/confirming_diagnosis.html

[34] Centers for Disease Control and Prevention. CDC and the Food Safety Modernization Act. September 16, 2013 http://www.cdc.gov/foodsafety/fsma.html#section399

[35] Food and Drug Administration Background on Food Safety Modernization Act. FSMA FACTS. July 12, 2011.

also required the FDA to enhance the foodborne illness surveillance systems by improving the collection, analysis, reporting, and usefulness of data on foodborne illness by coordinating across agencies and with state and local systems by sharing information, developing improved epidemiological tools, and expanding the capacities of these systems.[36] During an active investigation of a foodborne illness outbreak, or when the FDA determines that the following is necessary to prevent a foodborne illness outbreak, the FSMA permits the FDA to request that a farm identify potential immediate recipients, other than consumers, of any food that is or was adulterated or that presents a threat of serious adverse health consequences or death to humans or animals.[37]

The USDA's FSIS operates under the authority of the Federal Meat Inspection Act, the Poultry Products Inspection Act, and the Egg Products Inspection Act to inspect all poultry, livestock, and egg products, analyze these products for adulterants, and set food safety standards for processing facilities. FSIS also conducts epidemiological studies and risk assessments to provide science-based information for risk management and communication.[38]

Once a food is identified as contaminated, the FDA or FSIS will alert the public about the contamination and issue recalls of the contaminated food.[39,40] Voluntary or mandatory recall may occur due to the discovery of a contaminant or organism in food, which can cause illness, or the discovery of a major allergen in a food product that is misbranded due to failure to disclose the ingredient on the label. The FSMA gave the FDA enhanced capabilities to issue a mandatory recall when a company fails to voluntarily recall unsafe food. The FSMA also permits the FDA to suspend the registration of a food facility that the agency determines poses a reasonable probability of serious adverse health consequences.[41] Under its new authority, the FDA issued its first food seizure order in September 2011 after inspections found rodent and insect infestation at a food storage and processing facility in Washington state.[42]

Food Allergens

Congress identified the eight major food allergens responsible for 90% of all food allergy reactions as: milk, eggs, fish, crustacean shellfish, tree nuts, wheat,

---

[36] 21 USC 2224.

[37] 21 USC 2223.

[38] United States Department of Agriculture Food Safety and Inspection Service. Factbook. Chapter 9. http://www.usda.gov/factbook/chapter9.htm

[39] Food and Drug Administration. http://www.fda.gov/Food/ResourcesForYou/Consumers/ucm180323.htm#federal

[40] United States Department of Agriculture. http://www.usda.gov/factbook/chapter9.htm

[41] Food and Drug Administration Background on Food Safety Modernization Act. FSMA FACTS. July 12, 2011.

[42] Food and Drug Administration. Press Announcement. FDA: U.S. Marshals Seize Foods Stored at Washington State Facility. October 11, 2011. http://www.fda.gov/NewsEvents/Newsroom/PressAnnouncements/ucm275204.htm

peanuts, and soybeans.[43] Food allergens are permitted in food products regulated by both the FDA and USDA as long as food companies disclose their inclusion on the food label. See Chapter 6 on this labeling requirement.

The CDC found that food allergies affect approximately 4% to 6% of children in the United States and that this is of increasingly greater concern.[44] The FSMA required HHS and the Department of Education to develop voluntary guidelines to manage the risk of food allergy and anaphylaxis in schools and early childhood education programs.[45] In response to this requirement, the CDC and the Department of Education created the "Voluntary Guidelines for Managing Food Allergies In Schools and Early Care and Education Programs." The guidelines provide practical information and planning steps for school-related administrators and staff to address food allergy management and prevention plans in their schools.[46]

Food Additives and Generally Recognized As Safe

In 1958, Congress passed the Food Additives Amendment, which required manufacturers of new food additives to establish the safety of the additives before they could be introduced into the food supply. Now food ingredients are categorized as either "food additives" or "generally recognized as safe." Food additives are defined as substances for which the intended use results or may reasonably be expected to result, directly or indirectly, in their becoming a component of food or otherwise affecting the characteristics of food.[47] Food companies must obtain FDA approval before marketing a food with a food additive.[48] The FDA generally issues a food additive regulation prescribing its approved use and thereafter the food additive will be deemed unsafe only if it does not conform to the terms of the regulation.[49]

An ingredient is exempt from the definition of food additive if it is "generally recognized as safe," or GRAS. A substance may be considered GRAS based on the views of "experts qualified by scientific training and experience to evaluate the safety of substances."[50] This may occur through two methods. First, for

---

[43] 21 USCS § 321(q)(q)(1).

[44] Centers for Disease Control and Prevention. Food Allergies in Schools. October 31, 2013. http://www.cdc.gov/healthyyouth/foodallergies/index.htm

[45] 21 USC 2205.

[46] Centers for Disease Control and Prevention. Voluntary Guidelines for Managing Food Allergies in Schools and Early Care and Education Programs. http://www.cdc.gov/healthyyouth/foodallergies/pdf/13_243135_A_Food_Allergy_Web_508.pdf

[47] 21 CFR 170.3.

[48] 21 CFR 570.30.

[49] Food and Drug Administration. Determining the Regulatory Status of a Food Ingredient. http://www.fda.gov/Food/IngredientsPackagingLabeling/FoodAdditivesIngredients/ucm228269.htm

[50] 21 CFR 170.30

substances used in food prior to January 1, 1958, an ingredient could have been declared GRAS through experience based on common knowledge about the substance throughout the scientific community.[51] Salt and pepper are examples of ingredients with GRAS status through this mechanism. Second, an ingredient can be declared GRAS through studies published in peer-reviewed journals, which may be corroborated by other data and information, the opinion of an "expert panel" convened for this purpose, or the recommendation of an authoritative body such as the National Academy of Sciences.[52,53]

In 1969, President Richard Nixon convened a White House Conference on Food, Nutrition, and Health. Much of the conference focused on topics such as hunger, malnutrition, and nutrition education.[54] However, in response to the FDA's 1969 decision to remove various cyclamate salts (nonnutritive sweeteners) from the GRAS list after studies revealed bladder tumors in rats fed with them, President Nixon additionally directed the FDA to re-examine the safety of GRAS substances.[55] The FDA announced that it would undertake a comprehensive study of GRAS substances in 1970 to evaluate the available safety information and determine whether each item should be confirmed as GRAS or be subject to a food additive regulation.[56] The FDA created administrative procedures and convened the Select Committee on GRAS Substances to make independent scientific determinations.[57] By 1982, the Select Committee had produced 151 detailed reports covering over 400 substances.[58]

Thereafter, GRAS affirmation involved the FDA's formal rulemaking procedure, which the agency found to be resource intensive. When a food company petitioned the FDA to confirm an ingredient should be GRAS based on its own determination that this was the case, the FDA had to engage in the following activities: (1) publish a notice in the Federal Register; (2) request comments on the petitioned request; (3) conduct a comprehensive review of the petitioner's data and information and the comments received to determine whether the evidence established that the petitioned use of the substance is GRAS; (4) draft a detailed explanation of why the use is GRAS; and (5) publish that explanation in the Federal Register. In 1997, the FDA decided to permit food companies to

---

[51] 21 CFR 170.30

[52] 21 CFR 170.30

[53] 18938 Federal Register. 1997;62(74). Proposed Rules.

[54] White House Conference on Food Nutrition and Health. Final Report. Remarks of the President at the Open Plenary Session on the White House Conference on Food Nutrition and Health. Sheraton Park Hotel. December 2, 1969. www.nns.nih.gov/1969/full_report/White_House_Report2_S1a.pdf

[55] 62 Federal Register 18938, 18939 (April 17, 1997).

[56] 62 Federal Register 18938, 18939 (April 17, 1997).

[57] Food and Drug Administration. History of the GRAS List and SCOGS Reviews. http://www.fda.gov/Food/IngredientsPackagingLabeling/GRAS/SCOGS/ucm084142.htm

[58] Food and Drug Administration. History of the GRAS List and SCOGS Reviews. http://www.fda.gov/Food/IngredientsPackagingLabeling/GRAS/SCOGS/ucm084142.htm

self-declare an ingredient to be GRAS in order to avoid these steps and preserve its limited resources for other purposes.[59] The FDA thus proposed a rule to avoid this formal process. Although the 1997 proposed rule was never finalized or subject to a complete notice and comment rulemaking at that time, the FDA has functioned under this determination since then.[60]

Under the 1997 proposed rule program, the FDA permits companies to determine that a substance is GRAS and based on this conclusion, the company may market the food with the ingredient without first informing the FDA.[61] Instead of formally petitioning the FDA for GRAS verification, the company need only file a "GRAS exemption claim" describing the substance, the applicable conditions of use, and the basis for the GRAS determination; however, it does not need to submit the information or data upon which the determination was made.[62]

Several nonprofit groups sued the FDA in 2014, arguing that the GRAS exemption claim program is contrary to Congress's intent in passing statutory requirements related to GRAS status, deprives the public of the right to have its comments considered as required by the Administrative Procedure Act, exposes the public to potentially hazardous substances, and raises concerns about the integrity of the process and the food industry's determinations.[63] The parties settled the lawsuit, with the FDA agreeing to finalize a GRAS rule by August 2016.[64]

The FDA has the power to determine that a substance is not GRAS or no longer GRAS upon its own volition. The FDA must publish a notice in the Federal Register explaining its determination that a substance is not GRAS but rather is a food additive subject to regulatory oversight by the agency.[65] In 2013, the FDA determined that partially hydrogenated oils, which are the primary dietary source of trans fat, are not GRAS.

In the 1990s, studies emerged to indicate that the consumption of trans fat increases the risk of coronary heart disease. Denmark banned trans fat in 2003, New York City's Department of Health and Mental Hygiene banned its use in restaurant foods in 2006, and California followed suit in 2008.[66] The FDA initially

---

[59] 18938 Federal Register. 1997;62(74).Proposed Rules.

[60] 18938 Federal Register. 1997;62(74)Proposed Rules.

[61] U.S. Government Accountability Office. FDA Should Strengthen Its Oversight of Food Ingredients Determined to Be Generally Recognized as Safe (GRAS). GAO-10-246: Published: February 3, 2010. Publicly Released: March 5, 2010.

[62] 18938 Federal Register. 1997;62(74). Proposed Rules.

[63] *Center for Food Safety v. Sebelius et al.* Case No. 1:14-cv-267-RC. Complaint (D. DC March 13, 2014). http://www.centerforfoodsafety.org/files/2014-3-13-dkt-8--pls--am-compl_76904.pdf

[64] Center for Food Safety. Victory! CFS Wins First Step in Major Legal Battle to Protect Food Safety. October 20, 2014. http://www.centerforfoodsafety.org/press-releases/3550/victory-cfs-wins-first-step-in-major-legal-battle-to-protect-food-safety#

[65] 21 CFR 570.38.

[66] K. D. Brownell, J. L. Pomeranz. The Trans Fat Ban—Food Regulation and Long-Term Health. *New England Journal of Medicine*. 2014;370:1773–1775.

addressed concerns over partially hydrogenated oils by requiring the disclosure of the trans fat content of food on the Nutrition Facts Panel in 2006.[67]

In 2013 the FDA issued a notice in the Federal Register, stating that it found that partially hydrogenated oils are "no longer GRAS under any condition of use in food and therefore are food additives."[68] The agency noted that partially hydrogenated oils have been used in food for many years based on the food industry's self-determination that such use is GRAS.[69] The agency thus sought comments on its conclusion that food manufacturers should no longer be permitted to sell partially hydrogenated oils, "either directly or as ingredients in another food product, without prior FDA approval for use as a food additive."[70] The FDA received over 1,500 comments.[71] In June 2015, the agency finalized its determination that partially hydrogenated oils are not GRAS for use in human food. The FDA gave food manufacturers three years to remove partially hydrogenated oils from their products but is permitting food companies to petition the agency to request an exemption for specific uses.

Caffeine is another substance with questionable GRAS status when added to food. See Box 5.1 for more information on caffeine and its GRAS designation.

Color Additives

A color additive is a dye, pigment, or other substance made by a process of synthesis or that is extracted, isolated, or otherwise derived from a vegetable, animal, mineral, or other source and that, when added or applied to a food is capable of imparting color to it.[72] The FDA is responsible for determining the safety of color additives based on its own independent analysis, as well as the scientific data submitted to it by the company proposing to introduce the additive into the food supply.[73] The FDA defined "safe" in the context of color additives to mean "that there is convincing evidence that establishes with reasonable certainty that no harm will result from the intended use of the color additive."[74] In addition, the FDA passed a specific regulation noting that if the information from qualified scientists suggests the possibility that a color additive has induced cancer when ingested, "no regulation may issue which

[67] 21 CFR 101.9(c)(2)(ii).

[68] 78 Federal Register 67169 (November 8, 2013).

[69] 78 Federal Register 67169 (November 8, 2013).

[70] 78 Federal Register 67169 (November 8, 2013).

[71] Docket ID: FDA-2013-N-1317. Regulations.gov. http://www.regulations.gov/#!docketDetail;D=FDA-2013-N-1317

[72] 21 CFR 70.3(f).

[73] Food and Drug Administration. Overview of Food Ingredients, Additives & Colors. April 2010. http://www.fda.gov/Food/IngredientsPackagingLabeling/FoodAdditivesIngredients/ucm094211.htm

[74] 21 CFR 70.3(i).

BOX 5.1

GRAS and Caffeine

In the 1970s, the Select Committee on GRAS substances analyzed caffeine as a commercially added food ingredient (but not caffeine that naturally occurs in food such as coffee and tea). In 1978, the committee concluded that:

> "A. While no evidence in the available information on caffeine demonstrates a hazard to the public when it is used in cola type beverages at levels that are now current and in the manner now practiced, uncertainties exist requiring that additional studies be conducted.
>
> B. It is inappropriate to include caffeine among the substances generally recognized as safe (GRAS). At current levels of consumption of cola-type beverages, the dose of caffeine can approximate that known to induce such pharmacological effects as central nervous system stimulation."[a]

The FDA lists caffeine as GRAS "when used in cola-type beverages in accordance with good manufacturing practices,"[b] at "0.02%" of the product, or in concentrations no greater than 200 parts per million.[c] However, food manufacturers started adding much larger amounts of caffeine to beverages such as alcoholic drinks and energy drinks, and additionally began adding caffeine to various foods, such as waffles, gum, and snack foods.[d] This addition of caffeine is not required to be disclosed on the food label so companies can add caffeine without notifying consumers of its existence in the product or of the amount of caffeine included. Some beverage companies voluntarily disclose the amount of caffeine in their products.[e]

Although the Alcohol and Tobacco Tax and Trade Bureau regulates the labeling of alcoholic beverages, the FDA has the authority to evaluate the safety of ingredients added to alcoholic beverages.[f] In 2009,[g] the FDA sent letters to the manufacturers of caffeinated alcoholic beverages noting that the GRAS regulation "does not confer GRAS status to the use of caffeine in ... alcoholic beverages or at higher use levels" and that the agency did not sanction this use.[h] The FDA requested companies to provide data and information supporting the conclusion that their company's' use of caffeine in an alcoholic beverage was GRAS or sanctioned by the FDA. In 2010, four companies were still producing caffeinated alcoholic beverages.[i] The FDA sent official Warning Letters to these companies and all four stated that they had ceased production or shipment of the products.[j] (See Chapter 6 for further discussion of the FDA's authority to address food labeling violations, including its use of Warning Letters.)

In 2013, the FDA notified food manufacturers that it would investigate the safety of additional caffeine in food products (such as waffles and syrup) and particularly its effects on children and adolescents.[k] The agency noted that it was prepared to go through the regulatory process but sought industry's "voluntary restraint."[l] In the wake of this announcement, one company announced that it would discontinue production of its caffeinated gum; the FDA commended the company and has taken no formal action on caffeine labeling or its GRAS status since then.[m]

In addition to the public health concerns over mixing alcohol with caffeine, consuming extreme levels of caffeine on its own has health consequences. Energy drinks containing several times the amount of caffeine in cola-type products are sold nationally.[n] A study by HHS revealed that emergency room visits involving energy drinks alone or mixed with other substances increased tenfold from 2005 to 2009.[o] Eleven percent of these visits involved youth aged 12–17 years, and the vast majority of these (75%) were due to energy drink consumption alone. The American Academy of Pediatrics' position is that caffeine and energy drinks "have no place in the diet of children and adolescents," and the American Medical Association supports banning the marketing of energy drinks to youth under the age of 18 years.[p]

In July 2013, the United States Senate Committee on Commerce, Science and Transportation held a hearing on the potential health risks associated with the consumption of energy drinks by children and teenagers; thereafter, Senators Edward J. Markey (Massachusetts), John D. Rockefeller (West Virginia), Richard J. Durbin (Illinois), and Richard Blumenthal (Connecticut) followed up with reports and letters.[q] The Senators wrote letters to energy drink manufacturers urging them to commit to voluntary measures not to market their products to youth. Several of the big energy drink companies have refused to abide by the Senators' requests to limit marketing to adolescents.[r] These products remain legal for youth to purchase (except in one county in New York State), so the First Amendment stands as a barrier to government prohibitions on related marketing practices (see Chapter Seven). State and local governments could ban the sale, as opposed to the marketing, of energy drinks to youth pursuant to their police power, as discussed in Chapter 9.

[a]Food and Drug Administration. Database of Select Committee on GRAS Substances (SCOGS) Reviews. Caffeine. 1978. http://www.accessdata.fda.gov/scripts/fcn/fcnDetailNavigation.cfm?rpt=scogsListing&id=42

[b]Good Manufacturing Practices are the FDA's descriptions of the methods, equipment, facilities, and controls for producing processed food (and dietary supplements) to ensure proper quality, packaging and labeling.

[c]21 CFR 182.1180.

[d]Food and Drug Administration. For Consumers. FDA to Investigate Added Caffeine. May 3, 2013. http://www.fda.gov/ForConsumers/ConsumerUpdates/ucm350570.htm

[e]J. L. Pomeranz, C. Munsell, and J. L. Harris. Energy Drinks: An Emerging Public Health Hazard for Youth. *Journal of Public Health Policy.* 2013;34(2):254–271.

[f]Alcohol and Tobacco Tax and Trade Bureau. Alcohol Beverages with Added Caffeine. August 21, 2014. http://www.ttb.gov/main_pages/caffeine-added.shtml

[g]FDA to Examine the Safety of Caffeinated Alcoholic Beverages. November 13, 2009. http://www.fda.gov/ForConsumers/ConsumerUpdates/ucm190364.htm

[h]Food and Drug Administration. Food. Background Information: Caffeinated Alcoholic Beverages. Nov 13, 2009.Caffeinated Alcoholic Beverages Sample Letter #1

Caffeinated Alcoholic Beverages Sample Letter #2

Caffeinated Alcoholic Beverages Sample Letter #3 http://www.fda.gov/Food/IngredientsPackagingLabeling/FoodAdditivesIngredients/ucm233591.htm

[i]Food and Drug Administration. Food. Caffeinated Alcoholic Beverages. November 17, 2010. http://www.fda.gov/Food/IngredientsPackagingLabeling/FoodAdditivesIngredients/ucm190366.htm

[j]Food and Drug Administration. News & Events. Update on Caffeinated Alcoholic Beverages. November 24, 2010. http://www.fda.gov/NewsEvents/PublicHealthFocus/ucm234900.htm

[k]Food and Drug Administration. For Consumers. FDA to Investigate Added Caffeine. May 3, 2013. http://www.fda.gov/ForConsumers/ConsumerUpdates/ucm350570.htm

[l]Food and Drug Administration. For Consumers. FDA to Investigate Added Caffeine. May 3, 2013. http://www.fda.gov/ForConsumers/ConsumerUpdates/ucm350570.htm

[m]Food and Drug Administration. Food. Added Caffeine in Gum. http://www.fda.gov/Food/IngredientsPackagingLabeling/FoodAdditivesIngredients/ucm396885.htm

(*continued*)

BOX 5.1
Continued

[n] J. L. Pomeranz, C. Munsell, J. L. Harris. Energy Drinks: An Emerging Public Health Hazard for Youth. *Journal of Public Health Policy.* 2013;34(2):254–271.

[o] Substance Abuse and Mental Health Services Administration. Center for Behavioral Health Statistics and Quality. *The DAWN Report: Emergency Department Visits Involving Energy Drinks.* November 22, 2011. Rockville, Maryland.

[p] Staff of Senator Edward J. Markey (D-MA) in coordination with the staff of Senators Richard J. Durbin (D-IL), and Richard Blumenthal (D-CT). Buzz Kill: A Survey of Popular Energy Drinks Finds Majority of the Market Unwilling to Make Commitments to Protect Adolescents. January 2015. http://www.markey.senate.gov/imo/media/doc/2014-12-30-Report_BuzzKill_EnergyDrinks_ScreenV.pdf

[q] Staff of Senator Edward J. Markey (D-MA) in coordination with the staff of Senators Richard J. Durbin (D-IL), and Richard Blumenthal (D-CT). Buzz Kill: A Survey of Popular Energy Drinks Finds Majority of the Market Unwilling to Make Commitments to Protect Adolescents. January 2015. http://www.markey.senate.gov/imo/media/doc/2014-12-30-Report_BuzzKill_EnergyDrinks_ScreenV.pdf

[r] Staff of Senator Edward J. Markey (D-MA) in coordination with the staff of Senators Richard J. Durbin (D-IL), and Richard Blumenthal (D-CT). Buzz Kill: A Survey of Popular Energy Drinks Finds Majority of the Market Unwilling to Make Commitments to Protect Adolescents. January 2015. http://www.markey.senate.gov/imo/media/doc/2014-12-30-Report_BuzzKill_EnergyDrinks_ScreenV.pdf

permits its use."[75] The FDA may also confine its approval of color additives to certain foods.

Food companies seeking to introduce a new color additive for use in food must submit a petition for certification to the FDA or request an exemption from certification from the agency. Certifiable color additives are those that are synthetically made and are primarily derived from petroleum and coal sources.[76] Companies must submit a batch of the proposed synthetic color additive to the FDA. Examples of synthetic color additives approved for use in food include FD&C Blue No. 1, FD&C Red No. 40, and FD&C Yellow No. 5.[77] The category of color additives that are exempt from the certification process are those that are primarily derived from plant, animal, or mineral sources. Caramel color and annatto extract are examples of this second category approved for use in food.[78] Although they are not subject to certification requirements and companies do not need to submit batches to the FDA, companies must still comply with regulatory requirements. For example, grape color extract, derived from Concord

[75] 21 CFR 70.50.

[76] Food and Drug Administration. For Consumers. How Safe are Color Additives? December 10, 2007. http://www.fda.gov/ForConsumers/ConsumerUpdates/ucm048951.htm

[77] U.S. Government Printing Office. Electronic Code of Federal Regulations. Title 21, Chapter I, Subchapter A, Part 74. e-CFR Data is current as of December 23, 2014. http://www.ecfr.gov/cgi-bin/text-idx?c=ecfr&sid=3f6c9146ba54b1b84f17046e27197926&tpl=/ecfrbrowse/Title21/21cfr74_main_02.tpl

[78] Food and Drug Administration. For Industry. Color Additive Status List. List 4. December 2009. http://www.fda.gov/ForIndustry/ColorAdditives/ColorAdditiveInventories/ucm106626.htm

grapes, must comply with specifications regarding pesticide residues, and arsenic and lead levels, and is only approved for use in coloring "nonbeverage food."[79]

The FDA requires that food packaging disclose the presence of color additives. Any color additive, whether subject to, or exempt from certification is considered an "artificial color" or "artificial coloring" by the FDA.[80] Food manufacturers must list the full or abbreviated name of any FDA-certified color additive, such as FD&C Blue No. 1 or Blue 1. For noncertified color additives, manufacturers may state "Artificial Color," "Artificial Color Added," or "Color Added."[81,82]

Debates in Animal-based Food Production Safety

Modern food production practices include methods that have engendered safety concerns among scientists or the public and thus the appropriate government response and applicable laws are subject to debate. Two such examples include the use of synthetic growth hormones in dairy cows and subtherapeutic antibiotics in animal feed.

Synthetic Growth Hormones

Bovine somatotropin, also known as bovine growth hormone, is a protein hormone produced by the pituitary gland of cows. Cow milk contains naturally occurring bovine growth hormones. Scientists recognized that a synthetic form of this growth hormone could increase milk production and they created bioengineered forms, called recombinant bovine somatotropin (rbST) and recombinant bovine growth hormone, collectively referred to as rbST. The Monsanto company created an rbST that increased milk production and the company submitted a new animal drug application to the FDA. In November 1993, the FDA approved the new animal drug application providing for the subcutaneous use of rbST in lactating dairy cows for this purpose.[83] The FDA explained that it approved the drug after determining that it was safe and effective for dairy cows, that rbST-treated milk was safe for humans, and that the process would not have a significant impact on the environment.[84] The FDA and a panel of experts

---

[79] 21 CFR 73.169.

[80] 21 CFR 101.22(a)(4).

[81] 21 CFR 101.22(k).

[82] Food and Drug Administration. Overview of Food Ingredients, Additives & Colors. April 2010. http://www.fda.gov/Food/IngredientsPackagingLabeling/FoodAdditivesIngredients/ucm094211.htm

[83] Marion Nestle. *Safe Food: Bacteria, Biotechnology, and Bioterrorism.* Berkeley and Los Angeles, CA: University of California Press, 2003, p. 197.

[84] 59 Federal Register 6279, 6279–6280 (February 17, 1994).

recruited by the National Institutes of Health concluded that there was no significant difference between milk from rbST-treated and untreated cows.[85,86]

Members of the public were nonetheless concerned for several reasons.[87] First, Monsanto, the company that bioengineered rbST, was seen as exerting undue influence over the FDA, leading to theories of agency capture.[88] Further, critics argued that milk treated with rbST contained increased levels of an insulin-like growth factor substance, which had been theorized to stimulate premature growth and cancer in humans. Moreover, opponents argued that rbST increased the need for antibiotics in treated cows and the antibiotics remained in the milk, leading to a concern about antibiotic-resistant bacteria. Some dairy farmers, private companies such as Ben & Jerry's, and the State of Vermont wanted increased labeling requirements to allow consumers to distinguish between rbST-treated and untreated milk.[89]

The FDA argued that it did not have the authority to require mandatory labeling for milk from treated cows because it found rbST to be safe and the milk to be the same.[90] The FDA did, however, issue guidance for industry members who want to voluntarily label milk and milk products as being derived from cows not treated with rbST. Thus, the FDA explained that in order for labels to avoid being misleading, they must "disclose facts that are material in light of representations made about a product or facts that are material with respect to the consequences that may result from use of the product."[91] Therefore, the agency suggested the proper label should include the following two phrases or similar sentiment: This product is made "from cows not treated with rbST" and "No significant difference has been shown between milk derived from rbST-treated and non-rbST-treated cows."[92] This guidance remains in effect today. The scientific debate surrounding rbST has died down for the most part, but food companies continue to distinguish their products through these labels.

Box 5.2 discusses The Case of Pink Slime.

---

[85] 59 Federal Register 6279, 6280 (February 17, 1994).

[86] Marion Nestle. *Safe Food: Bacteria, Biotechnology, and Bioterrorism*. Berkeley and Los Angeles, CA: University of California Press, 2003, p. 199.

[87] Marion Nestle. *Safe Food: Bacteria, Biotechnology, and Bioterrorism*. Berkeley and Los Angeles, CA: University of California Press, 2003, pp. 197–206.

[88] Agency capture, or regulatory capture, is theory that explains what happens when a regulatory agency acts in ways that benefit the industry it is supposed to be regulating, rather than the public's interest it is supposed to be protecting. Agency staff members are thus "captured by those they are ostensibly regulating." Clifford Rechtschaffen. Deterrence v. Cooperation and the Evolving Theory of Environmental Enforcement. 71 S. Cal. L. Rev. 1181, 1222 (1998).

[89] Marion Nestle. *Safe Food: Bacteria, Biotechonology, and Bioterrorism*. Berkeley and Los Angeles, CA: University of California Press, 2003, pp. 202–204.

[90] 59 Federal Register 6279, 6280 (February 17, 1994).

[91] 59 Federal Register 6279, 6280 (February 17, 1994).

[92] 59 Federal Register 6279, 6280 (February 17, 1994).

BOX 5.2

The Case of Pink Slime

"Lean Finely Textured Beef" (LFTB) made national headlines under the disparaging nickname, "pink slime," between 2009 and 2012. LFTB is a cheap, lean beef product used to make hamburgers. In the 1990s, the company Beef Products, Inc., was looking to expand its products to include inexpensive beef for burger patties.[a] The company turned "fatty slaughterhouse trimmings into usable lean beef" by "liquefying the fat and extracting the protein from the trimmings in a centrifuge."[b] This resulted in a product that was useable for burgers. However, LFTB was highly susceptible to E. coli and salmonella contamination, so the company added ammonia to kill the pathogens.[c] The FDA had approved ammonium hydroxide as a GRAS ingredient to be used in food produced according to Good Manufacturing Practices in 1974.[d] The USDA approved the resulting LFTB and its use in the school food program.[e]

The media began exposing LFTB as an ingredient in burgers, starting with a 2009 *New York Times* article and peaking in 2011, when celebrity chef Jamie Oliver displayed video footage on his television show of how pink slime was processed.[f] The meat processing industry launched a "Dude, It's BEEF" campaign in response, but this did not sway popular notions that pink slime was "disgusting."[g] Even though initial safety concerns were suppressed, several fast food restaurants announced that they would cease using LFTB, and a petition successfully encouraged the USDA to give schools the choice of whether to use it.[h,i] The USDA was quick to point out that there were no safety concerns and on March 22, 2012, the Under Secretary for Food Safety wrote on the USDA blog: "I believe it is important to distinguish people's concerns about how their food is made from their concerns about food safety. The process used to produce LFTB is safe and has been used for a very long time. And adding LFTB to ground beef does not make that ground beef any less safe to consume."[j]

The USDA does not require meat companies to label LFTB or ammonium hydroxide if they add it to their beef products, and the FDA does not require it to be labeled if it is used as part of the food's processing, rather than as an ingredient. However, some beef-product companies requested voluntary labeling measures by the USDA to appease consumers.[k] Other food products reportedly have ammonium hydroxide in them, but food companies do not publicize this fact.[l] Now that the hubbub has died down, some schools are bringing LFTB back[m] and it seems to have fallen off the radar of the press and food safety advocates.

[a]Michael Moss. Safety of Beef Processing Method Is Questioned. *The New York Times*. December 31, 2009. http://www.nytimes.com/2009/12/31/us/31meat.html?_r=2

[b]Michael Moss. Safety of Beef Processing Method Is Questioned. *The New York Times*. December 31, 2009. http://www.nytimes.com/2009/12/31/us/31meat.html?_r=2

[c]Michael Moss. Safety of Beef Processing Method Is Questioned. *The New York Times*. December 31, 2009. http://www.nytimes.com/2009/12/31/us/31meat.html?_r=2

[d]21 CFR 184.1139.

[e]United States Department of Agriculture. USDA Announces Additional Choices for Beef Products in the Upcoming School Year. News Release No. 0094.12 . March 15, 2012. http://www.usda.gov/wps/portal/usda/usdamediafb?contentid=2012/03/0094.xml&printable=true&contentidonly=true

[f]http://www.npr.org/blogs/thesalt/2012/03/09/148298678/is-it-safe-to-eat-pink-slime

[g]http://www.bbc.com/news/magazine-17615456

[h]Bettina Elias Siegel. How My 'Pink Slime' Petition Took Off. http://www.theguardian.com/commentisfree/cifamerica/2012/apr/06/pink-slime-rebellion-beef

(*continued*)

BOX 5.2
Continued

[i]United States Department of Agriculture. USDA Announces Additional Choices for Beef Products in the Upcoming School Year. News Release No. 0094.12 . March 15, 2012. http://www.usda.gov/wps/portal/usda/usdamediafb?contentid=2012/03/0094.xml&printable=true&contentidonly=true

[j]http://blogs.usda.gov/2012/03/22/setting-the-record-straight-on-beef/

[k]Jim Avila. BPI Endorses USDA Voluntary Labeling of LFTB or 'Pink Slime' April 3, 2012. http://abcnews.go.com/blogs/headlines/2012/04/bpi-endorses-usda-voluntary-labeling-of-lftb-or-pink-slime/

[l]Martinne Geller. Ammonia Used in Many Foods, Not Just "Pink Slime." Reuters. April 4, 2012. http://www.reuters.com/article/2012/04/04/us-food-ammonia-idUSBRE8331B420120404

[m]http://www.politico.com/story/2013/09/pink-slime-school-lunches-96502_Page2.html

Antibiotics in Meat

In the 1950s, the FDA approved the use of antibiotics in animal feed.[93] Farmers and ranchers engaged in animal husbandry use antibiotics to treat sick animals, as a preventive measure, and to increase an animal's weight gain beyond normal growth patterns. The use of antibiotics for nontreatment purposes is called subtherapeutic antibiotic use. Scientists inside and outside of the government have expressed concern about antibiotic resistance developing as a result of subtherapeutic antibiotic use in animals used for human food. The CDC defines antibiotic resistance as "the ability of bacteria or other microbes to resist the effects of an antibiotic."[94] This occurs when bacteria mutate in a way that reduces or eliminates the effectiveness of drugs designed to cure or prevent infections.[95]

In the 1970s, the FDA convened a Task Force to study subtherapeutic antibiotic use in animals. The Task Force found that this practice increased the prevalence of antibiotic resistance in humans and it recommended restrictions be placed on this practice.[96] In response to this recommendation, the FDA stated that it would propose a new rule that would limit the use of medically important antibiotics (those that are used in humans) for animal feed.[97] The FDA then proposed a regulation that would revoke the previously approved subtherapeutic uses of antibiotics in animal feed by the year 1975 "unless data are submitted which resolve conclusively the issues concerning their safety to man and animals and their effectiveness."[98] Pharmaceutical companies, agricultural groups, and

[93] *NRDC, Inc. v. United States FDA*, 760 F.3d 151, 153 (2nd Cir. 2014).

[94] Centers for Disease Control and Prevention. Antibiotic Resistance Questions & Answers http://www.cdc.gov/getsmart/antibiotic-use/antibiotic-resistance-faqs.html#define-antibiotic-resistance

[95] Centers for Disease Control and Prevention. Antibiotic Resistance Questions & Answers http://www.cdc.gov/getsmart/antibiotic-use/antibiotic-resistance-faqs.html#define-antibiotic-resistance

[96] 37 Federal Register 2444 (February 1, 1972).

[97] 37 Federal Register 2444 (February 1, 1972)..

[98] 21 CFR 558.15.

Congress sought to dissuade the FDA from engaging in this rulemaking.[99] The FDA stated that it would hold a hearing on the topic but, like the final rulemaking, this never came to fruition.

Countries in Europe, such as Sweden and Denmark, began banning antibiotics for nontherapeutic purposes in the 1980s and 1990s.[100] In 2001, the European Union began phasing out the use of antibiotics in animals for nonmedical purposes and by 2006, the European Union completely banned the use of antibiotics used for growth promotion in animal feed.[101] The United States has not acted in a similar manner.

Today, 80% of antibiotics used in the United States are given to livestock and poultry for nonmedical reasons to encourage faster growth.[102,103] Based on the history discussed above and research indicating that bacteria that develop resistance to antibiotics used in animal feed can pose a risk to human health, public-interest groups have petitioned the FDA to hold hearings and prohibit the use of certain antibiotics in animal feed.[104] The FDA initiated certain proceedings on this topic but changed course and decided to engage in a voluntary strategy "to promote the judicious use of medically important antimicrobial drugs in food animals."[105]

Several groups sued the FDA to try to require the agency to proceed with hearings to determine whether to withdraw approval for the inclusion of penicillin and tetracyclines in animal feed for subtherapeutic purposes. In 2014, the federal Second Circuit Court of Appeals found for the FDA in the case *Natural Resources Defense Council v. Food and Drug Administration*, in a 2–1 decision. In this case, the two questions presented to the court were whether the relevant statute and its implementing regulations require the FDA to proceed with withdrawal hearings for the antibiotics in animal feed because the FDA previously found that those uses are not safe for humans,[106] and second whether the FDA's

---

[99] Diana R. H. Winters. Intractable Delay and the Need to Amend the Petition Provisions of the FDCA (March 3, 2014). *Indiana Law Journal* 2015; 90: *1047*. Indiana University Robert H. McKinney School of Law Research Paper No. 2014-8. Available at SSRN: http://ssrn.com/abstract=2412662

[100] Carol Cogliani, Herman Goossens, and Christina Greko. Restricting Antimicrobial Use in Food Animals: Lessons from Europe. *Microbe*. 2011;6: 274–279.

[101] European Food Safety Authority. Antimicrobial Resistance http://www.efsa.europa.eu/en/topics/topic/amr.htm

[102] *NRDC, Inc. v. United States FDA*, 760 F.3d 151, 153 (2nd Cir. 2014).

[103] National Resources Defense Council. Food Farm Animals and Drugs. http://www.nrdc.org/food/saving-antibiotics.asp

[104] *NRDC, Inc. v. United States FDA*, 760 F.3d 151, 153 (2nd Cir. 2014).

[105] Food and Drug Administration. Animal & Veterinary FDA's Strategy on Antimicrobial Resistance—Questions and Answers. March 28, 2014. http://www.fda.gov/AnimalVeterinary/GuidanceComplianceEnforcement/GuidanceforIndustry/ucm216939.htm

[106] Food and Drug Administration. Animal & Veterinary FDA's Strategy on Antimicrobial Resistance—Questions and Answers. March 28, 2014. http://www.fda.gov/AnimalVeterinary/GuidanceComplianceEnforcement/GuidanceforIndustry/ucm216939.htm at 157–158.

decision to terminate such hearings was discretionary and if so whether it was arbitrary or capricious.[107]

The court found that the statutory text and context, the regulations, and background legal principles led to the conclusion that Congress did not require the FDA to hold hearings just because FDA officials have scientific concerns about the safety of drug use in animals and that the FDA retains the discretion to institute or terminate proceedings and to withdraw its approval by issuing or withdrawing notice for hearings.[108] The court explained that the FDA is only required to act to withdraw approval for the drugs *after* a hearing if the Secretary of HHS finds the drug is not shown to be safe.[109] The court also accepted the FDA's determination that its voluntary compliance program "offers greater prospect for immediate and significant reductions in animal antibiotic use than the pursuit of a potentially contentious withdrawal hearing."[110]

The FDA states that its current strategy is to work with industry "to help phase out the use of medically important antimicrobials in food animals for production purposes (e.g., to enhance growth or improve feed efficiency), and to bring the therapeutic uses of such drugs (to treat, control, or prevent specific diseases) under the oversight of licensed veterinarians."[111] Medically important antimicrobials are those that are important for treating human disease. In December 2013, the FDA issued a nonbinding guidance document to industry to promote the "judicious use" of medically important antimicrobial drugs in food animals and proposed a three-year phase-in period of the voluntary strategy.[112] In June 2014, the FDA announced that all 26 drug manufacturers affected by the guidance document "agreed to fully engage in the strategy by phasing out the use of medically important antimicrobials in food-producing animals for food production purposes and

---

[107] Food and Drug Administration. Animal & Veterinary FDA's Strategy on Antimicrobial Resistance—Questions and Answers. March 28, 2014. http://www.fda.gov/AnimalVeterinary/GuidanceComplianceEnforcement/GuidanceforIndustry/ucm216939.htm at 175.

[108] Food and Drug Administration. Animal & Veterinary FDA's Strategy on Antimicrobial Resistance—Questions and Answers. March 28, 2014. http://www.fda.gov/AnimalVeterinary/GuidanceComplianceEnforcement/GuidanceforIndustry/ucm216939.htm at 171–172.

[109] Food and Drug Administration. Animal & Veterinary FDA's Strategy on Antimicrobial Resistance—Questions and Answers. March 28, 2014. http://www.fda.gov/AnimalVeterinary/GuidanceComplianceEnforcement/GuidanceforIndustry/ucm216939.htm at 172.

[110] Food and Drug Administration. Animal & Veterinary FDA's Strategy on Antimicrobial Resistance—Questions and Answers. March 28, 2014. http://www.fda.gov/AnimalVeterinary/GuidanceComplianceEnforcement/GuidanceforIndustry/ucm216939.htm at 172.

[111] http://www.fda.gov/AnimalVeterinary/GuidanceComplianceEnforcement/GuidanceforIndustry/ucm216939.htm#question1

[112] New Animal Drugs and New Animal Drug Combination Products Administered in or on Medicated Feed or Drinking Water of Food-Producing Animals: Recommendations for Drug Sponsors for Voluntarily Aligning Product Use Conditions with GFI #209 (Guidance #213). December 2013. http://www.fda.gov/downloads/AnimalVeterinary/GuidanceComplianceEnforcement/GuidanceforIndustry/UCM299624.pdf

phasing in the oversight of a veterinarian for the remaining therapeutic uses of such drugs."[113]

Advocates argue that there are significant weaknesses in the FDA's voluntary program.[114] Several cited include (1) the program relies on voluntary compliance by drug companies and lacks a plan to address noncompliance; (2) the FDA will continue to allow livestock farmers to provide antibiotics to their entire herds and flocks through feed and water, for the purpose of preventing rather than treating infections; this will leave the use of antibiotics unabated under the banner of disease prevention instead of growth promotion; (3) the FDA relaxed the requirements for veterinary oversight by proposing to eliminate the federal framework and replace it with state-based veterinary licensing and practicing requirements; this would eliminate the federal requirement that veterinarians must see or examine the animal prior to directing livestock to receive antibiotics; and (4) the method the FDA will use to work with drug companies lacks transparency.[115]

President Obama issued an Executive Order on September 18, 2014, titled, Combating Antibiotic-Resistant Bacteria. He noted that the CDC estimates that approximately two million illnesses and 23,000 deaths are caused by antibiotic-resistant bacteria in the United States annually and ordered the federal government to work domestically and internationally to address this problem in all facets of health.[116] The Executive Order established the Task Force for Combating Antibiotic-Resistant Bacteria, to be co-chaired by the Secretaries of Defense, Agriculture, and HHS, and required them to submit a five-year National Action Plan to the President that outlines a National Strategy for Combating Antibiotic-Resistant Bacteria. Among other items, the Task Force agencies are ordered to analyze antibiotic resistance in all types of healthcare, emergency, and nursing care delivery facilities and develop new antibacterial drugs, diagnostics, vaccines, and novel therapeutics for both the public and agricultural sectors. Relevant to food policy, the FDA is instructed to coordinate with the USDA to "continue taking steps to eliminate the use of medically important classes of antibiotics for growth promotion purposes in food-producing animals." Finally, the Executive Order states that the USDA, EPA, and FDA shall strengthen their coordination on this topic.

---

[113] FDA Secures Full Industry Engagement on Antimicrobial Resistance Strategy. June 30, 2014. http://www.fda.gov/AnimalVeterinary/NewsEvents/CVMUpdates/ucm403285.htm

[114] Diana R. H. Winters. The inadequacy of voluntary measures to reduce the use of antimicrobials in animal feed. Petrie Flom Center Harvard Law School. October 4, 2014. http://blogs.law.harvard.edu/billofhealth/2014/10/04/the-inadequacy-of-voluntary-measures-to-reduce-the-use-of-antimicrobials-in-animal-feed/#more-12972

[115] Lisa Heinzerling. The FDA's Continuing Incapacity on Livestock Antibiotics. *Stanford Environmental Law Journal*. 2014;33(3): 325–350.

[116] Executive Order. Combating Antibiotic-Resistant Bacteria. September 18, 2014. http://www.whitehouse.gov/the-press-office/2014/09/18/executive-order-combating-antibiotic-resistant-bacteria

The use of antibiotics in animal feed is an ongoing issue and the subject of much continued debate.[117,118,119] Congress members have introduced bills in both the House[120] and the Senate[121] to address the topic. It remains to be seen whether the FDA's voluntary program can address the issue successfully.

State and Local Control

State and local governments sometimes attempt to regulate farming techniques in an effort to address food safety and other issues such as environmental concerns. Preemption can be a barrier to state and local governments acting in this manner. The federal laws discussed above may preempt states from enacting their own requirements and states have preempted local governments from addressing farming practices in their own communities. Three examples of state and local governments attempting to address animal production and farming practices are discussed in this section.

CONCENTRATED ANIMAL FEEDING OPERATION LAWS

The industrialization of farming in the 1970s led to the creation of Animal Feeding Operations (AFOs), which are production operations where animals are raised in confined spaces for 45 days or more in any 12-month period. In AFOs, animals do not graze but rather are fed and are kept in close proximity to other animals, to their urine and excrement, and to dead animals.[122] A Concentrated Animal Feeding Operation (CAFO) is a type of AFO that meets additional criteria created by the EPA based on the number of animals and the facility's contribution of pollutants.[123] CAFOs tend to be industrial-scale productions. The EPA is the primary federal regulator of CAFOs and individual states have additional laws.

The National Association of Local Boards of Health issued a report noting that the increase in CAFOs has led to growing environmental problems in many

---

[117] Duff Wilson and Mimi Dwyer. Veterinarians Face Conflicting Allegiances to Animals, Farmers—and Drug Companies. Dec. 23, 2014, http://www.reuters.com/investigates/special-report/farmaceuticals-the-drugs-fed-to-farm-animals-and-the-risks-posed-to-humans/

[118] Public Broadcasting System. Frontline. Modern Meat. Is Your Meat Safe? Antibiotic Debate Overview. http://www.pbs.org/wgbh/pages/frontline/shows/meat/safe/overview.html

[119] Ruth Reichl. The FDA's Blatant Failure on Food. July 30, 2014 http://www.nytimes.com/2014/07/31/opinion/the-fda-blatant-failure-on-food.html?emc=eta1

[120] HR1150: Preservation of Antibiotics for Medical Treatment Act of 2013 (introduced March 14, 2013).

[121] S 1256: Preventing Antibiotic Resistance Act of 2013 (introduced June 27, 2013).

[122] Environmental Protection Agency. What is a CAFO? http://www.epa.gov/rgytgrnj/water/cafo/index.htm

[123] Environmental Protection Agency. Animal Feeding Operations Overview. http://water.epa.gov/polwaste/npdes/afo/index.cfm

communities.[124] A great many of these problems stem from the fact that CAFOs have difficulty storing or managing the excess manure, which can negatively affect ground and surface water quality and create air pollution. There are pathogens on animal manure and emissions from degrading manure and other processes produce air pollutants, including ammonia, hydrogen sulfide, methane, particulate matter, and greenhouse gases; these can negatively affect air quality in the surrounding communities and contribute to climate change. Due to health and safety concerns, many local governments have tried to regulate CAFOs. One barrier has been that all 50 states have some form of a "right-to-farm" law, which provides legal protections to farmers if they abide by certain basic requirements determined by each state. As a consequence, local governments have had mixed results in their ability to regulate CAFOs within their communities. For example, Missouri does not preempt local public health regulations so a Linn County, Missouri permitting scheme for CAFOs was not preempted.[125] However, a Fort Worth County, Iowa regulation that sought to address public health issues from CAFOs was found to be preempted by Iowa's laws regulating land use for animal farms.[126] Some states have created stricter or looser right-to-farm regulations in the face of CAFOs. This is largely in response to ongoing debates regarding whether to categorize and regulate CAFOs as agricultural or industrial uses, and whether stricter rules are necessary to protect the surrounding community or whether those rules could hurt farmers.[127]

EGG FARMER LAW

The California legislature passed a law banning the sale of shelled eggs within California unless the producers or handlers abide by state requirements. The law mandates that egg farmers implement the salmonella prevention measures required by the FDA, implement a salmonella environmental monitoring program, and maintain a vaccination program.[128] The California law additionally prohibits egg farmers from confining egg-laying hens in an enclosure that does not provide a minimum square inches of floor space per bird or allow them to stand up, lay down, or turn around freely.[129] The California legislature's intent in passing the law was "to protect California consumers from the deleterious, health, safety, and welfare effects of the sale and consumption of eggs derived from egg-laying hens that are exposed to

---

[124] Carrie Hribar. National Association of Local Boards of Health. Understanding Concentrated Animal Feeding Operations and Their Impact on Communities. 2010. Mark Schultz, Ed..

[125] *Borron v. Farrenkopf*, 5 S.W.3d 618 (Court of Appeals of Missouri, Western District 1999).

[126] *Worth County Friends of Agriculture. v. Worth County*, 688 N.W.2d 257 (Iowa 2004).

[127] Tom Henry. Stricter rules for agriculture debated. *Toledo Blade*. August 31, 2014. http://www.toledoblade.com/local/2014/08/31/Stricter-rules-for-agriculture-debated.html

[128] *Missouri v. Harris*, 2014 U.S. Dist. LEXIS 141337, *14 (E.D. CA 2014).

[129] *Missouri v. Harris*, 2014 U.S. Dist. LEXIS 141337, *15 (E.D. CA 2014).

significant stress and may result in increased exposure to disease pathogens including salmonella."[130] The law went into effect in January 2015. Several states with egg farmers who sell their eggs in California sued California to prevent enforcement of the law, arguing that it violated the Commerce Clause and was preempted by the Federal Egg Products Inspection Act. The case was dismissed on procedural grounds (discussed in Chapter 8) so the court did not analyze the substantive claims. It remains to be seen whether other plaintiffs will be able to challenge the state law successfully based on these or other substantive legal arguments.

GENETIC ENGINEERING LAW

Maui County, Hawaii passed an ordinance through a ballot referendum in November 2014 that placed a moratorium on the knowing propagation, cultivation, raising, growing, or testing of genetically engineered (GE) organisms within the County of Maui. The moratorium can only be amended or repealed by the Maui County Council by two-thirds vote.[131] The purpose of the law was to address the finding that the GE operations and practices that occur in Maui County are unique, and therefore, "pose different circumstances, risks, and concerns" than GE food production farming because they include "the cultivation of GE seed crops, experimental GE test crops, and extensive pesticide use including the testing of experimental pesticides."[132] The text of the law states that these practices may be "causing irreparable harm to the people, Environment, and Public Trust Resources."[133] Agricultural organizations, including Monsanto, sued Maui County to enjoin the operation of the law. The plaintiffs argued that the moratorium will harm the local economy, especially local farmers, and will harm the seed companies that rely on the unique climate of Maui to breed seeds. The plaintiffs filed a lawsuit arguing that the law violates the regulatory schemes enacted by the USDA, FDA, EPA, and the State of Hawaii for genetically engineered organisms and is thus preempted by federal and state law. Further it argues that the law violates the Commerce Clause and that the Maui Charter does not permit it to exact penalties.[134] In March 2015, the court enjoined Maui

---

[130] *Missouri v. Harris*, 2014 U.S. Dist. LEXIS 141337, *16 (E.D. CA 2014) (quoting Cal. Health & Safety Code § 25995).

[131] Chapter 20.39 of the Maui County Code. Moratorium on the Cultivation of Genetically Engineered Organisms. Sec. 5 and Sec. 6. http://www.shakamovement.org/law/

[132] A Bill Placing a Moratorium on the Cultivation of Genetically Engineered Organisms. http://www.shakamovement.org/law/

[133] A Bill Placing a Moratorium on the Cultivation of Genetically Engineered Organisms. http://www.shakamovement.org/law/

[134] *Robert Ito Farm, Inc. v. County of Maui.* Complaint for Declaratory and Injunctive Relieve. Civ. No. 1:13-cv-00511 (D. Hawaii November 13, 2014). Available: http://www.civilbeat.com/2014/11/monsanto-agrigenetics-sue-to-invalidate-maui-county-gmo-farming-ban/ and http://www.slideshare.net/civilbeat/complaint-41532329?ref=http://www.civilbeat.com/2014/11/monsanto-agrigenetics-sue-to-invalidate-maui-county-gmo-farming-ban/

County from enforcing the ordinance until the court ruled on the merits of the dispute, which is expected later in 2015.[135]

Given the extensive federal framework for agricultural safety issues, states have had a more difficult time addressing concerns within their communities in this context than in other areas of food policy. Chapter 9 discusses numerous state and local opportunities to address the modern food environment in other ways.

Questions and Exercises for Classroom Discussion

Consider the FSMA's requirement to designate certain foods as high-risk. Food companies do not want their foods to qualify as high-risk. Review a food company and a food trade organization's response to the FDA's request for comments on Regulations.gov: http://www.regulations.gov/#!docketBrowser;rpp=25;po=0;dct=PS;D=FDA-2014-N-0053;refD=FDA-2014-N-0053-0003. What methods does the food industry use to criticize the requirement? Do you agree? What do you think of the requirement in the first place?

What should the FDA's GRAS rule permit in terms of a company's ability to self-declare an ingredient to be GRAS? Should the FDA be required to undertake the formal GRAS rulemaking? Why or why not?

The Pink Slime case is one where an effort to address safety issues led to what might just be considered a disgusting product. When is something just unseemly and when is it unsafe? Do you trust the government to make that distinction? Would any other entity be better to make that determination?

What is the most pressing food safety issue today? Is the government addressing it appropriately? Why or why not? What have other countries done? Should other countries' responses have an impact on how the United States responds to food safety concerns?

Section 105 of the Animal Drug User Fee Amendments of 2008 requires antimicrobial drug sponsors to report to the FDA the amount of antimicrobial drugs they sell or distribute for use in food-producing animals on an annual basis. (Note that these sales and distribution data do not directly correlate to actual use.) The FDA publishes yearly reports summarizing this data. The report for 2013, the year before the FDA implemented its judicial use strategy, shows increasing sales of antimicrobials, including those that are considered medically important.[136] Look up the report for the current year, compare it to years past, and analyze whether the FDA's judicial use strategy is working. What could the FDA do to improve the outcome?

---

[135] *Robert Ito Farm, Inc v. County of Maui*, 2015 U.S. Dist. LEXIS 34519 (D. Haw. March 19, 2015).

[136] Food and Drug Administration. 2013 Summary Report on Antimicrobials Sold or Distributed for Use in Food-Producing Animals. April 2015. http://www.fda.gov/downloads/ForIndustry/UserFees/AnimalDrugUserFeeActADUFA/UCM440584.pdf

6

Food Labeling

Introduction

Products of all kinds have labels on them. Many products are subject to standardized labeling requirements with a mixture of safety warnings, instructions, and factual information. Warnings generally describe risks that might not be obvious to a reasonable consumer, while instructions explain how to use the product and reduce any risk of injury if applicable.[1] Food products tend to have a great deal of information on the packaging. Outside of manufacturers' own marketing features, which are discussed in Chapter 7, the majority of this is factual information regulated or required by the federal government. Some of the safety-related warnings and related factual information on labeling was discussed in the previous chapter.

The Fair Packaging and Labeling Act (FPLA) was enacted in 1967 to ensure truthful and transparent labels over consumer products. FPLA requires that labels disclose the net contents, net quantity of each serving, and identity of commodity, and name and place of business of the product's manufacturer, packer, or distributor.[2] FPLA is administered by the Food and Drug Administration (FDA) for foods, drugs, and cosmetics and administered by the Federal Trade Commission (FTC) for all other consumer goods.[3]

This chapter reviews the First Amendment issues relevant to labels in the context of food. It delves into the food labeling authority and regulations administered by the FDA and the United States Department of Agriculture (USDA).

[1] Twerski Henderson. *Products Liability Problems and Process* (3rd ed.). New York, NY. Aspen Law & Business. 1997.

[2] Food and Drug Administration. Fair Packaging and Labeling Act. http://www.fda.gov/regulatoryinformation/legislation/ucm148722.htm

[3] Neal D. Fortin. *Food Regulation Law, Science, Policy, and Practice*. Hobokon, NJ: John Wiley & Sons Inc., 2009.

As noted earlier in the book, Congress granted the FDA primary authority over the majority of food products, while the USDA has authority over meat, poultry, and liquid, frozen, and dried egg products (shelled eggs are regulated by the FDA). Several statutes provide each agency with its specific authority relevant to this chapter. The FDA's authority over the safety and labeling of food stems from the Federal Food, Drug, and Cosmetic Act (FDCA), and its modern food labeling authority was granted to it by the Nutrition Labeling and Education Act (NLEA). The USDA's authority stems from the Federal Meat Inspection Act, the Poultry Products Inspection Act, and the Egg Products Inspection Act. Within the USDA, the Food Safety and Inspection Service has the primary authority to regulate labeling of USDA-regulated products. The USDA also administers the National Organic Program and Country of Origin Labeling program, both of which will be discussed.

The First Amendment and Labels

The First Amendment states that Congress shall make no law "abridging the freedom of speech."[4] As discussed in Chapter 2, the original purpose of the First Amendment was to protect the freedom of political speech, which has since been expanded to protect other "core" speech including religious speech, literature, and art. In the 1976 case, *Virginia State Board of Pharmacy v. Virginia Citizens Consumer Council*, the Supreme Court confirmed that commercial speech is likewise protected by the First Amendment, but to a somewhat lesser degree.

Commercial speech is considered speech that proposes a commercial transaction,[5] and in 1995, the Court explicitly included labeling within the definition.[6] The Court does permit the government to require commercial factual disclosures and to regulate false, deceptive, and misleading commercial speech.[7] As discussed in greater detail in Chapter 7, the government may ban commercial speech that is considered "inherently misleading" or that has been proven to be misleading to consumers.[8] However, if the speech is only "potentially misleading," which means that it can be presented in another way or can be explained through disclaimers or factual disclosures, it cannot be banned.[9] The government may only require that potentially misleading speech be presented in a non-misleading manner—often by requiring a factual disclosure requirement to cure the potential deception. In *Virginia Pharmacy*, the Court explained that the

---

[4] U.S. Constitution Amendment I.

[5] *Board. of Trustees v. Fox*, 492 U.S. 469 (1989).

[6] *Rubin v. Coors Brewing Co.*, 514 U.S. 476 (1995).

[7] *Virginia State Board of Pharmacy v. Virginia Citizens Consumer Council*, 425 U.S. 748 (1976).

[8] *In re R.M.J.*, 455 U.S. 191, 203 (1982).

[9] *In re R.M.J.*, 455 U.S. 191, 203 (1982).

government may appropriately require that commercial messages include "additional information, warnings, and disclaimers."[10]

The Supreme Court also permits the government to require commercial actors to disclose factual information about their products or services. This concept predates the commercial speech doctrine. In early cases addressing laws that sought to prevent adulteration and misbranding of food products, the Court explained that, "it is too plain for argument that a manufacturer or vendor has no constitutional right to sell goods without giving to the purchaser fair information of what it is that is being sold."[11] For example, in 1918, the Supreme Court upheld a state labeling law that required syrup manufacturers to disclose the percentage of each ingredient of which their "table syrup" was composed (in this case 85% corn syrup or glucose, 10% molasses, and 5% sorghum).[12] Thus, factual disclosure requirements are permitted in the commercial context and are a common requirement for food labels. Note that the requirement must relate to factual information—the government cannot require commercial actors to disclose ideological or subjective information on their labels (or otherwise).[13]

In two cases since *Virginia Pharmacy*, the Court upheld commercial disclosure requirements, both of them in the context of attorney advertisements.[14] In the first case, *Zauderer v. Office of Disciplinary Counsel*, the Court held that, "an advertiser's rights are adequately protected as long as disclosure requirements are reasonably related to the State's interest in preventing deception of consumers."[15] This means that commercial disclosure requirements must be reasonably related to the government's interest, which is the easiest level of test to pass for constitutional questions.

It is important to note that both *Zauderer* and the second case relied on the government's interest in preventing deception.[16] The Supreme Court has not heard a case where a commercial actor challenges a basic commercial disclosure where the government posits a different interest. This begs the question of whether the government can require factual disclosures that are not related to preventing consumer deception. Federal circuit courts have overwhelmingly held that other government rationales, such as safety and health, suffice under the reasonable relationship test;[17] however, one court found that "consumer curiosity" alone was

---

[10] *Virginia State Board of Pharmacy v. Virginia Citizens Consumer Council*, 425 U.S. 748, 772 n.24 (1976).

[11] *Corn Prods. Ref. Co. v. Eddy*, 249 U.S. 427, 431 (1919).

[12] *Corn Prods. Ref. Co. v. Eddy*, 249 U.S. 427, 431 (1919).

[13] *Entertainment Software Association v. Blagojevich*, 469 F.3d 641 (7th Cir. 2006).

[14] See *Milavetz, Gallop & Milavetz, P.A. v. United States*, 130 S. Ct. 1324 (2001); *Zauderer v. Office of Disciplinary Counsel*, 471 U.S. 626 (1985).

[15] *Zauderer v. Office of Disciplinary Counsel*, 471 U.S. 626 (1985).

[16] See *Milavetz, Gallop & Milavetz, P.A. v. United States*, 130 S. Ct. 1324 (2001).

[17] *American Meat Institute v. United States Department of Agriculture*, 2014 U.S. App. LEXIS 14398 (D.C. Cir. July 29, 2014); N.Y. State Rest. Ass'n v. N.Y.C. Bd. of Health, 556 F.3d 114, 132–34 (2d Cir. 2009); Envtl. Def. Ctr. v. EPA, 344 F.3d 832, 851 (9th Cir. 2003); Nat'l Elec. Mfrs. Ass'n v. Sorrell, 272 F.3d 104, 115 (2d Cir. 2001); Pharm. Care Mgmt. Ass'n v. Rowe, 429 F.3d 294, 310 n.8 (1st Cir. 2005).

insufficient.[18] There are many factual disclosure requirements in the food context that could arguably be related to preventing consumer deception or conversely could be based on a broader regulatory regime supporting a truthful and transparent marketplace. Future Supreme Court cases will need to flesh out this question.

The Food and Drug Administration's Authority over Food Labeling

The FDA has authority over all food products except for food regulated by the USDA: meat, poultry, and liquid, frozen, and dried egg products. The FDA, however, has jurisdiction over meat products with less than or equal to 3% meat,[19] while the USDA has jurisdiction over raw meat and all other meat products.[20] The USDA also administers the National Organic Program, which encompasses food regulated by the FDA.

The FDA's main labeling authority stems from the NLEA and applies to most of the food under its control. The FDA created a voluntary program for food retailers to provide nutrition information for raw fruit, vegetables, and fish at the point-of-purchase.[21] The FDA suggests that retailers place labels "affixed to the food or through labeling including shelf labels, signs, posters, brochures, notebooks, or leaflets that are readily available and in close proximity to the foods,"[22] for the 20 most consumed fruits, vegetables, and fish, as listed in the regulations.[23]

Nutrition Labeling and Education Act

The FDA has regulatory authority over the labeling of the majority of food and beverages for sale in the country. In 1990, Congress enacted the NLEA, which amended the Food, Drug and Cosmetic Act of 1938 (FDCA). By 1993, the FDA enacted most of the regulations carrying out the intent of the NLEA. These regulations expand and explain how the FDA will enforce NLEA requirements.

The NLEA authorized the FDA to regulate nutrition labeling and disclosure statements. The "label" is defined as "display of written, printed, or graphic matter upon the immediate container of any article," and which must also appear or be easily legible from the outside container or wrapper.[24] Labeling means all

---

[18] *International Dairy Foods Association v. Amestoy*, 92 F.3d 67, 74 (2d Cir. 1996).

[19] Neal D. Fortin. *Food Regulation Law, Science, Policy, and Practice*. Hobokon, NJ: John Wiley & Sons Inc., 2009, p. 39.

[20] United States Department of Agriculture. Food Safety and Inspection Service. Food Standards and Labeling Policy Book. August 2005. http://www.fsis.usda.gov/wps/wcm/connect/7c48be3e-e516-4ccf-a2d5-b95a128f04ae/Labeling_Policy_Book_082005.pdf?MOD=AJPERES

[21] 21 CFR 101.42.

[22] 21 CFR 101.45.

[23] 21 CFR 101.44.

[24] 21 USCS § 321 (m)

labels and other written, printed, or graphic matters upon or accompanying the article, container, or wrapper.[25] Thus, labeling includes things like shelf tags accompanying the food.

Instead of directly requiring or prohibiting certain practices, the NLEA specifies that certain labeling practices or lapses in labeling would render a food misbranded. The regulation states that a food designed for sale to consumers is considered misbranded if: it has a false or misleading label; it is misnamed; is an imitation but does not so state; the container is misleading, or does not disclose the name and place of business of the manufacturer, packer, or distributor; it does not state the quantity of the contents; required information is not prominently displayed; it misrepresents to be a food with a standard of identity; it does not disclose the ingredient list using common usual names of ingredients; it does not meet standards of quality prescribed by regulations (e.g., pasteurization); it misrepresents that it is for special dietary use; it does not list artificial flavoring, coloring, or chemical preservatives; or it does not disclose the eight major food allergens, nutrition information, or health and nutrition-related claims according to regulations.[26]

A few provisions are worth explaining. In terms of the major food allergens noted above, Congress passed the Food Allergen Labeling and Consumer Protection Act of 2004, which requires that the eight "major food allergens," defined as milk, eggs, fish, crustacean shellfish, tree nuts, wheat, peanuts, and soybeans,[27] must be explicitly disclosed on all food regulated by the FDA. The Act requires a statement that the product "Contains" the food source from which the allergen is derived to be printed immediately after or adjacent to the ingredient list, or the list of ingredients must include the common or usual name of the food allergen followed by the name of the food source in parentheses.[28]

FDA regulations require the ingredient list to disclose ingredients in descending order of predominance by weight until the product contains 2% or less by weight of an ingredient, in which case the manufacturer may use a quantifying statement, such as "Contains _ percent or less of ___."[29]

In terms of nutrition information, the product would be considered misbranded unless the Nutrition Facts Panel provides: the serving size based on the amount customarily consumed or common household measure; number of servings per container; total number of calories and total number of calories derived from the total fat; amount per serving of total fat, saturated fat, cholesterol, sodium, total carbohydrates, complex carbohydrates, sugars, dietary fiber, and total protein; and specific vitamins and minerals. The regulations permit the Secretary of Health and Human Services (HHS) (which by

---

[25] 21 USCS § 321(k)
[26] 21 USC 343.
[27] 21 USCS § 321(q)(q)(1).
[28] 21 USCS § 343(w).
[29] 21 CFR 101.4.

designation translates into the FDA) to specify other nutrients if such information "will assist consumers in maintaining healthy dietary practices."[30] The FDA is undertaking rulemaking, discussed below, that might amend some of these requirements.

When a food is misbranded the agency has limited recourse against the violator. Although it has the power to issue civil fines in the context of food safety (including missing allergen information), the FDA does not have the authority to issue fines in the context of false or misleading labels.[31] The vast majority of misbranding violations are thus met with a Warning Letter putting the company on notice that its label violated the NLEA.[32] Through Warning Letters, the FDA seeks voluntary compliance by the company to correct the labeling violation. The agency may alternatively hold a meeting with the violator to discuss the violation. After notice through a letter or meeting, the FDA may condemn and seize misbranded food if it is dangerous to health, or if the labeling is fraudulent, or materially misleading in a way that could injure or damage a purchaser or consumer.[33] This is rare in the typical misbranding context.

A final and not highly utilized option of limited availability to the FDA is for it to work with the United States Department of Justice (DOJ) to seek an injunction or initiate a criminal prosecution after providing notice through the letter or meeting.[34] The FDA is prohibited from reporting "minor violations" to the DOJ and it has little guidance to determine when a food-related violation rises to the level of criminality.[35] The FDCA gives the FDA leeway to determine otherwise, but Congress stated that the FDA should not elevate a violation when the "public interest will be adequately served by a suitable written notice or warning."[36] Thus, for the vast majority of cases, the FDA responds to labeling violations by issuing Warning Letters.

It is important to note that the FDA lacks the authority to compel a company responsible for a misleading claim to disclose the research or scientific data that presumably served as the basis for the claim.[37] These are called substantiation documents, and unlike other government entities such as the FTC and state attorneys general, the FDA cannot require companies to provide the agency with substantiation documents if the FDA questions a claim.[38] Rather, the FDA has the burden of conducting its own

---

[30] 21 USC 343(q).

[31] 21 USC § 333.

[32] J. L. Pomeranz. A Comprehensive Strategy to Overhaul FDA Authority for Misleading Food Labels. *American Journal of Law & Medicine*. 2013;39(4):617–647.

[33] 21 U.S.C. § 334.

[34] 21 USC 335.

[35] J. L. Pomeranz. A Comprehensive Strategy to Overhaul FDA Authority for Misleading Food Labels. *American Journal of Law & Medicine*. 2013;39(4):617–647.

[36] 21 U.S.C. § 336.

[37] U.S. Government Accountability Office. GAO-11-102. Food Labeling: FDA Needs To Reassess Its Approach to Protecting Consumers From False or Misleading Claims. 2011.

[38] J. L. Pomeranz. A Comprehensive Strategy to Overhaul FDA Authority for Misleading Food Labels. *American Journal of Law & Medicine*. 2013;39(4):617–647.

research if it questions information on a company's label. This is a very high burden and dissuades the FDA from addressing all potential labeling violations.

Proposed Food Label Changes

In 2014, the agency announced that it was updating the Nutrition Facts Panel. The original Nutrition Facts Panel is compared with the proposed revised Nutrition Facts Panel in Figure 6.1. The FDA issued a notice of the proposed changes and sought public comments. The FDA received almost 8,000 comments, all of which the agency is tasked with reviewing.[39]

The FDA's major proposed changes in 2014 are reviewed in Box 6.1. It is important to note that the NLEA requires that serving size information be based on Reference Amounts Customarily Consumed (RACCs).[40] As such, the FDA defines "serving" and "serving size" as an amount of food customarily consumed per eating occasion.[41] The FDA established two sets of RACCs, one for children younger than four years of age, and one for persons four years and older.[42] These amounts were based on surveys of food consumption conducted in 1977–1978 and 1987–1988. Because consumers of all ages eat larger portions of food now than at the time of these surveys, the FDA is proposing to update the RACCs, and thus, the serving sizes on nutrition labels, to reflect current consumption patterns. In 2015, the FDA added a proposal to include the percent daily value for added sugars on the Nutrition Facts Panel.

Health and Nutrition Related Claims

The FDA's regulations related to health and nutrition-related claims have been subject to scrutiny, but the agency is not planning to address these regulations directly. A Government Accountability Office 2011 report found that 86.9% of the claims on food packages are express or implied nutrient content claims, 5.5% are structure-function claims, 4.3% are health claims, and 0.4% are qualified health claims.[43] Each of these will be explained in turn.

Health claims characterize the relationship of a substance to a disease or health-related condition and must be based on a "significant scientific agreement" standard.[44] The FDA has a guidance document for industry explaining

---

[39] http://www.regulations.gov/#!docketDetail;D=FDA-2012-N-1210 http://www.regulations.gov/#!docketDetail;D=FDA-2004-N-0258

[40] 21 USC 343(q)(1)(A)(i).

[41] 9 CFR 317.309

[42] 9 CFR 317.312.

[43] U.S. Government Accountability Office. GAO-11-102. Food Labeling: FDA Needs to Reassess Its Approach to Protecting Consumers From False or Misleading Claims. 2011.

[44] 21 CFR 101.14.

FIGURE 6.1 Original Nutrition Facts Panel and Proposed Revised Nutrition Facts Panel.[a]

[a]FDA. Proposed Changes to the Nutrition Facts Label http://www.fda.gov/food/guidanceregulation/guidancedocumentsregulatoryinformation/labelingnutrition/ucm385663.htm

the agency's current thinking on the significant scientific agreement standard.[45] The FDA relies on an "evidence-based review system," which it defines as the systematic science-based evaluation of the strength of the evidence, to determine if in totality, the scientific evidence supports the determination that there is significant scientific agreement to support a claim.[46] Health claims may be express, such as "healthful diets with adequate folate may reduce a woman's risk of having a child with a brain or spinal cord defect,"[47] or implied, such as through a heart symbol.[48] A product may not bear a health claim if it contains "disqualifying nutrient levels" of total fat (13 grams), saturated fat (4 grams),

[45] Food and Drug Administration. Guidance for Industry: Evidence-Based Review System for the Scientific Evaluation of Health Claims—Final (January 2009). http://www.fda.gov/food/guidanceregulation/guidancedocumentsregulatoryinformation/labelingnutrition/ucm073332.htm.

[46] Food and Drug Administration. Guidance for Industry: Evidence-Based Review System for the Scientific Evaluation of Health Claims—Final (January 2009). http://www.fda.gov/food/guidanceregulation/guidancedocumentsregulatoryinformation/labelingnutrition/ucm073332.htm.

[47] 21 CFR 101.79.

[48] 21 CFR 101.14.

BOX 6.1

Proposed Changes to the Nutrition Facts Panel (2014)

Update Nutrition Information

- Require information about "added sugars" because consumers should reduce the amount of added sugar in their diets.
- Update daily values for nutrients like sodium, dietary fiber, and Vitamin D because they are used to calculate the Percent Daily Value, which is supposed to help consumers understand this information in the context of a total daily diet.
- Require manufacturers to declare on the label the amount of potassium and Vitamin D; calcium and iron would continue to be disclosed, and the disclosure of Vitamins A and Vitamin C would be voluntary.
- Remove the "Calories from Fat" entry; the type of fat is more important than the amount.

Updated Serving Size Requirements and New Labeling Requirements for Certain Package Sizes

- Update the Reference Amounts Customarily Consumed (RACCs) for both children younger than four years of age, and for persons four years and older to reflect current consumption patterns.
- Require that packaged foods customarily consumed in one sitting be labeled a single serving (e.g., a 20ounce bottle of soft drink).
- Require large packages that might be consumed in one or more sittings (e.g., a pint of ice cream) to provide dual column labels disclosing the calorie and nutrient information "per serving" and "per package." The proposed dual-column Nutrition Facts Panel to reflect per serving and per package information is in Figure 6.2.

Refresh the Design

- Emphasize important parts of the label relevant to the public health concerns of obesity, diabetes, and cardiovascular disease.
- Emphasize the Percent Daily Value.
- Edit the footnote to explain the meaning of the Percent Daily Value information.

Source: FDA. Proposed Changes to the Nutrition Facts Label http://www.fda.gov/food/guidanceregulation/guidancedocumentsregulatoryinformation/labelingnutrition/ucm385663.htm

cholesterol (60 milligrams) or sodium (480 milligrams).[49] Note there are no disqualifying nutrient levels of trans fat or added or total sugar.

A qualified health claim is permitted when credible emerging or limited scientific evidence supports a relationship between a food and reduced risk of a disease or health-related condition. These claims are similar in intent to health claims but with less evidence supporting the assertion, and must include a disclaimer such as, "very limited and preliminary scientific research suggests" and a

[49] 21 CFR 101.14.

Dual Column Format

Nutrition Facts

2 servings per container
Serving size 1 cup (255g)

	Per 1 cup		Per container	
Calories	**220**		**440**	
	% DV*		**% DV***	
Total Fat	**8%**	5g	**15%**	10g
Saturated Fat	**10%**	2g	**20%**	4g
Trans Fat		0g		0g
Cholesterol	**5%**	15mg	**10%**	30mg
Sodium	**10%**	240mg	**21%**	480mg
Total Carbs	**12%**	35g	**23%**	70g
Dietary Fiber	**21%**	6g	**43%**	12g
Sugars		7g		14g
Added Sugars		4g		8g
Protein		9g		18g
Vitamin D	25%	5mcg	50%	10mcg
Calcium	15%	200mg	30%	400mg
Iron	6%	1mg	10%	2mg
Potassium	10%	470mg	20%	940mg

* Footnote on Daily Values (DV) and calories reference to be inserted here.

FIGURE 6.2 Proposed Dual Column Nutrition Facts Panel.[a]

[a]FDA. Proposed Changes to the Nutrition Facts Label. Dual Column Format of the Nutrition Facts Label. http://www.fda.gov/downloads/Food/GuidanceRegulation/GuidanceDocumentsRegulatoryInformation/LabelingNutrition/UCM387440.jpg

notation that the "FDA concludes that there is little scientific evidence supporting this claim."[50] An example of such a claim is: "Very limited and preliminary scientific research suggests that eating one-half to one cup of tomatoes and/or tomato sauce a week may reduce the risk of prostate cancer. FDA concludes that there is little scientific evidence supporting this claim."[51] For this example, the FDA only permits the claim on cooked, raw, dried, canned tomatoes or tomato sauce that contains at least 8.37% salt-free tomato solids.[52]

---

[50] Food and Drug Administration. Summary of Qualified Health Claims Subject to Enforcement Discretion. http://www.fda.gov/food/ingredientspackaginglabeling/labelingnutrition/ucm073992.htm

[51] Food and Drug Administration. Summary of Qualified Health Claims Subject to Enforcement Discretion. http://www.fda.gov/food/ingredientspackaginglabeling/labelingnutrition/ucm073992.htm

[52] Food and Drug Administration. Summary of Qualified Health Claims Subject to Enforcement Discretion. http://www.fda.gov/food/ingredientspackaginglabeling/labelingnutrition/ucm073992.htm

Note that when the FDA promulgated the original regulations to carry out the NLEA, it did not allow qualified health claims. In comments to the proposed rules, dietary supplement manufacturers (who are subject to some of the same labeling requirements as manufacturers of conventional food) argued that the regulations only permitting health claims based on significant scientific agreement violated their First Amendment rights to communicate the science about weaker health connections related to their products. The FDA disagreed and responded that the First Amendment does not require "a more lenient standard of scientific validity" because the "FDA has a strong interest in ensuring that the information that appears on the food label is scientifically valid and believes that the standard it has adopted best furthers that interest."[53] The FDA adopted the final regulations requiring that health claims be supported by the significant scientific agreement standard. Marketers of dietary supplements sued the FDA, again arguing that the final rules violated their First Amendment rights. A federal appellate court agreed with the marketers and held that the proposed speech was only potentially misleading and thus the FDA could not ban health claims that failed to meet the more robust scientific standard.[54] Rather, the agency must allow a modified health claim or one with a clarifying disclaimer.[55] The FDA has since applied this rationale to food products.

Nutrient content claims characterize the level of a nutrient of the type required to be disclosed in nutrition labeling. There are several types of nutrient content claims and they all must be made in accordance with Reference Amounts Customarily Consumed or the Recommended Daily Value of the food or nutrient. Nutrient content claims may be express, such as "low sodium," or implied, which is when the claim about a food or ingredient suggests that a nutrient or ingredient is absent or present, such as "good source of oat bran."[56] They may also compare the level of a nutrient in the food with the level of a nutrient in a designated similar reference food or the same food type. These are called "relative claims."[57] For example, pretzels have "less sodium" than potato chips, or the claim, "reduced fat potato chips," implies that they are reduced fat as compared to standard potato chips. Other types of nutrient content claims are common terms such as "healthy" and "fortified."[58] These all must be made according to specific regulatory requirements. However, if the food contains more than the "disqualifying nutrient levels" of total fat, saturated fat, cholesterol, or sodium, it must also bear a statement related to the nutrient exceeding the specified level

[53] 59 FR 395, 421 (1994).

[54] *Pearson v. Shalala*, 164 F.3d 650, 655-656 (D.C. Cir. 1999).

[55] *Pearson v. Shalala*, 164 F.3d 650, 657-658 (D.C. Cir. 1999).

[56] 21 CFR 101.13.

[57] 21 CFR 101.13.

[58] Food and Drug Administration. Guidance for Industry: A Food Labeling Guide (10. Appendix B: Additional Requirements for Nutrient Content Claims). January 2013. http://www.fda.gov/food/guidanceregulation/guidancedocumentsregulatoryinformation/labelingnutrition/ucm064916.htm

present in the food; for example, if the nutrient exceeding the specified level is fat, the statement must say: "See nutrition information for fat content."[59]

The final category of claims has the least amount of FDA regulation. Structure-function claims describe the role of a nutrient or ingredient intended to affect or maintain normal structure or function in the body; for example, "calcium builds strong bones," or "fiber maintains bowel regularity."[60] Structure-function claims do not need preapproval and there are no specific requirements for their use on conventional foods, so the manufacturer alone is responsible for their accuracy.[61]

The result of this lenient permission for food manufacturers to use structure-function claims is that the FDA has less recourse against a questionable claim.[62] The penultimate example occurred when Kellogg's placed the claim on its Rice and Cocoa Krispies cereals, "Now Helps Support Your Child's IMMUNITY."[63] The FDA did not issue a warning letter or bring other action against Kellogg's for this questionable claim because it is considered a structure-function claim and also the FDA could not require Kellogg's to turn over its substantiation documents. The FTC, however, does not have similar restraints on its authority. It did investigate the claim and admonished Kellogg's to refrain from making misleading representations in the future.

The inclusion of high fructose corn syrup in food products has resulted in interesting and controversial labeling issues. These are described in Box 6.2.

Front-of-package Labeling for Processed Food Products

Between 2004 and 2008, several of the major food companies created their own front-of-package (FOP) symbols to highlight positive aspects of their products. For example, Kellogg's created "Nutrition at a Glance,"[64] General Mills created "Nutrition Highlights," PepsiCo launched Smart Spots, and Kraft created Sensible Solutions.[65] Hannaford grocery store also developed its own shelf tag

---

[59] 21 CFR 101.13.

[60] Food and Drug Administration. Label Claims for Conventional Foods and Dietary Supplements. December 2013. http://www.fda.gov/food/ingredientspackaginglabeling/labelingnutrition/ucm111447.htm

[61] Food and Drug Administration. Label Claims for Conventional Foods and Dietary Supplements. December 2013. http://www.fda.gov/food/ingredientspackaginglabeling/labelingnutrition/ucm111447.htm

[62] J. L. Pomeranz. A Comprehensive Strategy to Overhaul FDA Authority for Misleading Food Labels. *American Journal of Law & Medicine*. 2013;39(4):617–647.

[63] Bruce Horovitz. Critics Blast Kellogg's Claim that Cereals Can Boost Immunity. *USA Today*. November 6, 2009. http://www.usatoday.com/money/industries/food/2009-11-02-cereal-immunity-claim_N.htm.

[64] News Releases/Statements Attention Shoppers: Nutrition's Got a Brand New Look. September 18, 2007. http://newsroom.kelloggcompany.com/index.php?s=27529&item=76217

[65] Michele Tuttle. How Nutrition Symbols Influence Which Foods We Buy. *Food & Nutrition*. March 1, 2008. http://www.foodandnutrition.org/Online-Exclusives/2008/How-Nutrition-Symbols-Influence-Which-Foods-We-Buy/

BOX 6.2

High Fructose Corn Syrup and Labeling

One of the more controversial food ingredients involved in labeling issues is high fructose corn syrup (HFCS). HFCS initially is derived from the wet milling of corn and produced by a controlled enzymatic process that changes the corn starch through processing.[a] HFCS is shelf-stable and less expensive than sugar produced from beets or sugarcane in the United States. The majority of HFCS produced in the United States is used by the beverage industry.[b] In the early 2000s, emerging scientific research began to question whether there was a link between HFCS and obesity.[c] Although the science has moved to conclude that HFCS acts on the body similar to other sugars,[d] public opinion shifted toward a negative perception of HFCS. In surveys, consumers report that they try to avoid HFCS,[e] and some beverage companies began producing other versions of their soft drinks, while touting that these were made with "real sugar."[f] Two labeling issues resulted from this negative public perception.

First, food products containing HFCS and adorning a "natural" claim were subject to a great deal of litigation by consumers who claimed that this was a false assertion because they did not consider HFCS to be "natural."[g] Business trade groups, companies, consumers, and courts have requested that the FDA define the term "natural" to resolve this and other related disputes. Notably, the Sugar Association petitioned the FDA for clarification of the term "natural," presumably believing that sugar would be found to meet any such definition. Conversely, the Corn Refiners Association, a national trade group that represents producers of HFCS (among other corn products), submitted comments opposing such a clarification, stating that the FDA should not "waste scarce agency resources" to define the term, but rather should let the marketplace resolve the issue.[h] Notwithstanding all such requests, the FDA has declined to define the term "natural" beyond its statement that it will not "restrict the use of the term "natural" except for added color, synthetic substances, and flavors."[i]

A second controversy arose in response to the negative press associated with HFCS. The Corn Refiners Association began a media campaign titled, Sweet Surprise, to address and counter what it considered misinformation about HFCS in the media.[j] As part of this campaign, they started to call HFCS "corn sugar" and simultaneously petitioned the FDA to authorize "corn sugar" as an alternative name for HFCS.[k] The FDA, however, denied this request, explaining that FDA regulations already "describe and define corn sugar as 'dextrose.' " Further, the requested change would conflict with the FDA's regulatory approach on the "nomenclature of sugar and syrups," which "is that sugar is a solid, dried, and crystallized food; whereas syrup is an aqueous solution or liquid food."[l] Thus, HFCS remains the product's name and food containing it may continue to be labeled as "natural" under federal law.

[a]Peter S. Murano. *Understanding Food Science and Technology*. Belmont, CA: Thomson Wadsworth, 2003.

[b]United States Department of Agriculture. Economic Research Service. Sugar & Sweeteners. http://www.ers.usda.gov/topics/crops/sugar-sweeteners/background.aspx#.U-TipKOuCiO

[c]D. M. Klurfeld, J. Foreyt, T. J. Angelopoulos, J. M. Rippe. Lack of evidence for high fructose corn syrup as the cause of the obesity epidemic *International Journal of Obesity*. 2013;37: 771–773.

[d]Stanhope, K. L. Role of Fructose-containing Sugars in the Epidemics of Obesity and Metabolic Syndrome. *Annual Review of Medicine*. 2012;63: 329–343; Lustig, R. H. Fructose: Metabolic, Hedonic, and Societal Parallels With Ethanol. *Journal of the American Dietetic Association*, 2010; 110(9): 1307–1321.

[e]International Food Information Council Foundation. 2013 Food & Health Survey. *Food Insight*. April 1, 2013 http://old.foodinsight.org/LinkClick.aspx?fileticket=spavtJtVkzM%3d&tabid=1482.

(continued)

BOX 6.2
Continued

[f]PepsiCo. Pepsi-Cola Made With Real Sugar http://www.pepsicobeveragefacts.com/Home/Product?formula=35009*A9*01-01&form=RTD&size=20

[g]See Chapter 8, Litigation.

[h]Comments on the sugar association citizen petition re: definition of the term "Natural" for making claims on foods and beverages regulated by the Food and Drug Administration. November 14, 2006.

[i]58 FR 2302, 2407 (January 6, 1993).

[j]Sweet Surprise. http://sweetsurprise.com/

[k]Food and Drug Administration. Response to Petition from Corn Refiners Association to Authorize "Corn Sugar" as an Alternate Common or Usual Name for High Fructose Corn Syrup (HFCS). May 30, 2012. http://www.fda.gov/aboutfda/centersoffices/officeoffoods/cfsan/cfsanfoiaelectronicreadingroom/ucm305226.htm

[l]Food and Drug Administration. Response to Petition from Corn Refiners Association to Authorize "Corn Sugar" as an Alternate Common or Usual Name for High Fructose Corn Syrup (HFCS). May 30, 2012. http://www.fda.gov/aboutfda/centersoffices/officeoffoods/cfsan/cfsanfoiaelectronicreadingroom/ucm305226.htm

---

nutrition rating system.[66] The FDA reported receiving complaints about the diverse FOP labeling strategies.

In the 2009 Appropriations Act, Congress included funding for a study by the Institute of Medicine (IOM) to examine FOP nutrition symbols used by manufacturers, supermarkets, health organizations, and governments, to provide recommendations on "the overall merits of front-label nutrition icons, the advantages and disadvantages of various approaches, and the potential benefits of a single, standardized front label food guidance system" regulated by the FDA to best promote consumer health.[67] The IOM conducted a two-phase study and issued reports in 2010[68] and 2011,[69] analyzing various nutrition rating systems, relevant scientific research, and consumer comprehension and use of front-of-package systems.

The FDA engaged in efforts to address the proliferation of FOP schemes and support consumers' nutrition-related decisions. In 2009, Commissioner Margaret Hamburg announced that the FDA was: examining FOP schemes to determine whether any violate misbranding regulations; drafting a new regulation to provide a single set of FOP labels based on scientifically and nutritionally based

---

[66] Hannaford. Guiding Stars (developed 2006). http://www.hannaford.com/content.jsp?pageName=GuidingStars&leftNavArea=HealthLeftNav

[67] Explanatory Statement Submitted by Mr. Obey, Chairman of the House Committee on Appropriations, Regarding HR 1105, Omnibus Appropriations Act, 2009. Division F—Labor, Health and Human Services and Education, and Related Agencies Appropriations, p. 1398.

[68] Institute of Medicine. *Examination of Front-of-Package Nutrition Rating Systems and Symbols: Phase I Report*. Washington, DC: The National Academies Press; 2010.

[69] Institute of Medicine. *Front-of-Package Nutrition Rating Systems and Symbols: Promoting Healthier Choices*. Washington, DC: The National Academies Press; 2011.

science; conducting consumer research; and planning to reach out to food manufacturers, retailers, and other stakeholders to work together on this.[70] In March 2010, Commissioner Hamburg announced that the "FDA will soon issue new draft guidance relating to front-of-pack calorie and nutrient labeling."[71] This guidance has never been issued. Food manufacturers thus continue to use their own FOP schemes.

Preemption

The NLEA explicitly preempts state and local governments from directly or indirectly establishing requirements on food sold in interstate commerce that are not identical to the requirements of the NLEA.[72] There are two exceptions to this. First, state and local governments may petition the Secretary of HHS for an exemption to the NLEA if the request would not cause any food to be in violation of federal law, would not unduly burden interstate commerce, and is designed to address a particular need for information that is not met by the NLEA.[73] This is not a common occurrence.

Secondly, Congress explained that the preemption clause "shall not be construed to apply to any requirement respecting a statement in the labeling of food that provides for a warning concerning the safety of the food or component of the food."[74] This exception is the reason California's Proposition 65 is not preempted. "Prop 65," as it is called, notifies state residents of any products or chemicals known to the state to be associated with health hazards. It requires that warning signs, notices, menu stickers, or labels provide a warning in accordance with California regulations, such as: "WARNING: This product may contain a chemical known to the State of California to cause cancer, or birth defects or other reproductive harm."[75]

In 2014 and 2015, a California state legislator introduced a bill that would require labels on sugary drinks to state: "STATE OF CALIFORNIA SAFETY WARNING: Drinking beverages with added sugar(s) contributes to obesity, diabetes, and tooth decay."[76,77] This failed to pass both times, but the

---

[70] Transcript for FDA's media briefing on front-of-pack labeling. FDA position on front-of-package labeling. October 20, 2009. Remarks of Dr. Margaret Hamburg, Commissioner of Food and Drug Administration. www.fda.gov/downloads/NewsEvents/Newsroom/MediaTranscripts/UCM187809.pdf.

[71] Open Letter to Industry from Dr. Hamburg. March 3, 2010. http://www.fda.gov/Food/IngredientsPackagingLabeling/LabelingNutrition/ucm202733.htm

[72] 21 USC 343-1.

[73] 21 USC 343-1.

[74] 104 Stat. 2353, *6 (1990).

[75] California Code of Regulations, Title 27, Article 6, Clear and Reasonable Warnings § 25601 et seq.

[76] P. McGreevy. Health Warning Labels Proposed for Soda Sold in California. February 13, 2014. http://touch.latimes.com/#section/-1/article/p2p-79281799/

[77] California Senate Bill 203 (2015).

legislator remains interested in pursuing this policy. A similar bill, proposed in the New York State Assembly in 2014 and 2015, would require the warning: "SAFETY WARNING: DRINKING BEVERAGES WITH ADDED SUGAR CONTRIBUTES TO OBESITY, DIABETES AND TOOTH DECAY," to be placed on sugary-beverage containers, vending machines, and at the point of purchase, among other locations.[78,79] This bill is under consideration.

U.S. Department of Agriculture's Authority over Food Labeling

The USDA's Food Safety and Inspection Service (FSIS) is in charge of the labeling of meat and poultry products pursuant to the Federal Meat Inspection Act (FMIA).[80] Under this law, "label" is defined as "a display of any printing, embossing, stickers, seals, or other written, printed, or graphic matter upon the immediate container (not including package liners) of any product."[81] Labeling includes all labels and other written, printed, or graphic matter upon the article or any of its containers or wrappers, or accompanying such article.[82] Thus, shelf tags and accompanying material factor into labeling regulations. The USDA requires the following on meat and poultry product labels: the name of the product; ingredients in the product if it is fabricated from two or more ingredients; the name and place of business of the product's manufacturer, packer, or distributor; the net quantity of contents; and an official inspection legend,[83] which is a stamp stating that the product was inspected.

Meat and Poultry

The FMIA and Poultry Products Inspection Act (PPIA) prohibit misbranded labels for meat and poultry, which occurs if (1) the label is false or misleading; (2) the contents are offered for sale under the name of another food; (3) the product is an imitation of another food and does not so state; (4) the container is so made, formed, or filled as to be misleading; (5) the label lacks required company information and net weight; (6) the labeling is not prominent and conspicuous; (7) the product purports to be a food for which a definition and standard of identity has been prescribed and it does not conform to these; (8) the product

---

[78] New York Assembly Bill 10172 (2014).

[79] New York Assembly Bill 02320 (2015).

[80] United States Department of Agriculture. A Guide to Federal Food Labeling Requirements For Meat, Poultry, and Egg Products. August 2007. http://www.fsis.usda.gov/wps/wcm/connect/f4af7c74-2b9f-4484-bb16-fd8f9820012d/Labeling_Requirements_Guide.pdf?MOD=AJPERES

[81] 21 USCS § 601(o) (meat); 21 USCS § 453(s) poultry.

[82] 21 USCS § 601(p) (meat); 21 USCS § 453(s) poultry.

[83] 9 CFR 317.2(c).

misrepresents itself as a food with a standard of fill and does not meet it; (9) the label does not bear the product's common or usual name (provided it is not covered by a standard of identity) or declare ingredients by common or usual name; (10) the contents purport to be for special dietary uses but do not conform to FDA regulations; (11) fails to declare any artificial flavoring, artificial coloring, or chemical preservative; or (12) the package fails to bear the inspection legend and any other required information.[84,85]

Unlike for food labels regulated by the FDA under the NLEA, before a producer may introduce meat or poultry products into interstate commerce, FSIS must approve the product's label.[86] The producer must submit a label sketch to FSIS,[87] which reviews tens of thousands of labels each year.[88] Revised labels and those that conform to the generic labeling regulations do not need to be pre-reviewed by the agency.[89] FSIS requires that all proposed labels using "special statements and claims" must receive prior approval by the agency during the sketch label submission process.[90] These include logos, trademarks, symbols (e.g., American Heart Association heart), health claims, structure-function claims, nutrient content claims, claims regarding the raising of animals, front-of-package schemes (e.g., Facts Up Front), and specific statements such as organic, natural, and "made with whole grain."[91] Other claims can get generic approval including those with pre-approved nutrition definitions, poultry slaughtered in accordance with religious ritual (kosher or halal), and environmental claims.[92]

In December 2010, FSIS started requiring producers and retailers of major cuts of single-ingredient raw meat and poultry, as well as ground or chopped meat and poultry products, with or without added seasonings, to provide nutrition labels.[93] The required nutrition label mimics the requirements of the Nutrition Facts Panel established by the FDA.[94] Prior to this, the USDA's regulations required nutrition labels on the packages of most multi-ingredient and

---

[84] 21 USCS § 601(n) (meat).

[85] 21 USCS § 453(h) (poultry).

[86] United States Department of Agriculture. A Guide to Federal Food Labeling Requirements For Meat, Poultry, and Egg Products. August 2007. http://www.fsis.usda.gov/wps/wcm/connect/f4af7c74-2b9f-4484-bb16-fd8f9820012d/Labeling_Requirements_Guide.pdf?MOD=AJPERES

[87] 9 CFR 412.1

[88] 9 CFR 412.1

[89] 9 CFR 412.1

[90] 9 CFR 412.1

[91] United States Department of Agriculture. Food Safety and Inspection Service. Generic Label Approval. http://www.fsis.usda.gov/wps/wcm/connect/1364c48d-214b-41bf-bab8-6289f951cb31/Generic-Final-Rule-Overview-Industry.pdf?MOD=AJPERES

[92] United States Department of Agriculture. Food Safety and Inspection Service. Generic Label Approval. http://www.fsis.usda.gov/wps/wcm/connect/1364c48d-214b-41bf-bab8-6289f951cb31/Generic-Final-Rule-Overview-Industry.pdf?MOD=AJPERES

[93] Federal Register, 75(249): 82148.

[94] United States Department of Agriculture. Food Safety and Inspection Service. Nutrition Facts Panel—Examples. http://www.fsis.usda.gov/wps/wcm/connect/2e5394d2-b224-4f3b-818a-8a161771c9a9/Nutrition_Panel_Format.pdf?MOD=AJPERES

heat-processed meat and poultry products and it established guidelines for voluntary nutrition labeling of single-ingredient raw meat and poultry products and raw ground or chopped products.[95] Now major cuts, as well as ground and chopped meat and poultry, must have a nutrition label on the product. Retailers are required to provide point-of-purchase materials or nutrition labels for the same cuts; if they do not, they will be deemed misbranded under the FMIA and the PPIA.[96] Examples of major cuts of meat are chicken wings, turkey breast, and lamb rib roast; examples of minor cuts of meat include beef ribs and chicken tenders.[97] These are specified by the agency. Some exceptions apply for meat intended for export or further processing or meat that is not intended for sale to consumers.[98]

Retailers are required to place labeling on products packaged at the retailer (e.g., product name, handling statement, net weight, address, safe handling instructions, and the ingredients statement). Unlike producers,[99] retailers do not need prior approval for the addition of new information to their nutrition labels.[100]

FSIS regulations prohibit false or misleading labels, wrappers, packaging, and containers, including no statements, words, pictures, designs, or devices that convey any false impression or give any false indication of a location of origin for meat products or poultry products.[101,102] FSIS defines certain meat and poultry product terms so manufacturers can ensure their labels are truthful and not misleading. For example, in order for producers of meat and poultry products to state "free range" on a label, producers must demonstrate to the agency that the poultry has been allowed access to the outdoors. Further, hormones are not allowed in raising hogs or poultry, so the claim "no hormones added" only can be placed on the labels of pork or poultry when it is followed by a statement reading, "Federal regulations prohibit the use of hormones." The term "natural" may

---

[95] Federal Register, 75(249): 82148.

[96] Federal Register, 75(249): 82148.

[97] United States Department of Agriculture. Food Safety and Inspection Service. Nutrition Labeling of Single-Ingredient Products and Ground or Chopped Meat and Poultry Products http://www.fsis.usda.gov/wps/wcm/connect/092327ce-0b6f-47db-82e9-992e2350de73/Nutrition_Labeling_Overview.ppt?MOD=AJPERES

[98] United States Department of Agriculture. Food Safety and Inspection Service. Nutrition Labeling of Single-Ingredient Products and Ground or Chopped Meat and Poultry Products http://www.fsis.usda.gov/wps/wcm/connect/092327ce-0b6f-47db-82e9-992e2350de73/Nutrition_Labeling_Overview.ppt?MOD=AJPERES

[99] United States Department of Agriculture. Food Safety and Inspection Service. Nutrition Labeling of Single-Ingredient Products and Ground or Chopped Meat and Poultry Products http://www.fsis.usda.gov/wps/wcm/connect/092327ce-0b6f-47db-82e9-992e2350de73/Nutrition_Labeling_Overview.ppt?MOD=AJPERES

[100] United States Department of Agriculture Food Safety and Inspection Service. Nutrition Labeling - Questions and Answers http://www.fsis.usda.gov/wps/wcm/connect/d166536c-39d7-4331-b588-5dccdbe0d0f9/Nutrition_labeling_Q_A_041312.pdf?MOD=AJPERES

[101] 9 CFR 317.8 (a).

[102] 9 CFR 381.129

be used on a "product containing no artificial ingredient or added color and is only minimally processed," which means that it was "processed in a manner that does not fundamentally alter the product."[103] If a producer uses this term, the label must include a statement explaining the rationale, such as "No artificial ingredients" or "Minimally processed."[104] Moreover, FSIS requires a certain percentage of meat in products such as "chili con carne," spaghetti with meatballs, and "shepherds pie."[105]

FSIS has not issued regulations providing for the use of health claims or structure-function claims on meat or poultry products,[106] but it does have regulations expressly permitting the use of nutrient content claims and implied nutrient content claims.[107] The regulations are similar to those of the FDA. According to USDA regulations, the use of "free" or "low" before the name of a product implies that the product was specially processed, altered, formulated, or reformulated to lower, remove, or exclude the nutrient in the product (e.g., low sodium beef stew); otherwise, it must refer to all product types (e.g., chicken breast meat, a low sodium food).[108]

If a product is found to be misbranded, FSIS has the authority to rescind the use of the label; seize, condemn or detain the product;[109] request a product recall; issue press releases; issue fines; and in extreme cases, initiate criminal prosecution.[110] FSIS may also refuse to provide, or may withdraw, inspection service for a facility that produces a misbranded product.[111]

Eggs

Shelled eggs for retail sale must comply with FDA regulations. Egg products, which are dried, frozen, or liquid eggs, with or without added ingredients, are subject to USDA regulations and inspection provisions.[112] The Egg Products Inspection Act prohibits false or misleading labels.[113] The Fair Packaging and

---

[103] 9 CFR 381.129

[104] 9 CFR 381.129

[105] United States Department of Agriculture. Food Safety and Inspection Service. Food Standards and Labeling Policy Book. August 2005. http://www.fsis.usda.gov/wps/wcm/connect/7c48be3e-e516-4ccf-a2d5-b95a128f04ae/Labeling_Policy_Book_082005.pdf?MOD=AJPERES

[106] United States Department of Agriculture. A Guide to Federal Food Labeling Requirements For Meat, Poultry, and Egg Products. August 2007. http://www.fsis.usda.gov/wps/wcm/connect/f4af7c74-2b9f-4484-bb16-fd8f9820012d/Labeling_Requirements_Guide.pdf?MOD=AJPERES

[107] 9 CFR 317.313 (meat); 9 CFR 381.413 (poultry)

[108] 9 CFR 317.313 (meat); 9 CFR 381.413 (poultry)

[109] 21 USC 672; 21 USC 673; 21 U.S.C. § 467

[110] United States Department of Agriculture. A Guide to Federal Food Labeling Requirements For Meat, Poultry, and Egg Products. August 2007. http://www.fsis.usda.gov/wps/wcm/connect/f4af7c74-2b9f-4484-bb16-fd8f9820012d/Labeling_Requirements_Guide.pdf?MOD=AJPERES

[111] 21 USC 671; 21 U.S.C. § 467

[112] 7 CFR 94.2.

[113] 21 USCS § 1036

Labeling Act applies to egg products[114] and requires the basic information mentioned above.[115] For the most part, the eggs that come into contact with consumers are regulated by the FDA and have the familiar labeling.

Preemption

The federal laws administered by the USDA, Federal Meat Inspection Act, the Poultry Products Inspection Act, and the Egg Products Inspection Act preempt states from requiring different labeling than that required by federal law.[116] They all, however, permit states to enact identical requirements in order to exercise concurrent jurisdiction of enforcement to protect consumers against adulteration and misbranding.[117] States, territories, and the District of Columbia also may impose recordkeeping requirements that are the same as required by federal law.[118] Although they may not impose additional or different marking, labeling, packaging, or ingredient requirements than USDA regulations, they may exercise concurrent jurisdiction with the USDA for inspection purposes to prevent the distribution of adulterated or misbranded articles.[119]

National Organic Program

Congress passed the Organic Foods Production Act of 1990 in order to establish nationally consistent standards governing the marketing of agricultural products as organically produced.[120] USDA's Agricultural Marketing Service runs the National Organic Program. In order for products to be labeled as organic, they must be produced and handled without the use of synthetic chemicals, and in compliance with the organic plan agreed to by the producer/handler and the certifying agent.[121] The Agricultural Marketing Service explains that for crops, the "USDA organic seal verifies that irradiation, sewage sludge, synthetic fertilizers, prohibited pesticides, and genetically modified organisms were not used."[122] For

---

[114] 21 USCS § 1052

[115] United States Department of Agriculture. Guide to Federal Food Labeling Requirements For Meat, Poultry, and Egg Products. August 2007. http://www.fsis.usda.gov/wps/wcm/connect/f4af7c74-2b9f-4484-bb16-fd8f9820012d/Labeling_Requirements_Guide.pdf?MOD=AJPERES

[116] 21 U.S.C. § 678 (meat); 21 U.S.C. § 467(e) (poultry); 21 USC § 1052 (egg products).

[117] 21 U.S.C. § 678 (meat); 21 U.S.C. § 467(e) (poultry); 21 USC § 1052 (egg products).

[118] 21 U.S.C. § 678 (meat); 21 U.S.C. § 467(e) (poultry); 21 USC § 1052 (egg products).

[119] 21 U.S.C. § 678 (meat); 21 U.S.C. § 467(e) (poultry); 21 USC § 1052 (egg products).

[120] 7 U.S.C. 6501

[121] 7 USCS § 6504

[122] United States Department of Agriculture. Agricultural Marketing Service. http://www.ams.usda.gov/AMSv1.0/NOPOrganicStandards

livestock, the organic seal "verifies that producers met animal health and welfare standards, did not use antibiotics or growth hormones, used 100% organic feed, and provided animals with access to the outdoors."[123] No product may be labeled organic if it contains any amount of genetically modified organisms (GMOs) or is produced using genetic engineering.[124] The USDA is quite strict about this, so farmers must not only avoid GMOs but also must utilize crop spacing and timing methods to avoid cross-pollination with neighboring farms.

For multi-ingredient food products, the USDA's organic seal verifies that the product is comprised of 95% or more certified organic content. For products made with organic ingredients, at least 70% of the content must be organic (excluding water and salt) in order for the label to include a statement that the product is made with organic ingredients, food groups, or a combination of the two.[125] Such a label may list up to three ingredients or food groups, and the other agricultural ingredients must be produced without genetic engineering, sewage sludge, or ionizing radiation. The nonagricultural ingredients (e.g., baking soda) must be permitted according to the National List of Allowed and Prohibited Substances.[126] A farm or processing facility must be certified organic before it can label its products as organic. As of 2012, the USDA estimated that globally, approximately 30,000 organic farms and processing facilities are certified to the USDA organic standards.[127]

An entity that seeks to be an organic certifying agent must first be accredited by the USDA. The certifying agent is charged with ensuring that the proposed products meet USDA organic regulations and standards. On a yearly basis, the accredited certifying agent must verify that each certified organic farmer and food processor are complying with USDA regulations. The agent conducts on-site inspections and may conduct residue testing to screen for prohibited substances, such as synthetic pesticides.[128] The USDA also conducts its own investigations

---

[123] United States Department of Agriculture. Agricultural Marketing Service. http://www.ams.usda.gov/AMSv1.0/NOPOrganicStandards

[124] United States Department of Agriculture Blogs. Organics 101. May 17, 2013. http://blogs.usda.gov/2013/05/17/organic-101-can-gmos-be-used-in-organic-products/

[125] United States Department of Agriculture. Agricultural Marketing Service. National Organic Program. Products in the "Made With Organic ***" Labeling Category. NOP Document 5032. May 2, 2014. www.ams.usda.gov/AMSv1.0/getfile?dDocName=STELPRDC5107318

[126] United States Department of Agriculture. Agricultural Marketing Service. National Organic Program. Products in the "Made With Organic ***" Labeling Category. NOP Document 5032. May 2, 2014. www.ams.usda.gov/AMSv1.0/getfile?dDocName=STELPRDC5107318

[127] United States Department of Agriculture Agricultural Marketing Service. National Organic Program. Organic Certification & Accreditation. http://www.ams.usda.gov/AMSv1.0/ams.fetchTemplateData.do?template=TemplateN&navID=OrgCertLinkNOPOrganicStandards&rightNav1=OrgCertLinkNOPOrganicStandards&topNav=&leftNav=&page=NOPAccreditationandCertification&resultType=&acct=nopgeninfo

[128] United States Department of Agriculture. Agricultural Marketing Service. National Organic Program. Compliance and Enforcement. http://www.ams.usda.gov/AMSv1.0/ams.fetchTemplateData.do?template=TemplateE&navID=CompEnforceLinkNOPAboutUs&rightNav1=CompEnforceLinkNOPAboutUs&topNav=&leftNav=NationalOrganicProgram&page=NOPComplianceandEnforcement&resultType=&acct=nopgeninfo

and residue testing to ensure compliance with organic standards.[129] The agency also accepts and investigates complaints by consumers who believe that a product labeled "organic" does not meet national standards.[130] For violators of the National Organic Program, the USDA can issue notices of noncompliance, suspend or revoke the certification or accreditation of a once-certified or accredited entity, enter into settlement agreements, issue cease-and-desist letters to uncertified operations, and issue civil penalties to applicants for certification, as well as certified and uncertified operations (but not accredited certifying agents).[131]

Country of Origin Labeling

The USDA Agricultural Market Service is in charge of Country of Origin Labeling (COOL). COOL requirements were passed under the 2002 and 2008 Farm Bills. Regulations implementing each part of the legislation are divided by the type of covered commodity and were finalized years later, some not becoming effective until 2009.[132] COOL is required for fish and shellfish,[133] beef, veal, pork, lamb, chicken, goat, fresh and frozen fruit and vegetables (called Perishable Agricultural Commodities), macadamia nuts, pecans, peanuts, ginseng,[134] and honey. [135] COOL designations must be made to reflect where an animal was born, raised, and slaughtered so labels may designate up to three countries.[136] Processed foods with these ingredients such as hot dogs and fish sticks, and cooked versions of the covered commodities, such as roasted peanuts and canned tuna,[137] are exempt from COOL requirements.[138]

---

[129] United States Department of Agriculture. Organic Agriculture. http://www.usda.gov/wps/portal/usda/usdahome?contentidonly=true&contentid=organic-agriculture.html

[130] United States Department of Agriculture. Organic Agriculture. http://www.usda.gov/wps/portal/usda/usdahome?contentidonly=true&contentid=organic-agriculture.html

[131] National Organic Program. Enforcement Policy. NOP Document 4002. July 22, 2011. www.ams.usda.gov/AMSv1.0/getfile?dDocName=STELPRDC5087117

[132] Congressional Research Service. Country-of-Origin Labeling for Foods and the WTO Trade Dispute on Meat Labeling. September 16, 2013. http://fas.org/sgp/crs/misc/RS22955.pdf

[133] 7 CFR 60.300

[134] 7 CFR 65.400

[135] 7 CFR 52.54

[136] United States Department of Agriculture. Country of Origin Labeling for Meat and Chicken. http://www.fsis.usda.gov/wps/portal/fsis/topics/food-safety-education/get-answers/food-safety-fact-sheets/food-labeling/country-of-origin-labeling-for-meat-and-chicken/country-of-origin-labeling-for-meat-and-chicken

[137] United States Department of Agriculture. Cool. Country of Origin Labeling. Retailers and Consumers. October 2009. http://www.google.com/url?sa=t&rct=j&q=&esrc=s&source=web&cd=5&cad=rja&uact=8&ved=0CDwQFjAE&url=http%3A%2F%2F www.ams.usda.gov%2FAMSv1.0%2Fgetfile%3FdDocName%3DSTELPRDC5076163&ei=3QTdU-reB9GLyATLrYGgDw&usg=AFQjCNHwXOe8nwOW-uRKJfRBDKoRGkFl_g&sig2=IYxlq6AFoUk1m861ey88lg&bvm=bv.72197243,d.aWw

[138] Congressional Research Service. Country-of-Origin Labeling for Foods and the WTO Trade Dispute on Meat Labeling. September 16, 2013. http://fas.org/sgp/crs/misc/RS22955.pdf

Retailers licensed under the Perishable Agricultural Commodities Act[139] are required to provide COOL information through a typed, handwritten, or printed placard, sign, label, sticker, band, twist tie, pin tag, or other display.[140] Retailers and their suppliers are required to keep records upon which the COOL disclosure is based. Food service establishments are exempt from COOL requirements.[141]

COOL labeling is quite controversial. The USDA states that the "program is neither a food safety or traceability program but rather a consumer information program."[142] Proponents argue that COOL provides valuable information to consumers. Opponents argue that there is no strong evidence that consumers want this information, the costs to industry outweigh any interest in this information, it is a form of American protectionism, and it potentially undermines efforts to reduce trade barriers.[143] One impetus for COOL labeling seems to be based on concerns regarding past and future disease outbreaks from infected imported foods. These concerns relate to safety and might be akin to a criticism of the USDA's importation inspection controls.[144]

In 2009, Canada and Mexico challenged the COOL laws at the World Trade Organization (WTO), arguing that they distort trade by reducing the value and number of livestock shipped to the U.S. market, thereby violating WTO trade agreements by the United States.[145] The WTO established a panel to hear the complaints. In 2011, the WTO dispute settlement panel ruled that certain COOL requirements violate U.S. WTO commitments. The United States appealed and the appellate body found that the COOL laws partially violated the Technical Barriers to Trade (TBT) Agreement.[146] The United States informed the WTO Dispute Settlement Body that its final regulations corrected the violations of the TBT Agreement, bringing it into compliance with the findings of the Dispute

---

[139] United States Department of Agriculture. Country of Origin Labeling for Meat and Chicken. http://www.fsis.usda.gov/wps/portal/fsis/topics/food-safety-education/get-answers/food-safety-fact-sheets/food-labeling/country-of-origin-labeling-for-meat-and-chicken/country-of-origin-labeling-for-meat-and-chicken

[140] 7 CFR 65.400; 7 CFR 60.300

[141] Congressional Research Service. Country-of-Origin Labeling for Foods and the WTO Trade Dispute on Meat Labeling. September 16, 2013. http://fas.org/sgp/crs/misc/RS22955.pdf

[142] United States Department of Agriculture. Country of Origin Labeling for Meat and Chicken. http://www.fsis.usda.gov/wps/portal/fsis/topics/food-safety-education/get-answers/food-safety-fact-sheets/food-labeling/country-of-origin-labeling-for-meat-and-chicken/country-of-origin-labeling-for-meat-and-chicken

[143] Congressional Research Service. Country-of-Origin Labeling for Foods and the WTO Trade Dispute on Meat Labeling. September 16, 2013. http://fas.org/sgp/crs/misc/RS22955.pdf

[144] Daniel J. Ikenson. Uncool Rules: Second Thoughts on Mandatory Country of Origin Labeling. Cato Institute. January 16, 2004. http://www.cato.org/publications/free-trade-bulletin/uncool-rules-second-thoughts-mandatory-country-origin-labeling

[145] Congressional Research Service. Country-of-Origin Labeling for Foods and the WTO Trade Dispute on Meat Labeling. September 16, 2013. http://fas.org/sgp/crs/misc/RS22955.pdf.

[146] World Trade Organization. Dispute Settlement: Dispute DS384. United States — Certain Country of Origin Labelling (COOL) Requirements. http://www.wto.org/english/tratop_e/dispu_e/cases_e/ds384_e.htm

Settlement Body.[147] Canada disagreed, so compliance proceedings followed and a compliance panel was convened. Hearings were held, and in 2014, the WTO again ruled against the United States. In November 2014, the United States appealed this decision.[148]

After the USDA issued final regulations that required more precise information, a group of trade associations representing livestock producers, feedlot operators, and meat packers sued the USDA in U.S. federal district court, arguing that the regulation violated the original authorizing legislation and the First Amendment.[149] The case made its way to the federal appellate court, which acknowledged that the revised rules will have greater cost implications for the plaintiffs, but found that the government acted within its constitutional authority.[150] The court upheld the disclosure requirements under *Zauderer*, finding that addressing deception is not the only valid government rationale for a factual disclosure requirement.[151] The court determined that the government's interests in COOL labeling were substantial: "to enable consumers to choose American-made products; the demonstrated consumer interest in extending country-of-origin labeling to food products; and the individual health concerns and market impacts that can arise in the event of a food-borne illness outbreak."[152] The court thus found that COOL labeling was reasonably related to the government's interests, satisfying the *Zauderer* test, and not just enacted to satisfy consumer curiosity.

Restaurant Menu Labeling

Starting with New York City in 2006, state and local governments passed various menu labeling laws that required chain restaurants to disclose nutrition-related information on their menus, most commonly the disclosure of total calories next to each product. A history of this activity can be found in Chapter 9 on state and local control. As part of the Patient Protection and Affordable Care Act, Congress passed a federal menu labeling law in 2010 that amended the Nutrition Labeling and Education Act (NLEA) to include requirements for certain retailers. The

---

[147] World Trade Organization. Dispute Settlement: Dispute DS384. United States — Certain Country of Origin Labelling (COOL) Requirements. http://www.wto.org/english/tratop_e/dispu_e/cases_e/ds384_e.htm

[148] Damian Paletta, Paul Vieira. U.S. Appeals WTO Meat-Label Ruling Canadian Officials Implore U.S. to 'Live Up to International Trade Obligations.' *The Wall Street Journal.* November 28, 2014. http://www.wsj.com/articles/u-s-appeals-wto-meat-label-ruling-1417209053

[149] *American Meat Institute v. United States Department of Agriculture.* 2014 U.S. App. LEXIS 14398 (D.C. Cir. July 29, 2014).

[150] *American Meat Institute v. United States Department of Agriculture.* 2014 U.S. App. LEXIS 14398 (D.C. Cir. July 29, 2014).

[151] *American Meat Institute v. United States Department of Agriculture.* 2014 U.S. App. LEXIS 14398 (D.C. Cir. July 29, 2014).

[152] *American Meat Institute v. United States Department of Agriculture.* 2014 U.S. App. LEXIS 14398 (D.C. Cir. July 29, 2014) at *12.

federal law applies to vending machine operators who operate 20 or more vending machines where the customer cannot visually inspect the Nutrition Facts Panel. It also applies to restaurants and similar retail food establishments that are part of a chain with 20 or more locations doing business under the same name nationally (regardless of the type of ownership of the locations) and offering for sale substantially the same menu items.[153]

Vending machine operators must disclose the number of calories contained in each product for sale. Restaurants and similar establishments must disclose the total number of calories for each standard menu item on the menu, menu board, drive-through menu board, and on self-service items (e.g., salad bars). These retail establishments, but not vendors, must also note on the menu or menu board the following two statements: "2,000 calories a day is used for general nutrition advice, but calorie needs vary," and "Additional nutrition information available upon request." Upon consumer request, covered restaurants and similar establishments must also make additional nutrient information available, including the total number of calories derived from any source and derived from total fat, as well as the total fat, saturated fat, cholesterol, sodium, total carbohydrates, complex carbohydrates, sugars, dietary fiber, and total protein contained in each item.[154] Because the applicable regulation is the same one that applies to the Nutrition Facts Panel, this list may change when the FDA finalizes the amendments to the Nutrition Facts Panel.

The NLEA is administered by the FDA, so the agency was tasked with drafting regulations to carry out the federal law. Congress asked the agency to determine outstanding issues, including how the law would be enforced, whether the law applied to other retailers (e. g., grocers or movie theaters that sell prepared foods), and how to disclose nutrients when there is menu variability, such as when standard menu items come in different flavors, varieties, or combinations.

The FDA issued its Final Rule on December 1, 2014; covered food service establishments were originally required to comply within one year and vendors were given two years to comply. However, at the request of food businesses and trade associations, in July 2015, the FDA announced that it is giving food service establishments an additional year to comply. The FDA stated: "The FDA agrees additional time is necessary for the agency to provide further clarifying guidance to help facilitate efficient compliance across all covered businesses and for covered establishments to come into compliance with the final rule."[155] Therefore, all covered entities must comply with the regulations by December 1, 2016.

In the final regulations, the FDA fleshed out various requirements especially for food service establishments. First, the FDA clarified what

---

[153] 21 USC § 343(q)(5)(H).

[154] 21 USC § 343(q)(5)(H).

[155] FDA. FDA Statement on Extension of Menu Labeling Compliance Date July 9, 2015. http://www.fda.gov/Food/NewsEvents/ConstituentUpdates/ucm453529.htm

qualified as a "restaurant or similar retail food establishment."[156] The final regulations apply to entities with 20 or more locations that are restaurants, whether they are sit-down, quick service, take-out, or express (such as at an airport), cafeterias (such as at a university or workplace), coffee shops, superstores, grocery stores, convenience stores, and food facilities in entertainment venues such as movie theaters and bowling alleys. Noncovered entities include school cafeterias serving foods through USDA school lunch and breakfast programs, food trucks, planes, and trains.

The FDA also clarified that the labeling requirements apply to alcoholic beverages that are standard menu items. The FDA explained that alcoholic beverages are "food" under the Food Drug and Cosmetic Act (FDCA), which defines "food" to include "articles used for … drink for man," and the menu labeling requirements apply to "food that is a standard menu item."[157] The agency recognized that alcoholic beverages are regulated by the Alcohol and Tobacco Tax and Trade Bureau but noted the consistency with requiring labeling for these standard menu items just as the regulations apply to meat, poultry, and egg products that are regulated by the USDA.

The FDA further defined two phrases to explain coverage. Because the labeling requirements only apply to "standard menu items," the FDA determined that the following do not qualify as standard menu items and do not need to be labeled: condiments that are for general use, including those placed on the table or on or behind the counter; daily specials; temporary menu items; custom orders; food that is part of a customary market test; food that is offered for sale for fewer than 60 days per calendar year, or fewer than 90 consecutive days, in order to test consumer acceptance; and alcoholic beverages that are on display, such as behind a bar, and are not self-service items.[158]

The labeling requirements apply to "restaurant-type food," which the FDA defined as food that is: usually eaten on the premises, while walking away, or soon after arriving at another location. This includes food that is either served in the restaurant or similar establishment, or processed and prepared primarily in a retail establishment, ready for human consumption and offered for sale but not for immediate consumption in such establishment.[159] Examples include a muffin at a bakery, a self-service salad bar, and an ice-cream cone from a scoop shop.[160] This would not include grocery-store type items intended to be eaten over time or by several people, such as a whole cake, a loaf of bread, pounds of deli meats and cheeses, large-size deli salads, and foods bought from bulk bin cases

---

[156] 79 Federal Register 71156, 71186-71187 (December 1, 2014)

[157] 79 Federal Register 71156, 71186-71187 (December 1, 2014)

[158] 79 FR 71156, 71170.

[159] 21 CFR 101.11.

[160] Food and Drug Administration. Food. Questions and Answers on the Menu and Vending Machines Nutrition Labeling Requirements. November 26, 2014. http://www.fda.gov/Food/IngredientsPackagingLabeling/LabelingNutrition/ucm248731.htm

(e.g., nuts and olives).[161] For children's menus, the FDA also provided options for retailers to use as a substitute or in addition to the adult 2,000 calorie marker statement. One option reads: "1,200 to 1,400 calories a day is used for general nutrition advice for children ages 4 to 8 years and 1,400 to 2,000 calories a day for children ages 9 to 13 years, but calorie needs vary."[162]

The FDA's enforcement authority stems from its authority under the FDCA. The FDA explained that a food not labeled as required by the federal law will be deemed misbranded. Therefore, food service establishments and vendors may be subject to the same enforcement mechanisms as for misbranded food. The FDA stated that each case of enforcement will be made on a case-by-case basis and that it plans to issue guidance to assist covered establishments with compliance.[163]

Similar to other nutrition labeling regulated by the FDA, the NLEA preempts states from enacting nonidentical menu labeling requirements directed at establishments with 20 or more outlets nationally.[164] This means that a state cannot enact different requirements (e.g., listing sugar content on menu boards) and apply them to these same chain restaurants. States can, however, enact identical requirements covering these restaurants in order to allow the state government to enforce the menu label law on its own. States also may enact nonidentical or identical requirements applicable to restaurants with fewer than 20 locations nationally or entities not covered by the regulation, such as food trucks. However, retailers that are not covered by the federal law have the option of opting in to the federal requirements and thereby avoid nonidentical state mandates.[165] So, for example, if a state enacted a law that required restaurants with 10 locations nationally to abide by state menu labeling requirements, the affected restaurants within that state could opt-in to the federal requirements and thus avoid enforcement of the state law.

There are two exceptions to the preemption provision. First, as is the case for food product labels, states are not preempted from requiring a statement that "provides for a warning concerning the safety of the food or component of the food." A common example of this is that some states require notes on menus warning customers that consuming raw or undercooked seafood may pose an increased risk of foodborne illnesses. In June 2015, New York City's Department of Health and Mental Hygiene proposed a regulation to require food service establishments that are part of chains with more than 15 locations nationally to add a warning label identifying food items that contain "very high levels of

---

[161] Food and Drug Administration. Food. Questions and Answers on the Menu and Vending Machines Nutrition Labeling Requirements. November 26, 2014. http://www.fda.gov/Food/IngredientsPackagingLabeling/LabelingNutrition/ucm248731.htm

[162] 21 CFR 101.11.

[163] 79 FR 71156, 71242.

[164] 21 USCS § 343-1(a).

[165] 21 USC § 343(q)(5)(H).

sodium."[166] This would apply to combination meals and foods that per serving contain more than or equal to 2300 milligrams of sodium.

Second, a state may petition the FDA to request an exemption from the preemption provision. Such a proposal must address a particular need for information unmet by federal law and cannot require restaurants to violate federal requirements or unduly burden interstate commerce.[167] In 2011, Philadelphia, Pennsylvania petitioned the FDA to allow it to enforce its menu labeling law that, in addition to calories, requires the disclosure of total amounts of sodium, saturated fat, trans fat, and carbohydrates.[168] This is still pending.

Genetically Modified Organisms Debate in Food Labeling

Humans have been altering the genes of our food supply for 10,000 years. The FDA defines "genetic modification" as the alteration of the genotype of a plant using any technique, new or traditional, to add, delete, or change its hereditary traits (either through a single mutation that affects one gene or a major alteration that affect many genes).[169] The FDA explained: "Most, if not all, cultivated food crops have been genetically modified." Earlier methods included planting seeds from the best crops and cross-pollination, and these produced the product we think of today as corn on the cob. More recently, methods have evolved to include grafting, forced pollination, and radiation, with the newest method—genetic engineering—creating significant debate.[170]

Genetic engineering is also called biotechnology and foods produced through this method are referred to as genetically modified organisms (GMOs), genetically engineered, or bioengineered.[171] The goal of genetic modification is to develop a new plant variety that carries valued characteristics (such as larger fruit) or enhanced agronomic characteristics (such as hardiness).[172] Traditional modification techniques were time consuming and less exact; genetic engineering uses recombinant DNA techniques that offer more precise and efficient methods to achieve the same types of goals.[173] The FDA subjects GMOs to the same

---

[166] NYC Department of Health and Mental Hygiene, Board of Health, Notice of Public Hearing and Opportunity to Comment on Proposed Amendment to Article 81 of the New York City Health Code

http://www.nyc.gov/html/doh/downloads/pdf/notice/2015/noi-repeal-article81.pdf.

[167] 21 USCS § 343-1(b).

[168] City of Philadelphia. Department of Public Health Petition Requesting Exemption from Preemption for State Requirement. www.regulations.gov/contentStreamer?documentId=FDA-2011-P-0646-0001&attachmentNumber=1&disposition=attachment&contentType=pdf

[169] 57 FR 22984 (May 29, 1992).

[170] Pamela C. Ronald. Plant Engineers Sow Debate. Scientific American Classics. 2014.

[171] Marion Nestle. *Safe Food: Bacteria, Biotechnology, and Bioterrorism*. Berkeley and Los Angeles, CA::University of California Press; 2003, p. 139.

[172] 57 FR 22984 (May 29, 1992).

[173] 57 FR 22984 (May 29, 1992).

safety evaluation as other food, with the added requirement that developers of GMOs consult and meet with FDA before marketing their products.[174,175]

Debates about genetic modification can be traced back centuries. The process was early on discussed as being unnatural. More recently it has been criticized as posing risks for health, safety, agriculture, and the environment, and the manufacturers have been accused of fostering dependence on bioengineered seed for profit.[176,177,178] Proponents of GMOs argue that they are safe and can reduce reliance on synthetic insecticides and toxic herbicides, increase food production, and can be used to address hunger and malnutrition in developing countries.[179,180] These debates have resulted in significant efforts to increase the labeling of GMOs. A 2013 *New York Times* poll found that 93% of respondents wanted foods containing GMO ingredients to be labeled as such.[181]

In response to requests for increased labeling of GMO foods, the FDA has issued several documents. In a 1992 policy document, the FDA first noted that according to its regulations, if a food derived from a new plant variety differs from its traditional counterpart so that the common or usual name does not reveal material information, labeling must reflect this fact.[182] So, for example, if peanut proteins were added to tomatoes, an allergy alert label would have to be displayed on the tomato product. For the majority of foods developed with recombinant DNA techniques, however, the FDA would not require a label noting this fact.[183] The FDA explained:

> The agency is not aware of any information showing that foods derived by these new methods differ from other foods in any meaningful or uniform way, or that, as a class, foods developed by the new techniques present any different or greater safety concern than foods developed by traditional plant breeding. For this reason, the agency does not believe that the method of

---

[174] Food and Drug Administration. Food. Questions & Answers on Food from Genetically Engineered Plants. July 22, 2014. http://www.fda.gov/Food/FoodScienceResearch/Biotechnology/ucm346030.htm

[175] 57 FR 22984 (May 29, 1992).

[176] The Birth of the Great GMO Debate. Scientific American. Classics Agriculture. No. 22. May 2014.

[177] 9 V.S.A. § 3041 et seq. (2014).

[178] Marion Nestle. *Safe Food: Bacteria, Biotechnology, and Bioterrorism.* Berkeley and Los Angeles, CA: University of California Press. 2003, p. 139.

[179] The Birth of the Great GMO Debate. Scientific American. Classics Agriculture. No. 22. May 2014.

[180] Dan Charles. In A Grain Of Golden Rice, A World Of Controversy Over GMO Foods. National Public Radio. The Salt. March 7, 2013 http://www.npr.org/blogs/thesalt/2013/03/07/173611461/in-a-grain-of-golden-rice-a-world-of-controversy-over-gmo-foods

[181] Allison Kopicki. Strong Support for Labeling Modified Foods. *The New York Times.* July 27, 2013. http://www.nytimes.com/2013/07/28/science/strong-support-for-labeling-modified-foods.html

[182] 57 FR 22984 (May 29, 1992).

[183] 57 FR 22984 (May 29, 1992).

development of a new plant variety ... is normally material information within the meaning of [its regulations] and would not usually be required to be disclosed in labeling for the food.[184]

In 1993, the FDA requested information on a variety of labeling options.[185] And in 1999, the agency held hearings on the topic.[186] The FDA concluded that mandatory labeling was not necessary and issued guidance for voluntary labeling. The FDA determined that such labeling must be precise and not claim superiority for non-GMO foods, so it suggested the following as examples of statements it found permissible:

- "We do not use ingredients that were produced using biotechnology."
- "This oil is made from soybeans that were not genetically engineered."
- "Our tomato growers do not plant seeds developed using biotechnology."[187]

The agency cautioned against making statements that likely could not be accurate, such as proclaiming products to be "GMO-free," given that most plants have been genetically modified. Further, it noted that a statement would be misleading if it claimed that a food was not bioengineered when, in fact, there were no marketed bioengineered varieties in existence, such as is the case with green beans.[188]

Anti-GMO advocates seek increased labeling requirements. Maine and Connecticut passed GMO labeling laws that only become effective when a certain number of states pass similar laws. In 2014, Vermont passed the nation's first law that would require GMO-related labeling upon its effective date of July 1, 2016.[189] Vermont's law requires that foods sold in the state that are produced "entirely or partially" by genetic engineering must be labeled as such and the product's package, signage, and advertising cannot state that it is "natural," "naturally made," "naturally grown," "all natural," or use words of similar import.[190] The Grocery Manufacturers Association (GMA), along with the Snack

---

[184] 57 FR 22984 (May 29, 1992).

[185] 58 FR 25837 (April 28, 1993).

[186] Food and Drug Administration. Food. DRAFT Guidance for Industry: Voluntary Labeling Indicating Whether Foods Have or Have Not Been Developed Using Bioengineering; Draft Guidance. http://www.fda.gov/Food/GuidanceRegulation/GuidanceDocumentsRegulatoryInformation/ucm059098.htm

[187] Food and Drug Administration. Food. DRAFT Guidance for Industry: Voluntary Labeling Indicating Whether Foods Have or Have Not Been Developed Using Bioengineering; Draft Guidance. http://www.fda.gov/Food/GuidanceRegulation/GuidanceDocumentsRegulatoryInformation/ucm059098.htm

[188] Food and Drug Administration. Food. DRAFT Guidance for Industry: Voluntary Labeling Indicating Whether Foods Have or Have Not Been Developed Using Bioengineering; Draft Guidance. http://www.fda.gov/Food/GuidanceRegulation/GuidanceDocumentsRegulatoryInformation/ucm059098.htm

[189] 9 V.S.A. §§ 3041-3048 (2014).

[190] 9 V.S.A. §§ 3041-3048 (2014).

Food Association, International Dairy Foods Association, and the National Association of Manufacturers sued Vermont in federal district court to block enforcement of this law.[191] The GMA argues that Vermont's law "is a costly and misguided measure that will set the nation on a path toward a 50-state patchwork of GMO labeling policies that do nothing to advance the health and safety of consumers."[192] The case is being fought on First Amendment, Commerce Clause, and preemption grounds. In April 2015, the court issued an opinion denying both the state's motion to dismiss the case and the plaintiffs' request for an injunction; this permits both the lawsuit to proceed and the law to be enforced by its effective date of July 1, 2016.

A federal bill, Safe and Accurate Food Labeling Act of 2014, would establish premarket notification requirements for GMOs and would preempt any state or local requirements with respect to GMOs and GMO-labeling.[193] It also would authorize the Secretary of HHS to permit GMO labeling only upon the determination that there is a material difference between a food produced from, containing, or consisting of a GMO and a comparable non-GMO food, and that such a disclosure is necessary to protect public health and prevent the food label from being false or misleading. The bill states that the use of bioengineering does not, by itself, constitute a material difference. Food industry companies have engaged in substantial lobbying related to this bill.[194] At this point, there are no federal labeling requirements related to GMOs, although it remains to be seen whether this will change anytime soon.

Questions and Exercises for Classroom Discussion

Do you look at Country of Origin Labeling? Have you noticed whether a piece of fruit or bag of nuts you bought was grown locally or within the United States or in another country? Besides fear of contamination from outside the United States, what are some reasons consumers might want such information? Do you think the government's interests in requiring Country of Origin Labeling are legitimate?

---

[191] Grocery Manufacturers Association. Newsroom. GMA Files Lawsuit to Overturn Vermont's Unconstitutional Mandatory GMO Labeling Law. June 13, 2014. http://www.gmaonline.org/news-events/newsroom/gma-files-lawsuit-to-overturn-vermonts-unconstitutional-mandatory-gmo-label/

[192] Grocery Manufacturers Association. Newsroom. GMA Files Lawsuit to Overturn Vermont's Unconstitutional Mandatory GMO Labeling Law. June 13, 2014. http://www.gmaonline.org/news-events/newsroom/gma-files-lawsuit-to-overturn-vermonts-unconstitutional-mandatory-gmo-label/

[193] HR 4432 - Safe and Accurate Food Labeling Act of 2014113th Congress (2013-2014).

[194] Clients lobbying on HR 4432: Safe and Accurate Food Labeling Act of 2014. http://www.opensecrets.org/lobby/billsum.php?id=hr4432-113

Go into the FDA's Warning Letter Database and look for a food misbranding case: http://www.fda.gov/iceci/enforcementactions/WarningLetters/default.htm.[195] Read the warning letter. What are the violations? How serious is each violation in your opinion? What did the agency recommend the company do to fix the violation?

Identify some aspects of the food label regulated by the FDA that you think are potentially confusing to consumers or that studies have shown to be unclear. Create a proposal to the FDA that suggests the agency study these things, or if there are already studies to support your assertion, suggest the FDA change the label accordingly.

If available in your location, go to covered restaurants or similar retail food establishments and examine the calorie labels on the menus and menu boards. Are these clear and helpful? Would you have noticed them if you were not specifically looking for them? Ask to see the other nutrition information. Is there additional information that would be helpful there or on the menu boards? Could recommended serving sizes be captured somewhere within these requirements?

Read the City of Philadelphia's Petition Requesting Exemption from Preemption from the FDA for its menu labeling requirement: www.regulations.gov/contentStreamer?documentId=FDA-2011-P-0646-0001&attachmentNumber=1&disposition=attachment&contentType=pdf
Act as the FDA and write a response to Philadelphia. Recall that organic food may not contain GMO ingredients. Why or why not is this sufficient to address popular calls for GMO labeling? Do you think foods with GMO ingredients should be labeled as such? Why or why not?

Should consumer curiosity be enough to require information on food labels? Should there need to be a scientific basis, safety concerns, deception concerns, or other concerns behind labeling requirements?

---

[195] Food and Drug Administration. Inspections, Compliance, Enforcement, and Criminal Investigations. Warning Letters. http://www.fda.gov/iceci/enforcementactions/WarningLetters/default.htm

7

Food Marketing

Introduction

Most of us are exposed to food advertisements several times a day. Marketing, however, is a much broader term and includes all the processes, activities, and entities involved in creating, communicating, and delivering messages to various segments of society. When most people in public health talk about food marketing, they are referring to the wide range of activities that are responsible for the ultimate promotional communication directed at the public through advertising, school-based promotions, social media, point-of-purchase communications (e.g., packaging), and branding. The Institute of Medicine's key definitions regarding marketing and promotional activities can be found in Table 7.1.

The Federal Trade Commission (FTC) is the primary agency responsible for protecting consumers by preventing and addressing anticompetitive, unfair, and deceptive business practices, including marketing communications. State attorneys general have concurrent authority to function in this arena as discussed in Chapter 8 on litigation. Other government entities involved in this field include the Federal Communication Commission, which adopted rules that require television broadcasters, cable operators, and satellite providers to limit the amount of commercials on children's television programming to 10.5 minutes per hour on weekends and 12 minutes per hour on weekdays for an audience 12 years old and younger. This requirement is prorated for programs that are shorter than an hour.[1] Additionally, the Food and Drug Administration is in charge of food labels but does not address the marketing tactics employed on product packaging beyond health and nutrition-related claims, as discussed in Chapter 6. The FTC addresses unfair or deceptive marketing on packaging when it appears in

---

[1] Federal Communications Commission. Children's Educational Television. http://www.fcc.gov/guides/childrens-educational-television

TABLE 7.1
Institute of Medicine Definitions[a]

Term	Definition
Advertising	"A paid public presentation and promotion of ideas, goods or services by a sponsor that is intended to bring a product to the attention of consumers through a variety of media channels such as broadcast and cable television, radio, print, billboards, the Internet, or personal contact."[b]
Branding	"A marketing feature that provides a name or symbol that legally identifies a company, a single product, or a product line to differentiate it from other companies and products in the marketplace."[c]
Marketing	"An organizational function and a set of processes for creating, communicating and delivering value to customers and for managing customer relationships in ways that benefit an organization and its stakeholders. Marketing encompasses a wide range of activities including market research; analyzing the competition; positioning a new product; pricing products and services; and promoting them through advertising, consumer promotion, trade promotions, public relations, and sales."[d]
Promotion	"The means by which a business or company communicates with its target audience or customers to inform, persuade, or influence customers' purchase decisions."[e] This includes marketing in schools, on packages, in retail, sponsorships, viral, and social media.
Target Market	"A group of individuals to whom a company markets its products or ideas that are designed to satisfy their specific needs and preferences. Target markets may be segmented by demographic characteristics (e.g., age, gender, income, race, or ethnicity); psychographic characteristics (e.g., values, attitudes, beliefs, lifestyles); behavioral patterns (e.g., brand loyalty, product usage rates, price); and geographic characteristics (e.g., region, population density)."[f]

[a]Institute of Medicine. *Food Marketing to Children and Youth: Threat or Opportunity*? Glossary of Terms. December 5, 2005. http://www.iom.edu/~/media/Files/Report%20Files/2005/Food-Marketing-to-Children-and-Youth-Threat-or-Opportunity/KFMGlosssary2906.pdf

[b]Institute of Medicine. *Food Marketing to Children and Youth: Threat or Opportunity*? Glossary of Terms. December 5, 2005. http://www.iom.edu/~/media/Files/Report%20Files/2005/Food-Marketing-to-Children-and-Youth-Threat-or-Opportunity/KFMGlosssary2906.pdf

[c]Institute of Medicine. *Food Marketing to Children and Youth: Threat or Opportunity*? Glossary of Terms. December 5, 2005. http://www.iom.edu/~/media/Files/Report%20Files/2005/Food-Marketing-to-Children-and-Youth-Threat-or-Opportunity/KFMGlosssary2906.pdf

[d]Institute of Medicine. *Food Marketing to Children and Youth: Threat or Opportunity*? Glossary of Terms. December 5, 2005. http://www.iom.edu/~/media/Files/Report%20Files/2005/Food-Marketing-to-Children-and-Youth-Threat-or-Opportunity/KFMGlosssary2906.pdf

[e]Institute of Medicine. *Food Marketing to Children and Youth: Threat or Opportunity*? Glossary of Terms. December 5, 2005. http://www.iom.edu/~/media/Files/Report%20Files/2005/Food-Marketing-to-Children-and-Youth-Threat-or-Opportunity/KFMGlosssary2906.pdf

[f]Institute of Medicine. *Food Marketing to Children and Youth: Threat or Opportunity*? Glossary of Terms. December 5, 2005. http://www.iom.edu/~/media/Files/Report%20Files/2005/Food-Marketing-to-Children-and-Youth-Threat-or-Opportunity/KFMGlosssary2906.pdf

other marketing venues (e.g., a cereal box pictured in a commercial or on the company's website).

This chapter discusses food marketing directed at children, the government's ability to address these practices, First Amendment protections for food marketing, the food industry's self-regulatory efforts, and other government methods intended to influence the information environment.

Food Marketing to Children

Although the psychological evidence indicates that food marketing effects people of all ages, public health efforts are primarily focused on food marketing directed at children, because children are considered particularly vulnerable to such influences and do not necessarily have the ability to understand that unhealthy food is bad for them. Moreover, legal solutions to restrict marketing to adults are seen as paternalistic and have serious First Amendment implications. Conversely, many people consider protecting children to be a significantly more acceptable role for government to play.

Concerns over food marketing to children are not new. In 2004, Congress directed the Centers for Disease Control and Prevention (CDC) to support an evidence-based review on the effect that food marketing has on the diet and health of young people.[2] The CDC funded the Institute of Medicine (IOM) to conduct a comprehensive study. The IOM issued a seminal report, *Food Marketing to Children and Youth: Threat or Opportunity?*, in 2005. According to this report, the IOM found strong evidence that exposure to television advertising is associated with adiposity in youth ages 2–18 years, but the evidence did not establish a definite causal relationship between television advertising and adiposity. In terms of influence, the IOM found strong evidence that television advertising influences the food and beverage preferences, purchase requests, and short-term consumption of children ages 2–11 years. The IOM also found "moderate evidence" that television advertising influences the food and beverage beliefs of children ages 2–11 years. For these particular findings, there was insufficient evidence regarding youth 12–18 years old. Television advertising remains the most prominent method of marketing food to children.[3] At the time of the IOM report (2005), digital media were not being used to market as extensively as it is now. For example, Facebook was only just founded as a school-based social media platform in 2004[4] and Twitter did not yet exist. The IOM's finding that television advertising influences children's food and beverage preferences and purchase requests confirms that this food marketing strategy is effective.

It has been documented that the food industry utilizes a specific method of promotion to encourage children to request advertised products from their parents repeatedly.[5] This method is called the "pester power," or "the nag factor." The

---

[2] National Research Council. *Food Marketing to Children and Youth: Threat or Opportunity?* Washington, DC: The National Academies Press; 2006.

[3] Federal Trade Commission. Review of Food Marketing to Children and Adolescents—Follow-Up Report. December 2012. http://www.ftc.gov/sites/default/files/documents/reports/review-food-marketing-children-and-adolescents-follow-report/121221foodmarketingreport.pdf

[4] Sarah Phillips. A brief history of Facebook. *The Guardian*. July 24, 2007. http://www.theguardian.com/technology/2007/jul/25/media.newmedia

[5] Sarah Phillips. A brief history of Facebook. *The Guardian*. July 24, 2007. http://www.theguardian.com/technology/2007/jul/25/media.newmedia

American Psychological Association's Task Force on Advertising and Children found that marketers even employ child psychologists who apply principles of developmental psychology to effectively induce children to nag their parents to buy the advertised product.[6]

The IOM also concluded that "[m]ost children ages 8 years and under do not effectively comprehend the persuasive intent of marketing messages, and most children ages 4 years and under cannot consistently discriminate between television commercials and programming."[7] The American Psychological Association's Task Force similarly found that children younger than age 7–8 years are uniquely vulnerable to television advertising because they lack the ability to distinguish between claims intended to persuade them and truthful statements.[8]

Out of concern for the rising rates of obesity in the United States, in 2005, Congress directed the FTC to collect data on food marketing directed at youth.[9] To obtain the information sought by Congress, the FTC issued subpoenas to 44 food and beverage companies that market food to young people. In 2008, the FTC issued its report, *Marketing Food to Children and Adolescents: A Review of Industry Expenditures, Activities, and Self-Regulation*, on food marketing practices directed at youth 2 to 17 years old. Based on the companies' 2006 data, it originally reported that the industry spent $1.6 billion marketing to youth;[10] however, in its subsequent report the FTC corrected this to $2.1 billion to include the cost of premiums.[11] The primary method of communication remained traditional media, that is, television, radio, and print advertising. The second type of communication was through premiums, which mostly consisted of toy premiums provided with quick-service restaurant children's meals. This was followed by other promotional marketing, which included product placements, movie

---

[6] Sarah Phillips. A brief history of Facebook. *The Guardian*. July 24, 2007. http://www.theguardian.com/technology/2007/jul/25/media.newmedia

[7] Sarah Phillips. A brief history of Facebook. *The Guardian*. July 24, 2007. http://www.theguardian.com/technology/2007/jul/25/media.newmedia Executive Summary, p. 9.

[8] J. L. Pomeranz. Television food marketing to children revisited: the Federal Trade Commission has the constitutional and statutory authority to regulate. *Journal of Law Medicine and Ethics*. 2010;38: 98–116.

[9] Federal Trade Commission. Marketing Food To Children and Adolescents: A Review of Industry Expenditures, Activities, and Self-Regulation: A Federal Trade Commission Report To Congress. July 2008. http://www.ftc.gov/sites/default/files/documents/reports/marketing-food-children-and-adolescents-review-industry-expenditures-activities-and-self-regulation/p064504foodmktingreport.pdf

[10] Federal Trade Commission. Marketing Food To Children and Adolescents: A Review of Industry Expenditures, Activities, and Self-Regulation: A Federal Trade Commission Report To Congress. July 2008. http://www.ftc.gov/sites/default/files/documents/reports/marketing-food-children-and-adolescents-review-industry-expenditures-activities-and-self-regulation/p064504foodmktingreport.pdf

[11] Federal Trade Commission. Review of Food Marketing to Children and Adolescents—Follow-Up Report. December 2012. http://www.ftc.gov/sites/default/files/documents/reports/review-food-marketing-children-and-adolescents-follow-report/121221foodmarketingreport.pdf

theaters, video, video games, character or cross-promotion license fees, athletic sponsorships, celebrity endorsement fees, events, retail and packaging, schools, and, finally, the smallest percentage was dedicated to digital media. The vast majority of food marketing was for a short list of foods and beverages. In order of expenditure, they were: carbonated beverages, quick-service restaurant foods, breakfast cereal, juice and other noncarbonated beverages, snack foods, candy, and frozen desserts.

In December 2012, the FTC issued a follow-up report. The agency had subpoenaed 48 companies to create the subsequent report based on 2009 data. The FTC found that the industry spent $1.79 billion marketing to youth, with $1 billion directed at children ages 2–11 years, $1 billion directed at youth ages 12–17 years, and $263 million overlapping between the two age groups.[12] Three products accounted for 72% of all marketing: quick-service restaurant foods, carbonated beverages, and breakfast cereals. Most of the advertising for carbonated beverages was directed at youth 12–17 years old, and snack foods rounded out the top three list for children ages 2–11 years. Although overall spending had decreased since the 2008 report, it is noteworthy that spending on digital advertising increased. Digital marketing includes marketing on commercial websites, third-party Internet advertising (i.e., placement of banner advertising on other companies' websites), social media, and advergames.[13] Some of the reduced spending was the result of fewer in-store marketing promotions, as well as lower premium costs because restaurants reported selling fewer kids meals with toys to children, and the cost of these toys was less than in previous years.

Calls for Regulation

The World Health Organization has issued several reports on food marketing to children.[14] In 2010, it issued 12 recommendations to governments globally to reduce the exposure, impact, and power of food marketing directed at children by enacting policies to address the marketing of foods high in saturated fats, trans-fatty acids, free sugars, or salt, in all child-oriented settings such as schools, playgrounds, child health locations, and sporting and cultural events.[15]

---

[12] Federal Trade Commission. Review of Food Marketing to Children and Adolescents—Follow-Up Report. December 2012. http://www.ftc.gov/sites/default/files/documents/reports/review-food-marketing-children-and-adolescents-follow-report/121221foodmarketingreport.pdf

[13] J. L. Harris, S. E. Speers, M. B. Schwartz, K. D. Brownell. U.S. food company branded advergames on the Internet: Children's exposure and effects on snack consumption. *Journal of Children and Media*. 2012;6(1):51–68.

[14] World Health Organization. Publications related to marketing of food and non-alcoholic beverages to children. http://www.who.int/dietphysicalactivity/publications/marketing/en/

[15] World Health Organization. Set of recommendations on the marketing of foods and non-alcoholic beverages to children (2010). http://whqlibdoc.who.int/publications/2010/9789241500210_eng.pdf?ua=1

Several countries have implemented television marketing restrictions. Mexico is the only country that has banned television advertisements for sugary drinks and unhealthy food for all programming regardless of the age of the target audience; this ban is in place during weekday afternoons and evenings and most of the day and evening on weekends.[16] The Canadian province of Quebec prohibits all commercial advertising directed at children younger than 13 years of age.[17] The United Kingdom bans the marketing of food and beverages high in fat, salt, or sugar during television programming geared toward children aged 4 to 15 years.[18] Norway and Sweden also have restrictions.[19]

Conversely, the United States relies on a self-regulatory approach. Self-regulation is when an industry polices its own behaviors rather than being controlled by the government. Industries do this for various reasons, such as trying to avoid government regulation, trying to avoid litigation, a lack of adequate government regulation for certain issues typical of the industry, or it is in the industry's own best interest to self-regulate.[20] An example of the latter rationale is the Marine Stewardship Council, which created an "ecolabel and fishery certification program" to safeguard the world's fisheries from overfishing and create a sustainable seafood supply.[21] This is in the best interest of the seafood industry and consumers.

The U.S. self-regulatory structure for food marketing to children arose after several failed attempts at government regulation, discussed below in the section on the FTC. In addition to political barriers, the most significant difference between the United States and the rest of the world is the United States Constitution's First Amendment protection for commercial speech. This has hindered even the best efforts by government entities. Despite the fact that the government has not been able to successfully regulate food marketing directed at children, there is still an expectation that companies should not exploit children through marketing practices, and this expectation underlies self-regulatory efforts. This chapter discusses government and self-regulatory efforts to address food marketing to children. Because any government regulation takes shape

---

[16] British Broadcasting Corporation. Mexico restricts soft drink TV ads to fight obesity. July 16, 2014. http://www.bbc.com/news/world-latin-america-28325105

[17] Kim D. Raine, Tim Lobstein, Jane Landon, Monique Potvin Kent, Suzie Pellerin, Timothy Caulfield, Diane Finegood, Lyne Mongeau, Neil Neary, and John C Spence. Restricting Marketing to Children: Consensus on Policy Interventions to Address Obesity. *Journal of Public Health Policy.* 2013; 34(2): 239–253.

[18] Ofcom. HFSS Advertising Restrictions: Final Review. London: Ofcom; 2010. http://stakeholders.ofcom.org.uk/market-data-research/other/tv-research/hfss-final-review/

[19] http://www.economist.com/news/international/21590489-are-children-fair-game-sophisticated-and-relentless-marketing-techniques-many

[20] L. L. Sharma, S. P. Teret, K. D. Brownell. The Food Industry and Self-regulation: Standards to Promote Success and to Avoid Public Health Failures. *American Journal of Public Health.* 2010;100(2):240–246.

[21] Marine Stewardship Council http://www.msc.org/about-us/vision-mission

against the background of the Constitution, the First Amendment's protection for commercial communications will be described first.

The First Amendment

The First Amendment of the United States Constitution protects the people from the government's abridgment of the freedom of speech.[22] As discussed in Chapter 2, the original purpose of the First Amendment was to protect core speech such as political and religious communications. This type of speech is the most strictly protected. In 1976, the Supreme Court confirmed that commercial speech deserves First Amendment protection.[23] Commercial speech is defined as the proposal of a commercial transaction,[24] and includes advertising,[25] labeling,[26] and other types of commercial solicitations such as brochures.[27]

The 1976 case that served as the basis for the commercial speech doctrine, *Virginia State Board of Pharmacy v. Virginia Citizens Consumer Council*, stemmed from a state trying to use its licensing authority (discussed further in Chapter 9) to prohibit the dissemination of prescription drug price information in the state.[28] The Court struck down the ban, stating that consumers' interest in the free flow of commercial information, especially the poor, sick, and aged consumers in this case, "may be as keen, if not keener by far, than his interest in the day's most urgent political debate."[29] The Court found that commercial speech must be protected in order to enable economic decisions to be "intelligent and well informed" in our "predominantly free enterprise economy."[30] Although the Court protects commercial speech, it explained that the government may regulate false, deceptive, and misleading speech.[31]

The Court determined that commercial speech should be protected to an intermediate degree, which is less than the strict scrutiny bestowed on restrictions of core speech. In 1980, the Court created a four-pronged test called the *Central Hudson* test, named after the case in which it was created.[32] Under this test, courts first must "determine whether the expression is protected by the

---

22 U.S. Constitution Amendment I.

23 *Virginia State Board of Pharmacy v. Virginia Citizens Consumer Council*, 425 U.S. 748 (1976).

24 *Board of Trustees v. Fox*, 492 U.S. 469 (1989).

25 *Lorillard Tobacco Co. v. Reilly*, 533 US 525ʃ(2001).

26 *Rubin v. Coors Brewing Co.*, 514 U.S. 476 (1995).

27 Bolger, 463 US 60 (1983); see also, *Cincinnati v. Discovery Network*, 507 U.S. 410, 422 (1993).

28 *Virginia State Board of Pharmacy v. Virginia Citizens Consumer Council*, 425 U.S. 748 (1976).

29 *Virginia State Board of Pharmacy v. Virginia Citizens Consumer Council*, 425 U.S. 748 (1976) at 763–764.

30 *Virginia State Board of Pharmacy v. Virginia Citizens Consumer Council*, 425 U.S. 748 (1976) at 765.

31 *Virginia State Board of Pharmacy v. Virginia Citizens Consumer Council*, 425 U.S. 748 (1976).

32 *Central Hudson Gas & Electric Corp. v. Public Service Commission*, 447 U.S. 557 (1980).

First Amendment," which for commercial speech means it "must concern lawful activity and not be misleading."[33] Second, the court asks "whether the asserted governmental interest is substantial. If both inquiries yield positive answers, [it] must determine whether the regulation directly advances the governmental interest asserted," and fourth, whether or not the restriction on speech is "more extensive than is necessary to serve that interest."[34] No commercial speech restriction has passed this test in the Supreme Court since 1995.[35] The Court has seemed to bestow increasingly stricter protection to commercial speech since the inception of the doctrine.

A pivotal case related to marketing to children was the 2001 case of *Lorillard v. Reilly.* In this case, the Massachusetts Attorney General promulgated comprehensive regulations governing the advertising and sale of tobacco products in order to address the increased incidence of youth smoking.[36] The regulation prohibited outdoor tobacco advertisements within a 1,000-foot radius of a school or playground and restricted indoor tobacco advertising from being placed lower than five feet from the floor of a retail establishment located the same distance from schools or playgrounds.[37] The Supreme Court analyzed the constitutionality of these restrictions on commercial speech under the *Central Hudson* test.

The parties and the Court agreed that the proposed speech, tobacco advertisements, was protected commercial speech and that the state's interest in preventing tobacco use by minors was substantial, meeting parts one and two of the test. However, the Court found that the outdoor advertising restrictions failed the fourth prong of the test because their vast reach cut off substantial avenues of communication intended for adults, rendering them more extensive than necessary.[38] This is an important point: although the speech restriction was aimed at protecting children, because it interfered with the ability of tobacco companies to communicate with adults, the Court found it to be unconstitutional. The Court also found that the five-foot height requirement failed both prongs three and four because not all children are less than five feet tall and those who are have the ability to look up to see the signs.[39] Thus, the Court found that the restriction did not directly advance the government's interest and was more extensive than necessary.

Most recent commercial speech cases follow a similar course. As in *Lorillard v. Reilly,* the parties involved generally agree that truthful marketing communications constitute valid commercial speech, thus meeting the first prong of the

---

[33] *Central Hudson Gas & Electric Corp. v. Public Service Commission*, 447 U.S. 557 (1980) at 566.

[34] *Central Hudson Gas & Electric Corp. v. Public Service Commission*, 447 U.S. 557 (1980).

[35] J. L. Pomeranz. No Need to Break New Ground: A Response to the Supreme Court's Threat to Overhaul the Commercial Speech Doctrine. *Loyola of Los Angeles Law Review.* 2012;45:389–434.

[36] *Lorillard Tobacco Co. v. Reilly*, 533 U.S. 525, 533 (2001).

[37] *Lorillard Tobacco Co. v. Reilly*, 533 U.S. 525, 566 (2001).

[38] *Lorillard Tobacco Co. v. Reilly*, 533 U.S. 525, 566 (2001).

[39] *Lorillard Tobacco Co. v. Reilly*, 533 U.S. 525, 566 (2001).

Central Hudson test. Further, in the context of public health regulations, courts universally recognize the government's ability to regulate in order to promote public health, safety, and welfare,[40] so the court and the parties generally agree that the government's interest is substantial, thus meeting the second prong of the test. Commercial speech restrictions, therefore, generally fail either or both prongs three and four of the *Central Hudson* test.[41] At this juncture, it is unclear whether the government could devise a commercial speech restriction targeting truthful marketing practices that the Court would uphold in the future.

Two related issues need exploring in order to provide the full picture of the commercial speech doctrine as it relates to marketing to children. The first is that the foregoing relies on the existence of truthful advertising. What happens when an ad is false, deceptive, or misleading? The Supreme Court has interpreted the First Amendment to permit the government to regulate such speech, as discussed directly below. The second issue is that a different type of First Amendment analysis is relevant to public schools and this will be discussed below under School-based Marketing.

Recall that under prong one of the Central Hudson test, courts must ask whether the expression is protected by the First Amendment, which for commercial speech means it "must concern lawful activity and not be misleading."[42] An example of speech that would not be proposing a legal transaction would be an offer to sell alcohol to minors under 21 years of age, the legal drinking age nationally. This is important because food products are legally purchasable by children. Therefore, the commercial speech directed at them is constitutionally protected. Although the government would have a substantial interest in preventing obesity, diabetes, and unhealthy eating behaviors by restricting food marketing to children, the fact that food marketers have a constitutionally protected right to communicate with children and adults alike would lead the Court to be circumspect of such a restriction.

The government may ban a product,[43] however, or prohibit its purchase, possession, or use by minors.[44] These are regulations of conduct, described at greater length in Chapter 9 on state and local control. In some ways, regulating conduct, such as banning products, seems more extreme than banning speech about a product. But this choice was one made by the writers of the United States Constitution. The Supreme Court explained this as follows:

---

[40] *See e.g., Rubin v. Coors Brewing*, 514 U.S. 476, 485 (1995); *see also Florida Bar v. Went for It, Inc.* 515 U.S. 618, 625 (1995).

[41] *Sorrell v. IMS Health Inc.*, 131 S. Ct. 2653 (2011); see also, *Thompson v. Western States Medical Center*, 535 U.S. 357 (2002).

[42] *Central Hudson Gas & Electric Corp. v. Public Service Commission*, 447 U.S. 557, 566 (1980).

[43] *44 Liquormart*, 517 U.S. at 524 (THOMAS, J., concurring in part and concurring in judgment).

[44] *Lorillard Tobacco Co. v. Reilly*, 533 U.S. 525, 586 (2001) *JUSTICE THOMAS*, concurring in part and concurring in the judgment.

> The text of the First Amendment makes clear that the Constitution presumes that attempts to regulate speech are more dangerous than attempts to regulate conduct. That presumption accords with the essential role that the free flow of information plays in a democratic society. As a result, the First Amendment directs that government may not suppress speech as easily as it may suppress conduct, and that speech restrictions cannot be treated as simply another means that the government may use to achieve its ends.[45]

Thus, while banning food marketing directed at children is constitutionally difficult, governments can prohibit the purchase of certain products by children. This is significant because such a restriction would have the effect of making a proposal of a commercial transaction to a minor for that product unlawful commercial speech. Thus, if the government wanted to restrict speech about a product to children, it could do this if it made the product illegal for a minor to purchase. Such a restriction, however, would be subject to the *Central Hudson* test to determine if it cuts off more speech than necessary to adults, as in *Lorillard v. Reilly.*

The second reason why speech might not be protected is if it is misleading. This concept has been fleshed out in subsequent cases and is broader than just the term "misleading." The Court stated that the First Amendment protects "truthful" advertising;[46] thus, false statements intending to propose a commercial transaction are not protected. The Court also differentiated among three types of misleading speech: inherently misleading, actually misleading (i.e., proven to be misleading in practice), and potentially misleading.[47] The first, inherently misleading, is the most nebulous concept of the three. The Court has explained it as speech with no intrinsic meaning,[48] speech that is inherently likely to deceive,[49] or speech that conveys no information.[50] Inherently misleading speech rarely comes up in Supreme Court cases. The second type of misleading speech, actually misleading, is the most straightforward because it requires evidence of deception.[51] Courts look to the evidentiary record to determine whether people were actually misled or deceived. For both inherently and actually misleading commercial speech, the government may prohibit such speech entirely because it is not considered protected commercial speech. Thus, if the government restricts this speech, this should be upheld under the first prong of the *Central Hudson* test without a court having to go further to analyze the other prongs. One could envision the argument that it is deceptive to propose a commercial transaction

---

[45] *44 Liquormart, Inc. v. Rhode Island*, 517 U.S. 484, 512 (1996).

[46] *In re R. M. J.*, 455 U.S. 191, 203 (1982).

[47] *In re R. M. J.*, 455 U.S. 191, 203 (1982).

[48] *Friedman v. Rogers*, 440 U.S. 1, 4 (1979).

[49] *Central Hudson Gas & Electric Corp. v. Public Service Commission of New York*, 447 U.S. 557, 563 (1980) (*citing Friedman v. Rogers*, 440 U.S. 1, 13, 15–16).

[50] *Friedman v. Rogers*, 440 U.S. 1, 12 (1979).

[51] *Peel v. Atty. Registration & Disciplinary Commission*, 496 U.S. 91, 100-101 (1990).

to a young child because the recipient of the information does not have the cognitive capabilities to perceive persuasive intent, but nothing like this has been tested in court.

The third category, potentially misleading speech, is speech that "may be presented in a way that is not deceptive."[52] The Court has explained that when speech can be presented in another way that would cure the deception, the government cannot prohibit the speech, but rather can require disclaimers, disclosures, or further explanations to clarify the speech.[53] Thus, unlike the other two categories above, potentially misleading speech is considered protected by the First Amendment and may not be prohibited. If the government restricts potentially misleading speech, a court must review the remaining three prongs of the *Central Hudson* test in order to determine whether the challenged restriction on such speech is constitutional.[54] The Court highly favors additional information or "more speech" rather than speech restrictions or "enforced silence."[55] Thus, in most cases without evidence of deception, the Court favors government regulations that require commercial actors to increase their factual disclosures or disclaimers or to provide further explanation to cure the potential deception.[56]

Federal Trade Commission

The FTC has the primary authority to address nefarious business practices and commercial communications to protect consumers. The FTC has successfully brought individual cases addressing unfair and deceptive food marketing. It has less successfully attempted to enact regulations to restrict marketing to children and to lead cross-agency efforts proposing nutritionally strong voluntary guidelines.

The Federal Trade Commission Act prohibits unfair or deceptive acts or practices in or affecting commerce,[57] and pronounces that false advertisements are an unfair or deceptive act or practice.[58] There are two very distinct parts to this definition: unfair and deceptive. A bit of history is necessary to understand the authority the FTC has today as related to these two terms.

---

[52] *In re R. M. J.*, 455 U.S. 191, 203 (1982).

[53] *In re R. M. J.*, 455 U.S. 191, 203 (1982).

[54] *American Academy of Pain Management v. Joseph*, 353 F.3d 1099, 1107 (9th Cir. 2004); see also, *Mason v. Florida Bar*, 208 F.3d 952, 955 (11th Cir. 2000).

[55] *Whitney v. California*, 274 U.S. 357, 377 (1927) (Brandeis concurring).

[56] *Milavetz, Gallop & Milavetz, P.A. v. United States*, 130 S. Ct. 1324, (2010); see also, *Zauderer v. Office of Disciplinary Counsel*, 471 U.S. 626 (1985).

[57] 15 USCS § 45

[58] 15 USCS § 52

The FTC historically brought individual cases to address unfair and deceptive acts and practices. A consumer protection movement began in the 1960s, and in 1975, Congress passed the Magnuson-Moss Act granting the FTC substantive rulemaking authority. At that time, the FTC interpreted its unfairness authority to include considerations of "public policy, morality and ethics, and 'substantial injury to consumers.'"[59] The FTC began promulgating regulations to address problematic marketing practices. One such initiative was termed KidVid.[60]

In response to petitions by consumer protection groups, the FTC conducted an investigation and, in 1978, issued a report, which concluded that "there was sufficient evidence to suggest that both (1) the televised advertising of any product directed to children too young to understand the selling purpose of, or otherwise comprehend or evaluate commercials and (2) the televised advertising of sugared products to children of all ages may be unfair and deceptive within the meaning of section 5 of the FTC Act."[61] The FTC concluded that an appropriate remedy was necessary due to a concern over dental caries in children who consume sugary products. The agency issued a Notice of Proposed Rulemaking that same year, declaring its intent to hold a comprehensive rulemaking proceeding to address the marketing of sugary products to children on television.[62] The FTC was considering whether and how to ban television advertising of sugary products to very young children.[63]

There was political backlash to the proposed KidVid rulemaking and in May 1980, Congress enacted the FTC Improvements Act. This is in force today and states: "The Commission shall not have any authority to promulgate any rule in the children's advertising proceeding pending on the date of the enactment of the Federal Trade Commission Improvements Act of 1980 or in any substantially similar proceeding on the basis of a determination by the Commission that such advertising constitutes an unfair act or practice in or affecting commerce."[64] The FTC considered whether to continue under its deceptive authority but noted many issues, including legal and policy concerns, competing theories on cognitive development, and the reliability of a method to measure the cariogenicity of food advertised to children.[65] It terminated the proceedings in October 1981.

After this significant setback, the FTC went back to bringing individual cases. It issued a Policy Statement explaining what it considered its unfairness authority to be. In 1994, Congress codified the Commission's authority to declare unlawful an act or practice on the grounds that it is unfair if it "is likely to cause

---

[59] Stephen Calkins, FTC Unfairness: An Essay, 46 *Wayne L. Rev.* 1935 (2000).

[60] J. L. Pomeranz. Federal Trade Commission's Authority to Regulate Marketing to Children: Deceptive v. Unfair Rulemaking. *Health Matrix: Journal of Law-Medicine*. 2011;21:521–553.

[61] 46 Federal Register. 48710 (October 2, 1981).

[62] 46 Federal Register. 48710 (October 2, 1981).

[63] 43 Federal Register. 17967, 17969 (Apr. 27, 1978).

[64] 15 USCS § 57a(h).

[65] 46 Federal Register. 48710 (October 2, 1981).

substantial injury to consumers which is not reasonably avoidable by consumers themselves and not outweighed by countervailing benefits to consumers or to competition."[66] Congress added that the Commission may take into consideration whether the act or practice violates "established public policies as evidence to be considered with all other evidence," but that the public policy consideration "may not serve as a primary basis for such determination."[67]

In 1983, the FTC issued a Policy Statement characterizing its authority to address deceptive acts or practices. The policy sets forth three criteria for finding deception: (1) there must be a representation, omission, or practice that is likely to mislead a consumer; (2) that is analyzed from the perspective of a consumer acting reasonably in the circumstances; and (3) the representation, omission, or practice must be material.[68] This has not been codified but remains the FTC's policy.

When scrutinizing marketing practices directed at children, the FTC analyzes them from the perspective of the child. The FTC considers children to be a "specially susceptible group of people" and the advertisement will be measured by how it would impact them.[69] This is important because children do not often purchase all the products advertised to them. Thus, while the parent or another adult is usually the primary purchaser of food, the FTC looks to determine whether the marketing practice is false, deceptive, or unfair to the targeted audience. Over the years, the FTC has brought cases against food manufacturers for unfair or deceptive marketing directed at children, such as a television commercial that depicted bread "as an extraordinary food" for producing dramatic and impossible growth in children,[70] and a cereal commercial that represented that cereal alone would enable children to perform physical activities portrayed in the advertisements.[71] In one case brought against a vitamin manufacturer, the FTC argued that directing advertisement of a vitamin to children was in itself an unfair or deceptive practice because they are "unqualified by age and experience to decide for themselves whether or not they need or should use multiple vitamin supplements in general or an advertised brand in particular."[72] The agency also noted that the use of the Spiderman character to promote vitamins took "advantage of the trust relationship developed between children and the program character." Most cases settle and the companies agree to refrain from engaging in the challenged practice in the future.

---

[66] 15 USCS § 45(n).

[67] 15 USCS § 45(n).

[68] Federal Trade Commission. Policy Statement on Deception (1983), appended to Cliffdale Assoc., 103 F.T.C. 110, 174 (1984).

[69] Heinz W. Kirchner Trading as Universe Co., 63 F.T.C. 1282 (1963).

[70] *ITT Continental Baking Co., Inc. v. Federal Trade Commission,* 532 F.2d 207 (1976).

[71] *In the Matter of Kellogg Co,* 99 F.T.C. 8 (1982).

[72] In the Matter of *Hudson Pharmaceutical Corporation,* 89 F.T.C. 82 (1977).

In May 2009, Kellogg's placed a claim on its Rice and Cocoa Krispies cereals, "Now Helps Support Your Child's IMMUNITY."[73] The San Francisco City Attorney sent a letter to Kellogg's and to the Food and Drug Administration (FDA) voicing concern about the claim. Due to limitations in the FDA's authority, discussed in Chapter 6, the FDA did not act. The FTC, however, did investigate the claim, which it called "dubious" and "questionable."[74] Moreover, only a month before Kellogg's launched the "immunity" claim, it had agreed to settle another case brought by the FTC for falsely claiming that its Frosted Mini-Wheats cereal was "clinically shown to improve kids' attentiveness by nearly 20%."[75] The FTC modified and expanded its earlier order to require the company to refrain from misleading representations.

Although the FTC has the authority to enact regulations for deceptive marketing to children, it has thus far declined to do so. In addition to real and perceived First Amendment constraints, the FTC's Magnuson-Moss rulemaking authority imposes requirements that other federal agencies do not face, and which render the FTC's rulemaking process quite onerous and lengthy.[76] Thus, the FTC has focused on individual cases. The FTC also led a cross-agency collaboration to support voluntary food marketing guidelines. This also faced industry opposition, described next.

Interagency Working Group

In 2009, Congress directed the FTC, FDA, CDC, and the United States Department of Agriculture (USDA) to establish an Interagency Working Group on Food Marketed to Children to conduct a study and develop recommendations for standards for food marketing directed at children younger than 18 years of age. The Working Group was directed to consider both the positive and negative contributions of nutrients, ingredients, and food in preventing and contributing to obesity.[77] In April 2011, the Working Group released "proposed voluntary

---

[73] Bruce Horovitz. Critics Blast Kellogg's Claim That Cereals Can Boost Immunity. *USA Today*. November 6, 2009. http://www.usatoday.com/money/industries/food/2009-11-02-cereal-immunity-claim_N.htm.

[74] Federal Trade Commission. Press Release. FTC Investigation of Ad Claims that Rice Krispies Benefits Children's Immunity Leads to Stronger Order Against Kellogg. June 3, 2010. http://www.ftc.gov/news-events/press-releases/2010/06/ftc-investigation-ad-claims-rice-krispies-benefits-childrens.

[75] Federal Trade Commission. Press Release. FTC Investigation of Ad Claims that Rice Krispies Benefits Children's Immunity Leads to Stronger Order Against Kellogg. June 3, 2010. http://www.ftc.gov/news-events/press-releases/2010/06/ftc-investigation-ad-claims-rice-krispies-benefits-childrens.

[76] J. L. Pomeranz. Federal Trade Commission's Authority to Regulate Marketing to Children: Deceptive v. Unfair Rulemaking. *Health Matrix: Journal of Law-Medicine*. 2011;21:521–553.

[77] Interagency Working Group on Food Marketed to Children. Preliminary Proposed Nutrition Principles to Guide Industry Self-Regulatory Efforts, Request for Comments. http://www.

principles" with the goal to guide food marketers to take voluntary action to address childhood obesity.[78] The Working Group proposed both standards to assess whether a food product made "a meaningful contribution to a healthful diet" and specific targets to minimize foods marketed with saturated fat, trans fat, added sugars, and sodium.[79] The Working Group's goal was to shift the food most heavily marketed to children between 2 and 17 years old to meet the nutrition standards by the year 2016. The Working Group sought comments on its proposal and explicitly confirmed that these were not proposed regulations and that they were not calling for government regulation.[80]

There was extreme backlash from the food industry. Food companies and trade groups argued that the guidelines were backdoor regulations and claimed that the FTC would bring actions against violators.[81] False reports circulated that the FTC was banning the marketing and sale of foods not meeting the guidelines.[82] Food industry members lobbied against the standards, arguing that youth aged 12 to 17 years should not be included, and they hired First Amendment experts to argue that the guidelines were unconstitutional.[83]

The FTC issued a prepared statement to the House of Representatives in October 2011. It noted that it received considerable response to the proposed guidelines in the form of 29,000 comments, of which 28,000 were from a write-in campaign supporting the proposal.[84] Of the remaining substantively distinct comments, the positions were divided between favorable and unfavorable. The Commission acknowledged that the guidelines were strong and stricter than the contemporaneous industry self-regulatory mechanism called the Children's Food and Beverage Advertising Initiative (CFBAI). To address industry concerns,

---

google.com/url?sa=t&rct=j&q=&esrc=s&source=web&cd=1&ved=0CBoQFjAA&url=http%3A%2F%2Fcspinet.org%2Fnew%2Fpdf%2FIWG_food_marketing_proposed_guidelines_4.11.pdf&ei=VBS8U8m6NI7ksASy94CoBw&usg=AFQjCNFKlgdSgLtoFXmktbEWf18fpY625g&sig2=d3rWrLcBRPqWCBnc8Q647g&bvm=bv.70138588,d.cWc&cad=rja

[78] Federal Trade Commission. Interagency Working Group Seeks Input on Proposed Voluntary Principles for Marketing Food to Children. April 28, 2011. http://www.ftc.gov/news-events/press-releases/2011/04/interagency-working-group-seeks-input-proposed-voluntary

[79] Interagency Working Group on Food Marketed to Children. Preliminary Proposed Nutrition Principles to Guide Industry Self-Regulatory Efforts, Request for Comments.

[80] Federal Trade Commission. Interagency Working Group Seeks Input on Proposed Voluntary Principles for Marketing Food to Children. April 28, 2011. http://www.ftc.gov/news-events/press-releases/2011/04/interagency-working-group-seeks-input-proposed-voluntary

[81] David Vladeck. What's on the Table. Federal Trade Commission, Bureau of Consumer Protection. July 1, 2011. http://business.ftc.gov/blog/2011/07/whats-table

[82] David Vladeck. What's on the Table. Federal Trade Commission, Bureau of Consumer Protection. July 1, 2011. http://business.ftc.gov/blog/2011/07/whats-table

[83] Proponents of New Food Marketing Guidelines Fighting Back. *Adweek*. September 7, 2011. http://www.adweek.com/news/advertising-branding/proponents-new-food-marketing-guidelines-fighting-back-134649

[84] Federal Trade Commission. Prepared Statement. October 12, 2011. https://www.ftc.gov/sites/default/files/documents/public_statements/prepared-statement-federal-trade-commission-interagency-working-group-food-marketed-children/111012foodmarketing.pdf.

it stated that it was revising the guidelines to conform more closely to the CFBAI nutrition standards. While it was working on the revised guidelines, the FTC noted that they would not apply to marketing to youth 12–17 years old (outside of the school environment) or to food company sponsored community, charitable, entertainment, or sporting events and programs. Finally, the FTC noted that it "has neither the desire nor the authority to promulgate regulations governing the marketing of food to children. The Working Group's proposal is strictly voluntary. The Commission recognizes that some forms of regulatory action could raise First Amendment concerns."[85]

In response to the FTC's announcement that it was softening the Interagency Working Group guidelines, the Grocer Manufacturers Association (GMA), which is a trade organization that advocates on behalf of the major food and beverage manufacturers, said it would still not budge on its opposition.[86] The GMA urged Congress to require a cost-benefit analysis of the guidelines and also suggested that the better alternative to compromise was for industry to continue to use the CFBAI.

In December 2011, the House inserted language in the Consolidated Appropriations Act of 2012 stating that no money can be distributed to the Interagency Working Group unless it complied with an order to conduct a cost-benefit analysis.[87] Of course, a proper cost-benefit analysis cannot be performed for voluntary standards because there is no method to determine which groups will comply with which parts of the recommendations. The Interagency Working Group eventually disbanded and left the standards intact for potential future use. It is noteworthy that in the FTC's 2012 report on food marketing directed at children, the Commission expressed support for what it considered positive evolution of the CFBAI standards and growth in membership, described below.

Industry Self-regulatory Practices

In 2006, the Council of Better Business Bureaus launched the Children's Food and Beverage Advertising Initiative (CFBAI), which was first implemented in 2007 by 10 food and beverage companies. The early pledges were company-specific and intended to "shift the mix of foods in advertising" primarily directed to children to include healthy dietary choices or better-for-you foods.[88] Originally, each food

[85] Federal Trade Commission. Prepared Statement. October 12, 2011.

[86] Elaine Watson. Grocery Manufacturers Association: There is No Middle Ground on Kids Marketing Proposals. October 14, 2011. http://www.foodnavigator-usa.com/Markets/GMA-There-is-no-middle-ground-on-kids-marketing-proposals

[87] Marion Nestle. Congress Delays Setting Nutrition Standards for Kids—Again. December 19, 2011. http://www.theatlantic.com/health/archive/2011/12/congress-delays-setting-nutrition-standards-for-kids-again/250144/

[88] *CFBAI Program and Core Principles At A Glance.* June 2014. http://www.bbb.org/Global/Council_113/CFBAI/Program%20and%20Core%20Principles_for%20online%20access.pdf

company pledged to meet its own internal definition of what constituted healthy or better-for-you foods.

CFBAI applies to children younger than 12 years. Since its inception, CFBAI has updated its overall program and the companies have revised their pledges to address critics' concerns that they are not nutritionally rigorous and do not cover all venues or practices. CFBAI emphasizes that "it remains the primary responsibility of parents to guide their children's behavior in these areas," but notes that its industry members are voluntarily pursuing this initiative to assist parents.[89]

As of 2014, 17 food and beverage companies participate in the CFBAI. The commitments apply to television, radio, print, websites, video games, DVDs, mobile devices, licensed characters, product placement, and schools (prekindergarten through sixth grade).[90] For measured media, most companies employ the definition of "advertising primarily directed to children under age 12" to mean advertising for which children ages 2–11 constitute at least 35% of the audience at the time the media was purchased.[91] Therefore, family programming or programming intended for older children, but where younger children are in the audience, would not qualify. The pledges are not applicable to packaging, the retail environment, or sales, donations, or fundraising activities in elementary schools.[92]

All members of the CFBAI agreed to abide by a uniform nutrition criteria, which took effect on December 31, 2013 and applies according to the type of food product advertised. It is not uniform in nutrition criteria but uniform across companies.[93] An exception to this is that five companies say they do not advertise to children younger than 12 years at all: Coca-Cola, Ferrero USA, Nestle USA, Hershey, and Mars.[94] Familiar kid's foods that meet the criteria and are permitted to be advertised to children include such cereals as Lucky Charms, Chocolate Lucky Charms, Reese's Puffs, Trix, and Cocoa Pebbles.[95] Another example is McDonald's Happy Meals. Most variations of the Happy Meal qualify under the CFBAI[96] so the restaurant chain can advertise its most child-friendly product to

---

[89] *Enhanced Core Principles* (4th ed.). (January 2014). http://www.bbb.org/Global/Council_113/CFBAI/Enhanced%20Core%20Principles%20Fourth%20Edition%20with%20Appendix%20A.pdf

[90] *CFBAI Enhanced Core Principles.* http://www.bbb.org/Global/Council_113/CFBAI/Enhanced%20Core%20Principles%20Fourth%20Edition%20with%20Appendix%20A.pdf

[91] *CFBAI Enhanced Core Principles.* http://www.bbb.org/Global/Council_113/CFBAI/Enhanced%20Core%20Principles%20Fourth%20Edition%20with%20Appendix%20A.pdf

[92] *CFBAI Enhanced Core Principles.* http://www.bbb.org/Global/Council_113/CFBAI/Enhanced%20Core%20Principles%20Fourth%20Edition%20with%20Appendix%20A.pdf

[93] CFBAI's Uniform Nutrition Criteria Fact Sheet. June 2013. http://www.bbb.org/storage/16/documents/cfbai/CFBAI%20Uniform%20Nutrition%20Criteria%20Fact%20Sheet%20-FINAL.pdf

[94] CFBAI Program and Core Principles At A Glance. June 2014. http://www.bbb.org/Global/Council_113/CFBAI/Program%20and%20Core%20Principles_for%20online%20access.pdf

[95] CFBAI Product List. April 2014. http://www.bbb.org/Global/Council_113/CFBAI/CFBAI%20Product%20List%20April%202014_upload.pdf

[96] CFBAI Product List. April 2014. http://www.bbb.org/Global/Council_113/CFBAI/CFBAI%20Product%20List%20April%202014_upload.pdf

children without violating its commitment. The company also uses branded marketing to sell the experience of eating at McDonald's, so it might be less relevant which food is shown in the advertisement to draw customers to McDonald's.

One of the primary drawbacks of the CFBAI is that it does not apply within the retail environment. Food companies utilize a wide variety of marketing techniques on food packages that are directed at children, including the use of licensed characters (e.g., SpongeBob SquarePants and Dora the Explorer), company spokescharacters (e.g., the Lucky Charms Leprechaun, the Trix Rabbit, Tony the Tiger, and Snap, Crackle and Pop), celebrities, premiums, cross-promotions, tie-ins for movies and television shows, games, puzzles, contests, sweepstakes, and special colors, shapes, or flavors.[97] The CFBAI does not cover the retail environment so these remain unregulated and not subject to self-regulation. One could argue that it is deceptive and unfair to put characters on unhealthy food products because children are not in a position to determine whether they should be consuming these products, as in the Spiderman vitamin case, but neither the FTC nor any other government body has made such a claim.

Children shopping with an adult often use this opportunity to request a specific food. Sometimes the sighting in the store helps them recall the advertisement they saw on television. For example, Kraft has dozens of Lunchables varieties,[98] but only four of them meet the CFBAI criteria.[99] Thus, Kraft can advertise Lunchables on a children's television show, and although it would only display one of the four approved meals, the child would not necessarily be able to differentiate among them in the store because the product packaging displays child-oriented features no matter the nutritional quality of the content. Further, an adult in the supermarket would have no way to determine which of the dozens of Lunchables was the "healthier" one advertised in the television commercial. One report found that the CFBAI-approved Lunchables were more likely to be stocked on the highest shelves in the supermarket, above eye level of both children and adults.[100]

Federal Tax-based Efforts

Federal legislators have proposed a different approach to address food marketing directed at youth in all types of venues. U.S. Representative Rosa DeLauro from

[97] J. L. Pomeranz. Extending the Fantasy in the Supermarket: Where Unhealthy Food Promotions Meet Children and How the Government Can Intervene. *Indiana Health Law Review.* 2012;9:117–185.

[98] http://www.lunchablesparents.com/

[99] CFBAI Product List. April 2014. http://www.bbb.org/Global/Council_113/CFBAI/CFBAI%20Product%20List%20April%202014_upload.pdf

[100] Rudd Report. Food Marketing FACTS in Focus: Kraft Lunchables. April 2014. http://www.yaleruddcenter.org/resources/upload/docs/what/reports/RuddReport_Lunchables_4.14.pdf

Connecticut proposed a bill to amend the Internal Revenue Code, which contains federal tax law, to remove the tax deductibility of the marketing expenses for food of poor nutritional quality. Current law permits marketing expenses to be tax deductable as an ordinary business expense. This bill would remove that benefit for any type of marketing directed at youth under 18 years of age via any of nine venues or methods (e.g., labeling, celebrity endorsements, schools, Internet) for foods that are inconsistent with the Dietary Guidelines for Americans.[101]

United States Senators Richard Blumenthal from Connecticut and Thomas Harkin from Iowa proposed a similar law in the Senate, the "Stop Subsidizing Childhood Obesity Act," which would remove the tax deductibility of the marketing expenses related to food of poor nutritional quality or of a "brand primarily associated with food of poor nutritional quality that is primarily directed at children" younger than 14 years through the same nine venues and methods as in the DeLauro bill. The Senate bill would direct the Secretary of the Treasury to consult with the Secretary of Health and Human Services and the FTC to define "poor nutritional quality" and "directed at children," as used in the bill.[102] To date, such efforts have not passed.

School-based Marketing

The 2012 FTC Report found that the majority of food marketing in schools was directed at teens and consisted of carbonated beverages, juice, noncarbonated beverages, and restaurant food.[103] The USDA studied the issue of food marketing in schools and found that as of the 2010–2011 school year, only 10% of school districts nationally had a "strong policy" that restricted the marketing of unhealthy foods or beverages on school campuses.[104] It also found that despite the amount of money spent on marketing in schools as per the FTC's report, 67% of schools receive no compensation for the food marketing. In one study where schools were found to have received compensation, it was 0.01% of the schools' yearly operating budgets. Thus, the USDA concluded that there would not be a significant financial impact on schools if they prohibited food marketing.[105]

The Healthy, Hunger-Free Kids Act of 2010 required local education agencies that participate in the National School Lunch Program or the School Breakfast Program to develop or expand local school wellness policies to meet minimum standards designed to foster a school environment that promotes nutrition and health and reduces childhood obesity.[106] The USDA's proposed rules require that

---

[101] HR 2831 (July 25, 2013).
[102] S 2342 (May 15, 2014).
[103] Federal Trade Commission. 2012 Report.
[104] 79 Federal Register 10693, 10698 (February 26, 2014).
[105] 79 Federal Register 10693, 10698 (February 26, 2014).
[106] 79 Federal Register 10693, 10693 (February 26, 2014).

local education agencies include a requirement in their wellness plan policy that restricts the marketing of food and beverages in schools to those permitted to be sold on school campuses during the school day according to the Smart Snack requirements or a more restrictive standard adopted by the district.[107]

The USDA's proposed rule defined marketing as "advertising and other promotions in schools" but recognized the broader school-marketing context and sought comments on marketing in and on the school campus, including product sales, fundraising, and incentive programs; advertising in school facilities, buses, and publications; media-based advertising on school television and radio; food coupons; indirect advertising such as through corporate sponsored educational materials, teacher training, contests and incentives, grants, gifts, or event sponsorships; and market research via surveys, Internet panels, or Internet tracking.[108] However, many state legislatures concurrently proposed bills to permit school-based marketing in general. For example, legislators have proposed bills to grant local boards of education the ability to authorize commercial advertising on school buses,[109] or athletic fields and related structures and fences,[110] or on all school property, including real property and district vehicles.[111]

If a school education agency or state or local government would like to restrict marketing in public schools as per the Healthy Hunger-Free Kids Act or otherwise, they would be able to do so without violating the Constitution. Interestingly, the Supreme Court has explained that the objective of public education has a similar end-goal as the rationale for protecting the freedom of speech: "inculcation of fundamental values necessary to the maintenance of a democratic political system."[112] Both are considered "indispensable to the practice of self-government in the community and the nation."[113]

A public school is government property, but not all government property is treated the same for First Amendment purposes. Locations such as streets and public parks are considered public property, or "public forums," where the government can only institute time, place, and manner restrictions on speech. An example of such a restriction would be the government requiring a permit for a parade to take place on a certain day, street, and time in a community. These are locations where people traditionally assemble to discuss, debate, or protest the topics of the day.[114] A school, on the other hand, is considered a "nonpublic forum," in First Amendment parlance. Unless the government opens up a nonpublic forum for public debate, state and local governments and school officials

---

[107] 79 Federal Register 10693, 10698 (February 26, 2014).
[108] 79 Federal Register 10693, 10699 (February 26, 2014).
[109] GA HB 881 (2014).
[110] NY HB 7703 (2013).
[111] NH HB 1147 (2014).
[112] *Bethel School District v Fraser*, 478 US 675, 681 (1986).
[113] *Bethel School District v Fraser*, 478 US 675, 681 (1986).
[114] *Hazelwood School District v Kuhlmeier*, 484 US 260, 267 (1988).

may reserve a nonpublic forum for its intended purposes,[115] which in the case of schools is education.[116]

The Supreme Court has recognized that children are a captive audience while in school,[117] and courts defer to school authorities to determine which speech is appropriate for students.[118] A state or local education agency has the authority to preserve the property for its educational purpose and enact restrictions on speech in schools as long as the restrictions are "reasonable" and not an effort to suppress expression because the public officials disagree with the speaker's viewpoint.[119] For example, the Court held that school officials cannot ban students from wearing armbands that protest war in order to avoid the discomfort that may accompany an unpopular viewpoint.[120]

The Court has explained that, "control over access to a nonpublic forum can be based on subject matter and speaker identity so long as the distinctions drawn are reasonable in light of the purpose served by the forum and are viewpoint neutral."[121] Viewpoint neutral means that officials are not choosing certain viewpoints as acceptable or unacceptable to be expressed in the forum. For example, a school cannot permit a Republican candidate to speak at a pep rally about her political platform but exclude a Democratic candidate from speaking about his. (In reality a school would not want to permit any political debate because this could indicate that it is opening up the forum to be akin to a public forum, which limits school official's ability to control speech.[122]) What this means for food marketing in school is that the school district can exclude a class of speakers or a subject matter of speech to protect the students, such as banning all food marketing all together. Another method that would meet the Court's standard would be to restrict the marketing of all foods and beverages not permitted to be sold in school. This would be basing the marketing restriction on school food nutrition criteria rather than the viewpoint of the speech. This is the basis of the USDA's proposed wellness policy regulations.

Government Speech

The government does not have the resources but has the constitutional authority to counter unhealthy food messages with its own speech. Government speech is not subject to First Amendment constraints. The government may engage in

---

[115] *Perry Education Association v Perry Local Educators' Association*, 460 US 37, 46 (1983).
[116] *Bethel School District v Fraser*, 478 US 675, 685 (1986).
[117] *Bethel School District v Fraser*, 478 US 675, 684 (1986).
[118] *Hazelwood School District v Kuhlmeier*, 484 US 260 (1988).
[119] *Perry Education Association v Perry Local Educators' Association*, 460 US 37, 46 (1983).
[120] *Tinker v. Des Moines Independent Community School District*, 393 U.S. 503, 509 (1969).
[121] *United States v. Kokinda*, 497 U.S. 720, 730 (1990).
[122] *Perry Education Association v Perry Local Educators' Association*, 460 US 37, 45-46 (1983).

public health messaging and countermarketing campaigns. An example of the former was the national Five-A-Day For Better Health educational campaign, led by the CDC, to encourage fruit and vegetable consumption. Governments also can engage in countermarketing campaigns. For example, New York City launched a Pouring on the Pounds campaign, intended to highlight the health risks associated with drinking too many sugary beverages for both children and adults.[123] The goals of countermarketing include attempting to counter the impact of marketing of unhealthy food and beverage products and influencing public support for policy interventions. Outside of these and similar public health campaigns, most government entities do not have the resources to engage in effective or widespread government speech campaigns.

Questions and Exercises for Classroom Discussion

Locate child-directed food advertising. How healthy or unhealthy is the food product advertised? Where did you find it? Can you find any advertising by the companies that say they do not market to children younger than 12 years but seem to be targeting young children anyway?

What should the government's role in food marketing to children be? What do you think about the argument that it is parents' responsibility? What are some arguments in favor of and opposed to the government's role in supporting parents?

Do you think FTC Orders impact consumers, the company, or the company's sales? Are there methods to increase the weight they carry with consumers or the company?

Advergames are "online games designed to market a brand in a manner that is fun and engaging and to increase exposure and positive associations with the brand."[124] These games are often found on food companies' websites and contain a branded image. In light of the commercial speech doctrine and the Supreme Court case that found violent video games to be fully protected speech, how should a court analyze Advergames under the First Amendment?

---

[123] NYC Pouring on the Pounds Ad Campaign. http://www.nyc.gov/html/doh/html/living/sugarydrink-media.shtml

[124] J. L. Harris, S. E. Speers, M. B. Schwartz, K. D. Brownell. U.S. Food Company Branded Advergames on the Internet: Children's Exposure and Effects on Snack Consumption. *Journal of Children and Media*. 2012;6(1):51–68.

8

Litigation

Introduction

The legal system in the United States is based on the common law tradition. This tradition originated in England and is premised on the notion that judges interpret the law and apply the law to the facts of the case before them.[1] The law that applies to a particular case can be legislation, regulation, or case law. One unique aspect of the common law system is that judges refer to previous cases, called precedent, to determine how they should apply the law to the facts of a subsequent case. Legal precedent creates case law and is binding on judges in lower courts.

Litigation in the United States is relatively expensive and time consuming. A lawsuit is initiated by a plaintiff against a defendant. Both parties are typically represented by a lawyer or a team of lawyers depending on the significance of the case. The plaintiff files a Complaint with the court arguing that the defendant violated the law and this violation harmed the plaintiff. Most cases involve an individual or small group of related plaintiffs, but when a large group of people have the same complaint against a defendant, they initiate a class action lawsuit. In all civil litigation, the parties each file at least one brief detailing the facts of the case, presenting the court with the relevant law, and arguing why the court should find in their favor by applying the law to the facts of their case. If the case is not dismissed, which happens when the plaintiffs'

---

[1] The one exception in the United States is the state of Louisiana, which predominantly relies on the civil law tradition with its roots in ancient Roman law. Louisiana was a territory of France and Spain, where the civil law tradition exists and from which Louisiana's laws stem. (See, *Viterbo v. Friedlander*, 120 U.S. 707 (1887)). This method is based primarily on a civil code that is intended to capture a more comprehensive set of issues and refers less to case law. Litigation discussed in this chapter is based on the common law system.

arguments do not amount to an actual legal violation, the parties proceed to discovery. Discovery is the process of obtaining information and evidence from the opposing party. The parties exchange documents that substantively address the issues to be resolved in the case. The parties' respective legal counsel also may request the opposing party to answer written questions (interrogatories) or oral questions (at a deposition). Each of the parties then asks the judge to rule in its favor through a motion for summary judgment. If the parties agree on the facts of the case, the judge will apply the law to those facts and rule on the case. If the facts are in dispute, the case will go to trial before the same judge and the judge or a jury will decide which version of the facts is accurate. Often the parties will settle the case before trial due to the expense of litigation and the risks involved with losing. Parties can settle at any time over the course of the litigation, but most settle before trial. If the case goes to trial, the prevailing party may obtain damages, which is money, or injunctive relief, which is an order for the defendant to cease or refrain from acting in the manner found to violate the law. The losing party often appeals the case to a court of appeals, which examines the proceedings that transpired in the trial court to determine whether the law was applied appropriately to the facts of the case. If a party is dissatisfied with the outcome in the appellate court, it may petition the state's highest court if the case is in state court, or the United States Supreme Court, if it is in federal court. These courts determine whether they will hear the case and accept relatively few. It can take many years to get to a final resolution of just one case.

Litigation has played a starring role in legal disputes against, among, and by the food industry. This indicates that the law is unsettled or evolving in many areas. There are a number of reasons for this. First, many laws were enacted quite a few years ago and modern practices reveal gaps in the law or create conditions that either the food industry or consumers dislike. An example of this is the Nutrition Labeling and Education Act of 1990 (NLEA), under which many labeling disputes take place both between consumers and companies and between two different companies. Another reason for the increase in litigation is that the rise in obesity rates created new issues and led public health advocates to engage in a more in-depth examination of the food environment. Consumer advocacy groups, private plaintiffs, and a handful of state attorneys general seek to rectify situations they believe are unjust by using the court system. Finally, government entities have responded to the changes in the state and local food environment by enacting novel laws to regulate food businesses, which in turn sue the government entity to avoid enforcement of the law.

Several types of litigation will be explored below, including litigation against the food industry, litigation between food industry companies, litigation initiated by the food industry against individuals, and various types of litigation against the government.

Litigation Against the Food Industry

In order to initiate a lawsuit, the plaintiff must have a cause of action against the defendant. This means that the plaintiff must identify a law that the defendant violated and explain how this action harmed the plaintiff. Most cases initiated by private plaintiffs or state attorneys general against the food industry are brought pursuant to state consumer protection statutes. Every state and the District of Columbia has consumer protection statutes that are patterned after the Federal Trade Commission Act to varying degrees and that generally prohibit unfair and deceptive acts and practices.[2] Attorney general litigation is premised on protecting the public by forcing companies to change their marketing or business practices or by obtaining financial recovery to punish deceptive practices or to restore losses to the state or its citizens. Private plaintiffs, on the other hand, may seek personal financial gain, damages for losses incurred due to deceptive practices, or they may have loftier goals to protect the public. Consumer advocacy groups sometimes bring cases on behalf of individuals for the purpose of protecting the public and changing business practices. It is important to note that even though both attorneys general and private plaintiffs bring litigation under the same state consumer protection statutes, there are more procedural barriers to private plaintiffs initiating such lawsuits; as a consequence, attorney general lawsuits are generally more successful and can achieve broader reaching results—although they are rarer.[3] As discussed in Chapter 1, attorneys general have pre-litigation powers that they may utilize more often than litigation in the context of food marketing.

Private plaintiffs also sue according to common law theories of tort liability. This refers to case law that established the precedent for viable causes of action based on a civil, as opposed to criminal, wrongdoing. There are many types of torts, for example, that a defendant was negligent, or failed to warn of dangers inherent in the product, or manufactured a product defectively, thus causing injury. In very general terms, most torts require a plaintiff to show that the defendant owed the plaintiff some type of duty of care and breached that duty, which caused the plaintiff an actual loss or damage.[4]

One of the most notorious food-related cases, *Pelman v. McDonald's*, stemmed from a 2002 lawsuit by two teenagers from New York City against the restaurant company, McDonald's. The plaintiffs claimed that McDonald's advertising campaign and the company's failure to disclose certain facts about its food

---

[2] Glenn Kaplan and Chris Barry Smith. Patching the Holes in the Consumer Product Safety Net: Using State Unfair Practices Laws To Make Handguns and Other Consumer Goods Safer. *Yale Journal on Regulation*. 2000;17:253, 318.

[3] J. L. Pomeranz. Litigation to Address Misleading Food Label Claims and the Role of the State Attorneys General. *Regent University Law Review*. 2014;26:421–455.

[4] L.O. Gostin. *Public Health Law: Power, Duty, Restraint* (2nd ed.). Los Angeles: University of California Press; 2008, p. 184.

increased the likelihood that the teenagers and other consumers would develop poor health conditions such as obesity and diabetes as a consequence of consuming McDonald's food.[5] The public reaction to this novel lawsuit was decidedly negative. The plaintiffs were not able to certify a class, meaning the court found that the plaintiffs' claims did not support a class action, and the case was ultimately dismissed in 2010. However, *Pelman v. McDonald's* had farther reaching consequences than anyone could have expected for litigation against restaurants, as explored in Box 8.1.

The Nutrition Labeling and Education Act of 1990 (NLEA) has spurred a great deal of litigation.[6] The Food Drug and Cosmetic Act does not provide a private right of action, which means it does not permit a private plaintiff to sue a food company for violating the NLEA as a method to privately enforce the FDCA in the absence of FDA enforcement. Therefore, consumers and consumer advocates sue food companies under state consumer protection laws when they believe a company's action harmed them. The company's action may have violated the NLEA, but a legally viable claim is not that the violation itself harmed the plaintiff, but rather that the false or misleading label violated the state consumer protection law's prohibition on unfair and deceptive acts or practices. So, for example, a lawsuit arguing that a company's violation of the NLEA in and of itself harmed plaintiffs would likely get dismissed as was the case when plaintiffs sued Coca-Cola over its product, Diet Coke Plus. The plaintiffs argued that their harm was that they purchased a product that violated the FDA's regulation prohibiting the fortification, or addition of vitamins, to soda. The court dismissed the case finding that the plaintiffs suffered no damages.[7] Conversely, a legally viable claim is one in which the food company's label is false or deceptive, regardless of whether it violates the NLEA. Thus, a viable claim would be that they would not have purchased the product but for the deception and a court should allow this claim to go forward.

There are two other potential barriers to private plaintiffs seeking to address labeling deficiencies through litigation. The NLEA has a preemption provision that explicitly prohibits efforts that seek to compel manufacturers to label food in a manner that is "not identical to" the federal requirements.[8] Therefore, it is not a legally viable complaint for a plaintiff to argue that a different labeling scheme is necessary for the label to not be unfair or deceptive under the state consumer protection law. For example, if plaintiffs think a food company's "0 grams of trans fat" statement is deceptive because this number is based on the true amount rounded down, they do not have a legally viable argument that the company's

---

[5] *Pelman v. McDonald's Corp.*, 2003 U.S. Dist. LEXIS 15202 (S.D.N.Y. 2003).

[6] J. L. Pomeranz. Litigation to Address Misleading Food Label Claims and the Role of the State Attorneys General, *Regent University Law Review*. 2014;26:421.

[7] *Mason v. Coca-Cola Co.*, 774 F. Supp. 2d 699 (D.N.J. 2011).

[8] 21 U.S.C. § 343-1(a)(5).

BOX 8.1

How Litigation Against McDonald's Changed the Food Litigation Landscape

Two teenagers who ate at McDonald's several times a week, usually for lunch during the school day or on the way to or from school, sued the restaurant in 2002.[a] The plaintiffs' main causes of action were based on New York's consumer protection laws. They alleged that McDonald's misled the girls, through advertising campaigns and other publicity, to believe that its food products were nutritious and part of a healthy lifestyle if consumed on a daily basis. They also alleged that McDonald's failed to disclose the fact that certain foods were substantially less healthy due to processing and ingredient additives. The plaintiffs argued that as a result of McDonald's deceptive acts and practices, they suffered damages including an increased likelihood of developing obesity, diabetes, coronary heart disease, hypertension, and elevated cholesterol.

Lawyers representing McDonald's publicly opposed this litigation, telling the press that "if this case were allowed to proceed 'it would lead to an avalanche of litigation.' "[b] They also admonished the plaintiffs, stating: "Every responsible person understands what is in products such as hamburgers and fries, as well as the consequence to one's waistline, and potentially to one's health, of excessively eating those foods over a prolonged period of time."[c] The public seemed to agree with McDonald's. A CNN poll from 2003 found that 96% of the almost 50,000 respondents said that McDonald's should not be held responsible in court for an individual's obesity.[d]

In response to this litigation, the National Restaurant Association led a nationwide campaign urging state and federal legislators to adopt what were euphemistically called "Cheeseburger Bills," although the real names for the bills are more telling.[e] The first of these, the Personal Responsibility in Food Consumption Act, was first introduced in the United States House of Representatives in 2003.[f] This was followed by the Commonsense Consumption Act, introduced in the Senate in 2005. These bills, and the state bills that followed, sought to thwart the ability of potential plaintiffs to bring *Pelman*-like litigation in court. The representatives who introduced these bills argued that consumers had to take personal responsibility for their food intake,[g] and others argued that the laws were needed to protect businesses from frivolous litigation.[h]

Federal legislation never passed; however, the restaurant industry was much more successful at the state level due to intense lobbying efforts, which included drafting the legislation for state legislators.[i] By 2005, 20 states had passed common-sense consumption acts and by 2013, 25 states passed such laws. These effectively withdraw the ability of a plaintiff to bring a claim arguing that consuming products from food service establishments caused them poor health outcomes. Legal scholars who have analyzed all 25 laws explained the "point" of common-sense consumption laws "was not to prevent *frivolous* litigation, from which industry already had plentiful protection, but rather to limit legally and factually sound litigation, which might eventually have harmed industry's bottom line and forced it to change its practices."[j] By avoiding litigation, the restaurant industry also avoids plaintiffs' discovery into its food production practices. Although 25 states do not have common-sense consumption acts, the negative backlash from Pelman and the unsuccessful litigation itself discourage plaintiffs' lawyers from bringing similar cases.

[a] *Pelman v. McDonald's Corp.*, 2003 U.S. Dist. LEXIS 15202 (S.D.N.Y. 2003).

[b] Jonathan Wald. McDonald's obesity suit tossed. CNN. February 17, 2003. http://money.cnn.com/2003/01/22/news/companies/mcdonalds/

(*continued*)

BOX 8.1
Continued

[c]Jonathan Wald. McDonald's obesity suit tossed. CNN. February 17, 2003. http://money.cnn.com/2003/01/22/news/companies/mcdonalds/

[d]Jonathan Wald. McDonald's obesity suit tossed. CNN. February 17, 2003. Poll: http://money.cnn.com/POLLSERVER/results/2223.html

[e]M. Warner. The Food Industry Empire Strikes Back. *The New York Times*. July 7, 2005. http://www.nytimes.com/2005/07/07/business/07food.html?pagewanted=all&_r=1&

[f]David Burnett. Fast-Food Lawsuits and the Cheeseburger Bill: Critiquing Congress's Response to the Obesity Epidemic. *Virginia Journal of Social Policy and Law*. 2007;14:357.

[g]David Burnett. Fast-Food Lawsuits and the Cheeseburger Bill: Critiquing Congress's Response to the Obesity Epidemic. *Virginia Journal of Social Policy and Law*. 2007; 14:357.

[h]Cara L. Wilking and Richard A. Daynard. Beyond Cheeseburgers: The Impact of Commonsense Consumption Acts on Future Obesity-Related Lawsuits. *Food Drug Law Journal*. 2013;68:229.

[i]M. Warner. The Food Industry Empire Strikes Back. *The New York Times*. July 7, 2005. http://www.nytimes.com/2005/07/07/business/07food.html?pagewanted=all&_r=1&

[j]Cara L. Wilking and Richard A. Daynard. Beyond Cheeseburgers: The Impact of Commonsense Consumption Acts on Future Obesity-Related Lawsuits. *Food Drug Law Journal*. 2013;68:229, 237.

product should disclose the true amount of trans fat because the NLEA permits rounding down for amounts less than 0.5 grams. In such a case, the claim that defendant should label the product differently than as required by the NLEA is preempted.[9]

Sometimes a claim might not be preempted, but a court will decline to hear the case based on the doctrine of primary jurisdiction. This means that the issue in the litigation is one that the regulatory agency has not decided but it is one under that agency's purview. If this doctrine applies, the courts' perspective is that the agency has the primary jurisdiction to decide this novel or complex issue, rather than the courts.[10] The goal is to allow the agency to create the regulatory scheme and not have judges' decisions take the place of a scheme intended by the agency. Permitting such claims to go forward would be particularly problematic if different courts take on the same question and come to conflicting conclusions on how the food industry should act on the topic in dispute, leaving them with contradictory guidance going forward.

One method to avoid preemption or the doctrine of primary jurisdiction would to bring a lawsuit based on the broader marketing campaign, such as a television commercial that either uses the same misleading language as the label or that displays the product itself in the advertisement. As opposed to the FDCA, the Federal Trade Commission Act contains a savings clause expressly permitting litigation based on state statutes that prohibit unfair and deceptive marketing.[11]

[9] *Chacanaca v. The Quaker Oats Co.*, 752 F. Supp. 2d 1111, 1119-21 (NDCA 2010).
[10] *Ivie v. Kraft Foods Global Inc.*, 2013 U.S. Dist. LEXIS 25615 (N.D. CA February 25, 2013).
[11] 15 USC §57b(e).

A private plaintiff must have seen the commercial in question and under almost all state consumer protection acts, must have suffered an injury. Conversely, in all states the state attorney general can bring a lawsuit to protect the public from a deceptive advertisement without these additional requirements.

State attorneys general more rarely bring consumer protection litigation against food companies for unfair and deceptive marketing or labeling practices than do private plaintiffs, but when they do, they generally have more success and positively settle the case. For example, in 2010, 39 attorneys general brought an action against The Dannon Company for making health claims about their Activia and DanActive yogurt products that were not substantiated by scientific evidence.[12] Dannon settled the case for $21 million, which was the largest payment in a multistate settlement between attorneys general and a food producer as of that date. In comparison, it is interesting to note that the Federal Trade Commission (FTC) simultaneously brought charges against Dannon for the same violations. The FTC likewise settled the case but unlike the attorneys general, the agency's settlement involved Dannon agreeing to refrain from making unsubstantiated health claims about its two products in the future.[13] Attorneys general have agreed to similar types of settlements in the past that require companies to change their marketing practices.[14] In the Dannon case, the attorneys general and the FTC coordinated their efforts. Had the FTC not brought an action, the attorneys general likely also would have included a requirement for the company to refrain from such practices in their settlement agreement. Nevertheless, a large financial settlement is always considered a big win in the context of litigation.

Private plaintiffs' lawsuits against food companies have had mixed results in the pure litigation sense. The seminal case representing a true litigation win in the context of food labels is the 2008 case of *Williams v. Gerber*.[15] In this case, a private plaintiff sued Gerber under California consumer protection laws. She argued among other things that Gerber's Fruit Juice Snacks were deceptively labeled because the term "fruit juice" on the packaging was placed alongside images of oranges, peaches, strawberries, and cherries despite the fact that the product did not contain fruit juice from these fruit. The Ninth Circuit Court of

---

[12] Attorney General of Massachusetts. Massachusetts Attorney General Martha Coakley and 38 Other States Settle with Dannon for $21 Million Regarding Deceptive Advertising of Activia and DanActive Yogurt Products. December 15, 2010. http://www.mass.gov/ago/news-and-updates/press-releases/2010/ag-coakley-and-38-other-states-settle-with.html

[13] Federal Trade Commission. Dannon Agrees to Drop Exaggerated Health Claims for Activia Yogurt and DanActive Dairy Drink. December 15, 2010. http://www.ftc.gov/news-events/press-releases/2010/12/dannon-agrees-drop-exaggerated-health-claims-activia-yogurt

[14] California Attorney General. Brown Secures Agreement with American Spirit Cigarettes Maker over Alleged Misleading Marketing of Organic Tobacco Products. March 1, 2010. http://oag.ca.gov/news/press-releases/brown-secures-agreement-american-spirit-cigarettes-maker-over-alleged-misleading

[15] *Williams v. Gerber Prods. Co.*, 523 F.3d 934 (9th Cir. 2008).

Appeals agreed. It found that, "reasonable consumers should not be expected to look beyond misleading representations on the front of the box to discover the truth from the ingredient list in small print on the side of the box."[16] The court further stated: "We do not think that the FDA requires an ingredient list so that manufacturers can mislead consumers and then rely on the ingredient list to correct those misinterpretations and provide a shield for liability for the deception."[17] It is noteworthy that the California Attorney General wrote an amicus brief, or friend of the court brief, in support of the plaintiff. An amicus brief is filed by a non-party who has an interest in the outcome of the case and seeks to suggest the way the court should decide.

Many cases do not result in positive outcomes for private plaintiffs, such as when the plaintiff cannot point to any actual damages, as in the Diet Coke Plus case mentioned above, or because the court finds that the plaintiff's position is not akin to that of a "reasonable consumer." An example of this latter finding is a case in direct contrast to *Williams v. Gerber*: the 2009 case of *Sugawara v. PepsiCo*, also brought pursuant to California consumer protection law.[18] In that case, a private plaintiff sued the manufacturer of Cap'n Crunch with Crunchberries, arguing that the packaging and marketing campaign were deceptive. Specifically, the plaintiff alleged that the colorful pictures of Crunchberries, combined with use of the word berry in the product name, conveyed the message that the cereal contained real fruit. The district court disagreed that a reasonable consumer would have understood the product packaging or the term "Crunchberries" to indicate that "brightly colored cereal balls" contained real fruit.[19] It further stated: "As far as this Court has been made aware, there is no such fruit growing in the wild or occurring naturally in any part of the world."[20] Thus, the court dismissed the case, finding that because a reasonable consumer would not have been deceived by the term, the food company could not be found to have violated the consumer protection act.

Consumer advocacy groups sometimes pair up with individual plaintiffs to initiate lawsuits solely intended to change the food information environment. Courts call this acting like a "private attorney general" because the goal is to protect the public. These lawsuits do not necessarily define success by what happens in court, but rather whether the case pressures the company to change its behavior or rouses the public to put pressure on the company. This type of litigation can sometimes be viewed as a method of "regulating" the industry through the court

---

[16] *Williams v. Gerber Prods. Co.*, 523 F.3d 934, 939-940 (9th Cir. 2008).

[17] *Williams v. Gerber Prods. Co.*, 523 F.3d 934, 940 (9th Cir. 2008).

[18] *Sugawara v. PepsiCo, Inc.* 2009 U.S. Dist. LEXIS 43127, 69 U.C.C. Rep. Serv. 2d (Callaghan) 326 (E.D. CA 2009).

[19] *Sugawara v. PepsiCo, Inc.* 2009 U.S. Dist. LEXIS 43127 at *12, 69 U.C.C. Rep. Serv. 2d (Callaghan) 326 (E.D. CA 2009).

[20] *Sugawara v. PepsiCo, Inc.* 2009 U.S. Dist. LEXIS 43127 at *12, 69 U.C.C. Rep. Serv. 2d (Callaghan) 326 (E.D. CA 2009).

system and may be considered a form of activism rather than plaintiffs seeking to redress their grievances. Three diverse examples illustrate this strategy.

The first example is when a lawsuit is intended to encourage broader change, but the judge dismisses the case outright because there is no true legal violation stated in the Complaint. This occurred when a consumer advocacy group teamed up with a private plaintiff to sue McDonald's over the toys in Happy Meals. The lawsuit argued that McDonald's uses toys "to lure small children into McDonald's," which it alleged was unfair and deceptive marketing under state consumer protection laws.[21] The judge dismissed the case without writing an opinion, which means he thought there was no set of facts under which this claim could be found to violate the law. The lawsuit itself, however, was discussed in the media, which started a national conversation about toys in Happy Meals. Such a result is considered one positive outcome by the advocacy community.

The second example of activist litigation was more successful. In May 2003, a lawyer sued Kraft Foods seeking an injunction for the food company "to cease and desist from marketing and selling Oreo Cookies to children in the State of California, until such cookies contain no partially hydrogenated oil or other trans fat."[22] The lawyer's goal was to get trans fat out of the food supply. He hoped that a positive outcome with this case would have a "domino effect" and other food companies would remove it from their products.[23] The lawyer ended up withdrawing his own case because: "Just one day after the media coverage about the lawsuit began, Kraft announced that it would reduce or eliminate the trans fat in the Oreo."[24] Kraft and other companies later removed trans fat from many of their products due to the FDA's new labeling rule that required trans fat to be listed on the Nutrition Facts Panel by January 2006.[25]

The third strategy takes a long-term view that a few losses in court, in the end, still may result in an overall change. This is exemplified by litigation over the term "natural." Consumers and advocacy groups initiated a substantial amount of litigation related to the term "natural." The FDA has explained that it will not "restrict the use of the term 'natural' except for added color, synthetic substances, and flavors;"[26] however, it has not issued a final regulation defining the term. As a result, "All Natural," "100% Natural," and "Natural" were found on a wide variety of products, ranging from ice cream, juice, sugary beverages, and artificial sweetener, to creamer,

---

[21] Center for Science in the Public Interest. Litigation Project—Closed Cases. http://www.cspinet.org/litigation/closed.html

[22] Ban Trans Fats. The Oreo Case. http://www.bantransfats.com/theoreocase.html

[23] Ban Trans Fats. The Oreo Case. http://www.bantransfats.com/theoreocase.html

[24] Ban Trans Fats. The Oreo Case. http://www.bantransfats.com/theoreocase.html

[25] Lorraine Heller. Kraft Slashes Trans Fats in Time for Labeling Deadline. Food Navigator-USA. December 23, 2005. http://www.foodnavigator-usa.com/Suppliers2/Kraft-slashes-trans-fats-in-time-for-labeling-deadline

[26] 58 Fed. Reg. 2302, 2407 (Jan. 6, 1993).

cereal, and snacks.[27,28] Plaintiffs brought litigation over these products, arguing that ingredients such as high fructose corn syrup, alkalized cocoa, citric acid, and genetically modified organisms render the products not natural and thus the label is false.

This series of litigation had mixed results in court. Courts dismissed some cases based on the doctrine of primary jurisdiction while others allowed the case to go forward; one court found that the plaintiffs' claim was simply "rhetoric" and not based on any evidence.[29] After years of litigation ups and downs starting in 2003,[30] the tide seemed to turn in 2013 when two major food manufacturers were subject to class action lawsuits and settled for $4 and $9 million respectively—in both cases tied to "natural" claims on food containing genetically modified organisms. In 2013, the *Wall Street Journal* reported the use of the term, "natural," was down significantly, and that, amid the aforementioned lawsuits, a growing number of food and beverage companies were removing such claims from packages.[31] In 2014, more settlements followed.[32] As part of these settlement agreements, the companies agreed to remove the natural claims from the products. Consumer advocacy groups view this as the goal of the litigation and consider the label change a litigation "win." The plaintiffs involved in the class action lawsuits generally receive refunds for the products they purchased.[33]

Litigation Between Food Companies

Food companies sue each other for unfair competition through misleading advertising or labeling practices. These lawsuits are based on the theory that when a competitor's marketing campaign is false or misleading, it draws consumers away from the plaintiff's product in favor of the competitor's goods. Food companies do not have standing to bring actions under consumer protection statutes to

---

[27] Mike Esterl. Some Food Companies Ditch 'Natural' Label; Amid Lawsuits Over the Claim, More Producers Drop the Word. *The Wall Street Journal*. November 6, 2013.

[28] J. L. Pomeranz. Litigation to Address Misleading Food Label Claims and the Role of the State Attorneys General, *Regent University Law Review*. 2014; 26:421.

[29] J. L. Pomeranz. Litigation to Address Misleading Food Label Claims and the Role of the State Attorneys General, *Regent University Law Review*. 2014;26:421.

[30] Elaine Watson. PopChips Agrees $2.4m 'All-natural' Lawsuit Settlement; Settlements Also Likely in Kashi and Bear Naked Cases. Food Navigator-USA. February 26, 2014 http://www.foodnavigator-usa.com/Regulation/PopChips-agrees-2.4m-all-natural-lawsuit-settlement-settlements-also-likely-in-Kashi-and-Bear-Naked-cases

[31] Mike Esterl. Some Food Companies Ditch 'Natural' Label. *The Wall Street Journal*. November 6, 2013. http://online.wsj.com/news/articles/SB10001424052702304470504579163933732367084

[32] Elaine Watson. PopChips Agrees $2.4m 'All-natural' Lawsuit Settlement; Settlements Also Likely in Kashi and Bear Naked Cases. Food Navigator-USA. February 26, 2014.

[33] Elaine Watson. Judge Gives Initial Thumbs Up to $3.4m Settlement Over Trader Joe's 'All-natural' Claims. Food Navigator-USA. February 11, 2014. http://www.foodnavigator-usa.com/Regulation/Judge-gives-initial-thumbs-up-to-3.4m-settlement-over-Trader-Joe-s-all-natural-claims

argue that their competitors' marketing campaign is deceptive. Therefore, food companies generally bring litigation under a federal statute called the Lanham Act. The Act creates a cause of action for commercial competitors for false or misleading descriptions or representations that misrepresent the commercial actor's or another person's goods, services, or commercial activities.[34] This provides a food company a cause of action against a commercial competitor for false or misleading commercial advertising or promotion.[35] Unlike for consumer plaintiffs who bring actions pursuant to state law, the Lanham Act is a federal statute and as such is not subject to the FDCA's preemption provision.[36] Moreover, neither the FDCA nor the Lanham Act precludes the Lanham Act's enforcement, even if there is a conflict between the competitor's claims and the FDCA's provisions.[37]

POM Wonderful, a manufacturer of pomegranate juice, brought a series of Lanham Act lawsuits against its competitors. Perhaps the most famous case in this context is *POM Wonderful LLC v. Coca-Cola Co.* because it made its way to the Supreme Court. POM brought a Lanham Act claim against Coca-Cola for labeling its Minute Made juice blend containing 99.4% apple and grape juices, 0.3% pomegranate juice, 0.2% blueberry juice, and 0.1% raspberry juice, "POMEGRANATE BLUEBERRY," with a small subtitle "flavored blend of 5 juices."[38] POM argued that this deceived consumers to think the product predominantly consists of pomegranate and blueberry juice, which caused POM to lose sales on its products that do predominantly contain pomegranate juice. The FDA regulates the naming of juices and under its regulations, Coca-Cola's name was permissible. So if this was a private plaintiff's consumer protection case, courts would likely dismiss the case. However, in the context of the Lanham Act, the Supreme Court held that neither FDA regulations nor the FDCA precluded the private lawsuit and it could go forward.

The goal of Lanham Act litigation is not to vindicate the rights of consumers but rather to stop the false or misleading campaign or to provide damages to the plaintiff.[39] However, the food company's interests may overlap with those of consumers, so proper enforcement of the Lanham Act can indirectly benefit consumers. This is especially the case in the context of product adulteration, which is when a manufacturer dilutes or substitutes one food product for another and sells it at premium prices.[40] Product adulteration is common with certain products

[34] 15 USCS § 1125(a)(1).

[35] 15 USCS § 1125(a)(1).

[36] *POM Wonderful LLC v. Coca-Cola Co.*, 134 S. Ct. 2228 (2014).

[37] *POM Wonderful LLC v. Coca-Cola Co.*, 134 S. Ct. 2228 (2014).

[38] *POM Wonderful LLC v. Coca-Cola Co.*, 134 S. Ct. 2228 (2014).

[39] *POM Wonderful LLC v. Coca-Cola Co.*, 134 S. Ct. 2228 (2014).

[40] Michael T. Roberts. Cheaters Shouldn't Prosper and Consumers Shouldn't Suffer: The need for government enforcement against economic adulteration of 100% pomegranate juice and other imported food products. March 2010. Rolls Law Group, PC. http://works.bepress.com/michael_roberts/1/

that consumers specifically purchase for health benefits, such as juice, olive oil, and honey.[41] POM Wonderful sued a competitor, Purely Juice, arguing that the latter's juice labeled "100% pomegranate" was false and violated the Lanham Act.[42] POM conducted extensive laboratory analysis, which found that Purely's juice was, in fact, diluted, and thus the court granted POM's request for an injunction and ordered the defendant to cease its false advertising.[43] Because the FDA lacks enforcement authority and resources and its labeling requirements are weak in several areas,[44] it remains to be seen if future Lanham Act cases address deficiencies traditionally considered under the sole purview of the agency.

Litigation by the Food Industry Against Individuals

A rare type of litigation occurs when food companies sue individual persons. This is not common, but two noteworthy types of cases are explored here, both in the context of defamation. Defamation is the intentional false communication of information that harms a person or entity's reputation. This can be accomplished through spoken words, called slander, or written words, called libel. If the statement was truthful, it does not qualify as defamatory.

Several states have passed controversial laws that seek to shield the food and agricultural industry from negative public comments. The laws may target defamatory statements about the industry or whistle-blowing, which is the act of exposing misconduct or illegal activity occurring in an organization. These laws are sometimes called Veggie Libel, Food Libel, anti-whistleblower, or most commonly, "Ag-Gag" laws. One such law was the subject of a lawsuit by the cattle industry against the popular talk show host Oprah Winfrey and her guest.

In 1996, the British Ministry of Health announced that scientists had linked the consumption of beef infected with Bovine Spongiform Encephalopathy (BSE) with a fatal disease that affects the human brain, Creutzfeldt-Jakob Disease. BSE is widely referred to as "Mad Cow Disease," and is a deadly, degenerative brain condition in cattle that is likely to arise when cattle are fed contaminated ruminant-derived meat rendered from cattle and sheep. Oprah Winfrey hosted an episode of her talk show entitled, "Dangerous Food" to discuss Mad Cow Disease and whether it could occur in the United States.[45] Oprah famously stated on the

---

[41] Michael T. Roberts. Cheaters Shouldn't Prosper and Consumers Shouldn't Suffer: The need for government enforcement against economic adulteration of 100% pomegranate juice and other imported food products. March 2010. Rolls Law Group, PC. http://works.bepress.com/michael_roberts/1/

[42] *Pom Wonderful v. Organic Juice*, 769 F. Supp. 2d 188, 191 (S.D.N.Y. 2011).

[43] *Pom Wonderful v. Purely Juice*, 2008 U.S. Dist. LEXIS 55426 (C.D. Cal. July 17, 2008).

[44] J. L. Pomeranz. A Comprehensive Strategy to Overhaul FDA Authority for Misleading Food Labels. *American Journal of Law & Medicine*. 2013;39(4):617–647.

[45] *Engler v. Oprah Winfrey*, 201 F.3d 680 (5th Cir. 2000).

episode: "It has just stopped me cold from eating another burger! I'm stopped!"[46] One of the show's guests compared BSE to HIV-AIDS and opined that the government needed to institute a mandatory ban on ruminant-to-ruminant feeding (which it did months later). After the airing of the show, the cattle market in Texas and nationally "dropped drastically."[47]

Several Texas cattle ranchers sued Oprah Winfrey, her production company, and her guest alleging violation of the Texas False Disparagement of Perishable Food Products Act. Under this Act, "a person may be held liable for damages sustained by the producer of a perishable food product if that person knowingly disseminates false information to the public stating or implying that the producer's product is not safe for public consumption."[48] The Fifth Circuit Court of Appeals found that the statements on the show might have been "hyperbolic" and the show "melodramatized" but knowingly false information was not disseminated.[49] The case was dismissed.

The Texas legislature had passed the False Disparagement of Perishable Food Products Act in response to a segment that aired on the television show 60 Minutes about a carcinogenetic chemical sprayed on apples.[50] Apple sales dropped significantly and apple growers sued the show for the common law tort of product disparagement, also known as trade libel.[51] The Ninth Circuit found the apple growers were not able to prove the falsity of the statements. Unlike the Texas law, several state legislatures have proposed bills or passed laws specifically to address undercover reporting of questionable animal husbandry practices at factory farms. These are the subject of litigation against the government, discussed below.

The second defamation-related episode actually never made it to court. In 2013, a nutrition group sent a newsletter to elementary school children and their parents suggesting that children need to reduce consumption of sugary beverages including energy drinks. In addition, it warned of the dangers of young children consuming energy drinks.[52] Monster Beverage Company threatened to sue the nutritionist who sent the letter unless she retracted the statements.[53] Instead of heeding this scare tactic, the nutritionist contacted her United States Senator, Richard Blumenthal of Connecticut, an outspoken critic of energy drinks (and the former attorney general of the state). He urged Monster to apologize to the

---

[46] S.H. Verhovek. Talk of the Town: Burgers v. Oprah. *The New York Times*. January 21, 1998.

[47] *Engler v. Oprah Winfrey*, 201 F.3d 680, 683 (5th Cir. 2000).

[48] *Engler v. Oprah Winfrey*, 201 F.3d 680, 687 (5th Cir. 2000).

[49] *Engler v. Oprah Winfrey*, 201 F.3d 680, 687 (5th Cir. 2000).at 688-689.

[50] *Auvil v. CBS "60 Minutes"*, 67 F.3d 816, 819 (9th Cir 1995).

[51] *Auvil v. CBS "60 Minutes"*, 67 F.3d 816, 819 (9th Cir 1995).at 820.

[52] B. Meier. In a New Aisle, Energy Drinks Sidestep Some Rules. *The New York Times*. March 19, 2013.

[53] B. Meier. In a New Aisle, Energy Drinks Sidestep Some Rules. *The New York Times*. March 19, 2013.

nutritionist.[54] No further action is recorded to have occurred and the nutritionist expanded her message to include older children and teens.[55] The lesson here is that litigation can be used as a scare tactic. This can be especially problematic when a profitable corporation threatens to sue an individual because the costs associated with defending a lawsuit can be quite high and potentially damaging for a noncorporate entity.

Litigation Against the Government

The third type of litigation that impacts food policy is litigation against the government. Based on the Eleventh Amendment to the U.S. Constitution and early U.S. Supreme Court precedent, the state and federal governments are traditionally immune from lawsuits by persons.[56,57] The government must, therefore, provide consent to be sued and has done so in many contexts. This area of law is quite complex, but the important aspect for our purposes is that this "sovereign immunity" doctrine does not bar suits against the government that argue that the government is violating the federal Constitution. Moreover, the U.S. Constitution expressly recognizes lawsuits between two or more states.[58]

Lawsuits against the government in the context of food policy have been initiated by one government entity against another, by public interest groups against the government, and by the food industry against the government. Recall that litigation can take many years and the final outcome may not be realized until after one or more appeals to higher courts. Several of the more cutting-edge cases discussed below are in the earliest stages of litigation, meaning that by the time this book went to print, they had only been heard by district courts. These are discussed to provide information on the types of litigation being initiated against the government in the context of food, but those interested in the substantive outcome of the litigation may find it beneficial to look up the result of any appeal.

Government Entity v. Government Entity

State and local governments may sue one another to address laws or actions deemed harmful to the plaintiff government and its residents. Recall, for example, the case of *Cleveland v. the State of Ohio*, discussed in Chapter 2, where the

---

[54] B. Meier. In a New Aisle, Energy Drinks Sidestep Some Rules. *The New York Times*. March 19, 2013.

[55] G. B. Hladky. Monster Beverage Now In Legal War with San Francisco, While Connecticut Nutritionist Keeps Calling for Ban on Energy Drink Sales to Kids. *Los Angeles Times*. May 6, 2013.

[56] *Cohen v. Virginia*, 19 U.S. 264 (1821); United States v. McLemore, 45 U.S. 286 (1846).

[57] U.S. Constitution Amendment XI.

[58] U.S. Constitutino Article III, Section 2.

state preempted the ability of local jurisdictions to regulate food service operations in order to overturn Cleveland's trans fat ban; the city successfully sued the state for violating its grant of Home Rule authority.[59]

Sometimes a state sues another state when it determines that a law passed by the defendant state will hurt the plaintiff state. These lawsuits are brought and defended through the states' attorneys general. State attorneys general may bring an action against another state pursuant to their *parens patriae* authority to assert the "quasi-sovereign interests" of their state, as discussed in Chapter 1. In these cases, the states' claims are related to vindicating the physical and economic health and well-being "of its residents in general."[60]

In *Missouri v. Harris*, several states, through their attorneys general, sued California for banning the sale of shelled eggs within California if the producers or handlers do not abide by a California law containing specific provisions aimed at preventing salmonella contamination and regulating the confinement of egg-laying hens.[61] The law applies to egg farmers within and outside of the state and the states that sued each have residents who are egg farmers and sell their eggs in California. The federal district court that heard the case found that the attorneys general did not assert a quasi-sovereign interest because the only parties that could potentially be injured by California's law are the egg farmers subject to the law, and not the broader residents within the plaintiff states. The court dismissed the case stating that the plaintiffs were not bringing the action on behalf of a substantial segment of the population and thus they did not have a unique interest apart from that of the egg farmers themselves. Therefore, the court found that the state attorneys general lacked standing, and it dismissed the case on procedural grounds without examining the substantive complaints regarding the law. The egg farmers may choose to sue separately.

Public v. Government

In 2012, California passed a law prohibiting the sale in California of products that are "the result of force feeding a bird for the purpose of enlarging the bird's liver beyond normal size."[62] The product at issue, called foie gras, is considered a delicacy. Canadian, New York, and California businesses involved in the production and sale of foie gras in California sued the state in federal district court to prevent enforcement of the law. The court found that the plaintiffs had standing because they asserted that they lost millions of dollars because they ceased selling

---

[59] *Cleveland v. State of Ohio*, 989 NE.2d 1072 (Oh. Ct. App. 2013).

[60] *Alfred L. Snap & Son, Inc v Puerto Rico*, 458 US 592, 607 (1982).

[61] *Missouri v. Harris*, 2014 U.S. Dist. LEXIS 141337 (E.D. CA 2014).

[62] *Association des Eleveurs de Canards et d'Oies du Quebec v. Harris*, Case No. 2:12-cv-5735-SVW-RW (CD CA. January 7, 2015) (quoting 2 Cal. Health & Safety Code § 25982).

their foie gras products in California to avoid facing prosecution.[63] Plaintiffs alleged that the foie gras ban was preempted by the Poultry Products Inspections Act (PPIA), which regulates poultry and poultry products including foie gras. PPIA expressly preempts state laws that impose marking, labeling, packaging, or ingredient requirements that are in addition to or different from federal law. The court found that the California law did impose an ingredient requirement that varied from federal law and as such it enjoined the enforcement of the foie gras ban in 2015.[64] Chefs in California rejoiced, while animal rights activists continue to protest the practice.[65]

In another example, as mentioned above, several states passed anti-whistleblower or "Ag-Gag" laws that criminalize the undercover investigation of animal abuses on factory farms.[66] These laws proliferated after videos of food-related animals being abused surfaced through undercover investigations.[67] In June 2015, North Carolina become the eighth state to have such a law when the state legislators overrode their governor's veto.[68] In response to Idaho's law, the Animal Legal Defense Fund and other nonprofit organizations, agricultural experts, and journalists sued Idaho arguing that the Ag-Gag law is unconstitutional.[69] The plaintiffs argued that the law violates the First Amendment because it implicates protected speech and further that it violates the Equal Protection Clause because it unfairly targets whistleblowers and was passed with "animus" toward this group. The plaintiffs also argued that the law is preempted by several federal statutes that encourage the very same whistleblowing activity that the Idaho law criminalizes. Just as this book went to press, the court granted the plaintiffs' motion for summary judgment on both the First Amendment and Equal Protection counts, citing Upton Sinclair's *The Jungle*.

Food Industry v. Government Entity

The food industry often sues the government after the latter passes a novel law. This means that state or local governments need to consider the potential for litigation when, in an effort to support public health, they enact laws that regulate an industry. All states have an attorney general whose office is responsible for

---

[63] *Association des Eleveurs de Canards et d'Oies du Quebec v. Harris,* Case No. 2:12-cv-5735-SVW-RW (CD CA. January 7, 2015).

[64] *Association des Eleveurs de Canards et d'Oies du Quebec v. Harris,* Case No. 2:12-cv-5735-SVW-RW (CD CA. January 7, 2015).

[65] National Public Radio. In California, Foie Gras Is Back On The Menu. January 10, 2015 http://www.npr.org/2015/01/10/376381103/in-california-fois-gras-is-back-on-the-menu

[66] The Editorial Board. Eating With Our Eyes Closed. *The New York Times.* April 9, 2013.

[67] Farm Forward. Exposing Ag-Gag. http://www.farmforward.com/features/ag-gag

[68] Farm Forward. Exposing Ag-Gag. http://www.farmforward.com/features/ag-gag

[69] *Animal Legal Defense Fund v. Otter,* Case No. 1:14-cv-00104-BLW (Memorandum Decision and Order) (D. Idaho September 4, 2014).

defending the state government in such matters. Additionally, approximately 30 state health agencies have their own legal department that employs attorneys.[70] There are approximately 89,000 local governments in the United States,[71] which have much more diverse structures than the state governments. Several local governments, however, have taken novel approaches to food policy and have been sued by the food industry. The litigation against New York City for the nation's first menu label law exemplifies a typical lawsuit of this kind.

New York City was sued several times for laws enacted by the Department of Health and Mental Hygiene under Mayor Bloomberg's administration (2002–2013). As discussed in more detail in Chapter 9, New York City was the first location to pass a trans fat ban, menu label law, and sugary beverage serving-size restriction. Various sectors of the food industry sued the city to prevent enforcement of the latter two laws. The lawsuit related to the serving size restriction is premised on separation of powers issues and is discussed in the next chapter. The lawsuit based on the menu label law represents common arguments industry makes in response to public health laws, especially those regulating food and tob acco.[72,73,74]

In 2006, the New York City Board of Health adopted an amendment to its health code enacting the nation's first menu label law.[75] The New York State Restaurant Association (NYSRA) challenged the law in federal district court based on two allegations: that the law was preempted by the NLEA and that the law violated the First Amendment.[76] The court found that this original ordinance was, in fact, preempted by the NLEA because it tied the requirement to voluntary disclosures; the court ruled in favor of the NYSRA without addressing the First Amendment claims.[77] New York City amended the law to correct the violation and adopted the revised law on January 22, 2008. The new regulation required covered food service establishments to disclose the calorie content of their food products directly on the menu or menu board. The NYSRA again filed a lawsuit, alleging that this, too, was preempted by the NLEA and violated the First Amendment.

---

[70] Association of State and Territorial Health Officials. Public Health Responsibilities. Key findings on State Public Health Agency Responsibilities from the 2010 Profile of State Public Health Survey. http://www.astho.org/research/data-and-analysis/2010-profile-survey-slide-decks/chapter-1—state-public-health-agency-responsibilities/

[71] Census Bureau Reports. There Are 89,004 Local Governments in the United States. August 30, 2012. http://www.census.gov/newsroom/releases/archives/governments/cb12-161.html

[72] *Lorillard Tobacco Co. v. Reilly*, 533 U.S. 525 (2001).

[73] *Philip Morris USA, Inc. v. City & County of San Francisco*, 345 Fed. Appx. 276 (9th Cir. 2009).

[74] *National Association of Tobacco Outlets, Inc. v. City of Providence*, 731 F.3d 71 (1st Cir. 2013).

[75] New York City Health Code § 81.50.

[76] J. L. Pomeranz. Compelled Speech Under the Commercial Speech Doctrine: The Case of Menu Label Laws. *Journal of Health Care Law & Policy*. 2009;12:159–194.

[77] *New York State Restaurant Association v. New York City Board of Health*, 509 F. Supp. 2d 351 (S.D.N.Y. 2007).

In the New York City menu label case, the industry first argued that the NLEA preempted the law.[78] Prior to the federal menu labeling law which was enacted in 2010, however, the NLEA did not preempt mandatory disclosures in food retail establishments. So at this time, the NLEA's preemption provision did not apply to restaurants. The NYSRA also argued that the menu label law impermissibly compelled speech. As discussed in the chapter on labeling, the First Amendment permits government to require commercial entities to disclose factual information about the products for sale in the marketplace. Thus, the district court found in favor of the city and ordered covered food service establishments to comply with the regulation. The NYSRA appealed this decision to the United States Court of Appeals for the Second Circuit. It is noteworthy that the FDA submitted an amicus brief in support of New York City. In February 2009, the court upheld the menu label law. At this point, other local governments around the country enacted menu label laws, including Seattle King County,[79] and San Francisco and Santa Clara, California.[80]

The claims that local government action is preempted and violates the regulated industry's First Amendment rights are typical of public health-related litigation. Although courts are technically supposed to lean toward state and local law not being preempted according to Supreme Court precedent, many opportunities remain for a court to find a law is preempted. As discussed in Chapter 2, even if the federal law does not expressly preempt state or local law, a court could find that they conflict or that the federal government intended to occupy the field and thus it is technically preempted anyway. Thus, it makes sense that the food industry would argue in court that a state or local law is preempted.

The second argument, that the action violates the First Amendment is also very typical in public health litigation. In fact, many of the seminal Supreme Court cases on commercial speech involve industry challenges to public health laws. This is because many laws aimed at protecting public health implicate businesses' interests in some manner. Since the Supreme Court created the commercial speech doctrine in 1976, corporations have argued for increased First Amendment protections for commercial speech. As such, they often contend that regulations involving any type of communication violate their First Amendment rights. Creative lawyers can argue that most public health regulations involve speech or expression of some sort. For example, the tobacco industry unsuccessfully claimed that a city's ban of tobacco sales in pharmacies unconstitutionally

---

[78] J. L. Pomeranz. Compelled Speech Under the Commercial Speech Doctrine: The Case of Menu Label Laws. *Journal of Health Care Law & Policy.* 2009;12:159–194.

[79] King County, Washington. Nutrition labeling in King County. http://www.kingcounty.gov/healthservices/health/nutrition/healthyeating/%7e/media/health/publichealth/documents/boh/reg0802.ashx

[80] San Francisco, California Health Code § 468 (2008); Santa Clara, California, Ordinance NS 300.793 (2008).

suppressed "its speech because the product itself is a form of advertisement."[81] The ban was upheld as a regulation of conduct. Regulations of conduct are discussed further in Chapter 9.

Questions and Exercises for Classroom Discussion

Has litigation against the food industry been successful in changing food marketing strategies?

Has the food industry's litigation against the government been successful in discouraging local governments from enacting novel food policy laws?

Are there certain lawsuits you think would be effective to support public health in the context of food?

Why do you think the state attorneys general brought the case against California to address its shelled egg laws? Do you think they considered this a violation of their states quasi-sovereign interests?

Students should read Orin S. Kerr. How to Read a Legal Opinion. *The Green Bag.* 2007;1(1):51–63 (cited in legal databases: 11 GREEN BAG 2D 51) and a recent food case. In class, students explain what the case was about, analyze the parties' claims, and discuss how the outcome and the alternative outcome could impact public health.

Find a current news story about a food labeling litigation case. Why is this case in court? Is litigation the best method to address the issue? What is your opinion about the merits of this case?

---

[81] *Philip Morris USA v. City & County of San Francisco,* 2008 U.S. Dist. LEXIS 101933 (N.D. CA 2008).

9

State and Local Control of the Food Environment

Introduction

State governments have broad authority to impact the food environment. As discussed in Chapter 2, the United States Constitution reserves for the states those powers that are not exclusively granted to the federal government. State governments act pursuant to their police power to enact laws and regulations to protect, preserve, and promote the health, safety, and general welfare of their populations.[1] Through this police power, states may support population interests at the expense of individual interests through various legal mechanisms, including zoning land, licensing persons, and directly regulating retailers, products, and services. States also have the power to tax and spend and to disseminate health warnings and information. All of these powers confer on states a substantial ability to influence diverse aspects of the food environment.

The Constitution does not refer to local governments. States originally created local governments to perform administrative duties for the state, such as property assessment.[2] These duties expanded in the early part of the 1900s. Today there are over 89,000 local governments[3] with varying degrees of authority. The state government determines the extent to which a local government has the power to structure its own government, exercise functional powers of local control, engage in financial activities such as taxation, and employ personnel.[4]

---

[1] L. O. Gostin. *Public Health Law: Power, Duty, Restraint* (2nd ed.). Los Angeles: University of California Press; 2008, pp. 92–93.

[2] National League of Cities. Local Governments. http://www.nlc.org/build-skills-and-networks/resources/cities-101/city-structures/local-us-governments

[3] U.S. Census Bureau. Census Bureau Reports There Are 89,004 Local Governments in the United States, August 30, 2012. http://www.census.gov/newsroom/releases/archives/governments/cb12-161.html

[4] National League of Cities. Local Government Authority. http://www.nlc.org/build-skills-and-networks/resources/cities-101/city-powers/local-government-authority

Unless indicated otherwise, this chapter refers to state governments' authority to include local governments to the extent that the state permits the local government to act in the manner described. Because local governments have a diverse range of responsibilities, it is not possible to categorically describe their authorities or limitations.

The Authority of State and Local Governments

As discussed in Chapter 1, each state has a state health agency that performs a wide range of duties. There are also approximately 2,800 local health departments.[5] Local health departments are involved with food through the regulation, inspection, and licensing of food service establishments, food safety education, population-based nutrition services, and the administration of the Special Supplemental Nutrition Program for Women, Infants, and Children (WIC).[6] Local health departments are also involved in policy and advocacy activities related to obesity and chronic disease and food safety.

State and local governments address food related issues through their police power over health, safety, and welfare.[7] Strategies that fall under this rubric include zoning, licensing, health inspection of food service establishments, and direct controls. As long as government initiatives do not violate the constitutional rights of the regulated entity, courts generally defer to the government's determinations of how best to further public health.[8] Still, when government regulates pursuant to its police power, the action must be rationally related to a legitimate government interest. The government's interest in protecting public health is generally accepted as legitimate.[9] A state's specific interest in regulating food retailers and restaurants might stem from the goals of food safety, sanitation, or encouraging nutritious choices. The government must employ a rational method to further its interests, so regulations cannot be unreasonable or arbitrary.[10] This means that not every conceivable restriction is legally feasible. The more effectively a regulation negatively influences purchase decisions, the more likely food companies or retailers will challenge the ordinance in court.

---

[5] National Association of County and City Health Officials. The National Profile of Local Health Departments. http://nacchoprofilestudy.org/wp-content/uploads/2014/02/2013_National_Profile021014.pdf

[6] National Association of County and City Health Officials. The National Profile of Local Health Departments. http://nacchoprofilestudy.org/wp-content/uploads/2014/02/2013_National_Profile021014.pdf

[7] *Jacobson v. Massachusetts*, 197 U.S. 11 (1905).

[8] *Gundling v. Chicago*, 177 U.S. 183 (1900).

[9] *Jacobson v. Massachusetts*, 197 U.S. 11 (1905).

[10] *Schmidinger v. Chicago*, 226 U.S. 578 (1913).

Zoning and Licensing

State and local governments have the authority to alter the food retail environment, including where and how restaurants, grocery stores, and convenience stores are located and how they can function using their zoning and licensing authorities. One concern for many people in the United States is that they live in locations without reasonable access to full-service grocery stores. Such stores tend to stock fresh produce and meats more often than convenience stores or gas station stores, which generally sell less healthy foods and can be more expensive. Areas without ready access to healthy food sources are called "food deserts," and they may exist in both rural and urban neighborhoods. Rural food deserts denote lack of access to a full-service supermarket due to the distance one must travel to get there. Lack of affordable and feasible transportation options can be an impediment to such shopping trips. Urban food deserts are marked by low access to a supermarket and may result in corner stores and fast food restaurants filling the void. The USDA Economic Research Service (ERS) tracks food deserts by looking at the distance those in low-income census tracts live from supermarkets; it uses 1 mile in urban areas and 10 miles in rural areas to demarcate those who are far from a supermarket.[11] Using 2010 data, the USDA ERS found there are 8,959 food deserts in the 50 states.[12]

The Centers for Disease Control and Prevention (CDC) has found that, "Supermarkets and full-service grocery stores have a larger selection of healthy food (e.g., fruits and vegetables) at lower prices compared with smaller grocery stores and convenience stores. However, research suggests that low-income, minority, and rural communities have fewer supermarkets as compared with more affluent areas."[13] Many state and local zoning and licensing options discussed in this section attempt to address the issue of access. Cost-related concerns are addressed below.

Zoning is a method of regulating land use and the built environment while licensing is a method of regulating persons and business operations. Both methods stem from the government's police power and can be utilized to further public health interests. Generally, zoning is prospective and attaches to land, meaning that it applies to future building and land use, while licensing requirements can be implemented at any time and attach to the licensed person or business.[14] Each will be discussed in turn.

---

[11] USDA. ERS. Food Access Research Atlas. Documentation. Last updated March 11, 2015. http://www.ers.usda.gov/data-products/food-access-research-atlas/documentation.aspx

[12] USDA. ERS. Food Access Research Atlas. Documentation. Last updated March 11, 2015. http://www.ers.usda.gov/data-products/food-access-research-atlas/documentation.aspx

[13] http://www.cdc.gov/mmwr/preview/mmwrhtml/rr5807a1.htm

[14] Heather Wooten, Ian McLaughlin, Lisa Chen, Christine Fry,Catherine Mongeon, and Samantha Graff. Zoning and Licensing to Regulate the Retail Environment and Achieve Public Health Goals. *Duke Forum For Law & Social Change*. 2013;5:65–96

State governments generally delegate their zoning authority to local governments, which are the primary zoning authority.[15] They use this power to divide land into permitted, unpermitted, or conditionally permitted uses; thus, the zoning authority can issue a permit to use the land in the manner desired, deny the permit, or grant the permit subject to certain conditions such as having adequate parking. Governments also use their zoning authority to create zones or districts that designate these permissions in certain locations, such as residential, business, industrial, retail, tourism, parks, hospitals, or schools. Zoning laws may also prescribe the size and height of buildings, the density of certain businesses, and the size, height, and location of business signs and billboards.

The seminal case on zoning is *Village of Euclid, Ohio v. Ambler Realty Co.*, under which the U.S. Supreme Court declared the zoning authority to be a valid use of the government's "flexible" police powers unless the ordinance is "clearly arbitrary and unreasonable, having no substantial relation to the public health, safety, morals, or general welfare."[16] The government's use of its zoning authority must have a rational basis, so when it passes zoning ordinances it provides the rationale for the decision. In that case, the Court upheld the village's comprehensive zoning plan, explaining that dividing the land into different districts "bears a rational relation to the health and safety of the community."[17] The most common rationales utilized by government are to protect public health or safety.[18]

Many zoning ordinances shape the food environment, especially as related to fast food establishments. For example, some towns ban drive-through passageways to lessen street congestion for traffic safety and air pollution from idling cars; others ban formula restaurants (e.g., McDonald's) or formula businesses (e.g., the Gap) to preserve a quaint, unique, or historic district.[19] Local governments also have established quotas on the number of fast food outlets permitted within a district or regulated fast-food outlet density, spacing, or distance from other uses. For example, Detroit, Michigan passed a zoning ordinance that bans fast food establishments from locating within 500 feet of a school.[20] Such ordinances are generally instituted for a dispersion rationale[21] or to minimize nuisances such as litter, noise, loitering, or odors.[22]

---

[15] J. S. Mair, M. W. Pierce, and S. P. Teret. The Use of Zoning to Restrict Fast Food Outlets: A Potential Strategy to Combat Obesity. October 2005. http://www.publichealthlaw.net/Zoning%20Fast%20Food%20Outlets.pdf

[16] *Euclid v. Ambler Realty Co.*, 272 U.S. 365, 395, 397 (1926).

[17] *Euclid v. Ambler Realty Co.*, 272 U.S. 365, 391 (1926).

[18] J. S. Mair, M. W. Pierce, and S. P. Teret. The Use of Zoning to Restrict Fast Food Outlets: A Potential Strategy to Combat Obesity. October 2005.

[19] J. S. Mair, M. W. Pierce, and S. P. Teret. The Use of Zoning to Restrict Fast Food Outlets: A Potential Strategy to Combat Obesity. October 2005.

[20] Detroit Zoning Ordinances. Sec. 61-12-96; Sec. 61-12-228.

[21] Detroit Zoning Ordinances. Sec. 61-12-96; Sec. 61-12-228.

[22] J. S. Mair, M. W. Pierce, and S. P. Teret. The Use of Zoning to Restrict Fast Food Outlets: A Potential Strategy to Combat Obesity. October 2005.

A 2008 ordinance in Los Angeles proclaimed that the city would not issue any more permits for fast food restaurants in certain zones of the city specifically to address the "over-concentration of fast food restaurants," which the city found to be "detrimental to the health and welfare of the people of the community."[23] The city also noted that fast food establishments negatively impact pedestrian activity, traffic, neighborhood aesthetics, and the environment. The moratorium on new fast food restaurants was supposed to take effect for one year starting in 2008, but it remains in place as of 2015. It is noteworthy that although the particular location within Los Angeles where the ordinance is effective has one of the highest obesity rates in the city, the City Council did not cite this as a rationale for the moratorium. At the time of this writing, an obesity-prevention rationale has not been utilized to support zoning efforts.

Local communities also might regulate commercial signage, such as a zoning ordinance in Braintree, Massachusetts that prohibits roof signs, limits window signs to 20% of total window space, and prohibits ground signs from being taller or larger than a prescribed size and distance from the ground. The city's rationale is to improve aesthetics and traffic safety in the town.[24]

Local governments also might zone areas to attract full-service supermarkets[25] or to encourage farmers' markets to locate within a community to support a positive food environment.[26] For example, Portland, Oregon updated its Urban Food Zoning Code to permit market gardens, community gardens, and food membership distribution sites in all of the city's zones.[27] It also regulated farmers' markets as "temporary uses" to address frequency, location, and other issues. Communities can provide incentives for such businesses to locate in the designated area by coupling the supportive zoning measure with financial incentives such as tax benefits or loans.[28,29]

Licensing, on the other hand, regulates people or business operations. State governments typically require people in certain professions to obtain licenses to engage in a profession or a type of work, such as attorneys, doctors,

---

[23] Los Angeles Ordinance 180103. http://cityplanning.lacity.org/Code_Studies/Misc/FastFoodInterim.pdf

[24] Town of Braintree, Zoning Bylaws § 135. http://ecode360.com/14708382

[25] Centers for Disease Control and Prevention. Recommended Community Strategies and Measurements to Prevent Obesity in the United States. *MMWF.* July 24, 2009 / 58(RR07);1–26. http://www.cdc.gov/mmwr/preview/mmwrhtml/rr5807a1.htm

[26] The City of Portland Oregon. Urban Food Zoning Code Update Approved by City Council on June 13th (June 13, 2012). http://www.portlandoregon.gov/bps/article/402598

[27] The City of Portland Oregon. Urban Food Zoning Code Update Approved by City Council on June 13th (June 13, 2012). http://www.portlandoregon.gov/bps/article/402598

[28] Centers for Disease Control and Prevention. Recommended Community Strategies and Measurements to Prevent Obesity in the United States. *MMWF.* July 24, 2009 / 58(RR07);1–26. http://www.cdc.gov/mmwr/preview/mmwrhtml/rr5807a1.htm

[29] New York City Planning Department. FRESH Food Stores—Approved! May 11, 2011. http://www.nyc.gov/html/dcp/html/fresh/index.shtml

acupuncturists, and plumbers. State and local governments also require licenses for certain business practices in order to collect taxes or maintain more control over the operation than general retail establishments.[30] Many jurisdictions place conditions on the license in order to ensure the retailer operates according to the government's specifications. This has two primary functions. First, the government can tie requirements into the retailer's abidance with the conditions and second, if the retailer does not abide by the conditions, the government can withdraw the license. The threat of losing one's license to operate, and thus losing one's business, is often a stronger deterrent to violating the law than the threat of a fine alone. Finally, governments often impose licensing fees that can be used to cover the costs of implementing, inspecting, and enforcing the licensing laws.[31]

Licensing ordinances have been applied to the food environment, although this is less common than zoning.[32] However, licensing can provide a more flexible approach because new requirements can be established on previously existing and new businesses. Further, zoning agencies do not generally see their role as inspecting locations for compliance with substantive health-related provisions. Licensing also can accomplish some of the more operational zoning regulations discussed above; specifically, the signage limitations could be achieved through a license that conditions the operation of a business on it abiding by the signage requirements. Licensing also has the potential to go farther than zoning in terms of regulating in-store practices. For example, Minneapolis, Minnesota has a strong licensing program to support health-oriented corner grocery stores. The program is operated out of the Minneapolis Health Department and is funded by the state. It requires that grocery stores (defined to include stores selling necessity and non-necessity food and household items) be licensed by the department and offer for sale on a continual basis, at least three varieties of qualifying (and non-expired or spoiled) food in each of the following four staple food groups: (1) vegetables and/or fruits, (2) meat, poultry, fish, and/or vegetable proteins, (3) bread and/or cereal, and (4) dairy products and/or substitutes, with at least five varieties of perishable food in the first category and at least two varieties of perishable food in all subsequent categories.[33]

Licensing is commonly used to regulate tobacco retailers, who routinely agree to certain conditions such as posting signs regarding the legal age of purchase,

---

[30] Heather Wooten, Ian McLaughlin, Lisa Chen, Christine Fry,Catherine Mongeon, and Samantha Graff. Zoning and Licensing to Regulate the Retail Environment and Achieve Public Health Goals. *Duke Forum for Law & Social Change*. 2013;5:65–96.

[31] Heather Wooten, Ian McLaughlin, Lisa Chen, Christine Fry,Catherine Mongeon, and Samantha Graff. Zoning and Licensing to Regulate the Retail Environment and Achieve Public Health Goals. *Duke Forum for Law & Social Change*. 2013;5:65–96.

[32] Heather Wooten, Ian McLaughlin, Lisa Chen, Christine Fry,Catherine Mongeon, and Samantha Graff. Zoning and Licensing to Regulate the Retail Environment and Achieve Public Health Goals. *Duke Forum for Law & Social Change*. 2013;5:65–96.

[33] Minneapolis, Minnesota, Code of Ordinances Title 10. Chapter 203.20.

not selling single cigarettes, and not selling tobacco out of vending machines.[34] In the food context, one could imagine similar types of conditions intended to support a healthier food environment that could be included in a license, such as agreeing to have junk food-free check-out aisles or not selling soda in vending machines. It is important to note that a government entity cannot require a retailer to agree to unconstitutional conditions as part of the licensing requirement. For example, the government could not condition a license on the prohibition that the retailer refrain from promoting its low prices for unhealthy foods, because such a prohibition would violate the First Amendment.[35]

Directly Regulating Conduct

Recall the discussion of the commercial speech doctrine in Chapter 7. Although it is quite difficult for the government to restrict speech, it can regulate conduct much more easily. In the 2001 case of *Lorillard v. Reilly*, in addition to advertising restrictions, Massachusetts banned self-service tobacco displays to require that "tobacco products be placed out of the reach of all consumers in a location accessible only to salespersons."[36] The regulations' stated purpose was to minimize customer access without proper age verification to prevent minors from obtaining tobacco products. The Court assumed that the tobacco companies that challenged the law had "a cognizable speech interest in a particular means of displaying their products," but it found the regulations withstood First Amendment scrutiny.[37] The Court differentiated between a regulation that restricts speech and one that regulates conduct. It sustained the regulations stating that, "Massachusetts' sales practices provisions regulate conduct that may have a communicative component, but Massachusetts seeks to regulate the placement of tobacco products for reasons unrelated to the communication of ideas."[38] Because the regulation of the location of product displays was found to be a restriction of conduct and not the suppression of speech, the restriction fell out from under the purview of the commercial speech doctrine and thus was not subject to the *Central Hudson* test. Rather, the Court looked to a different analytical framework for restrictions on "expressive conduct."

"Expressive conduct" is *behavior* that has a communicative component. For example, flag burning to protest a war is considered expressive conduct.[39] On the other hand, conduct that must be accompanied by speech to explain its meaning is

---

[34] See e.g., City of Milwaukee. Cigarette Business Information. Cigarette and Tobacco License. http://city.milwaukee.gov/ImageLibrary/Groups/ccLicenses/cigarette.pdf

[35] *Virginia State Board of Pharmacy v. Virginia Citizens Consumer Council*, 425 U.S. 748 (1976).

[36] *Lorillard v. Reilly*, 533 U.S. 525, 567 (2001).

[37] *Lorillard v. Reilly*, 533 U.S. 525, 569 (2001).

[38] *Lorillard v. Reilly*, 533 U.S. 525, 570 (2001).

[39] *Spence v. Washington*, 418 U.S. 405 (1974).

not expressive. The government may regulate expressive conduct as long as it furthers an important or substantial government interest and any incidental restriction on communications is no greater than necessary.[40] The government must also leave open "alternative avenues for vendors to convey information about products and for would-be customers to inspect products before purchase."[41] In *Lorillard v. Reilly*, the Court assumed for purposes of the case that there was an expressive component to displaying the tobacco products in a certain manner; however, Massachusetts was regulating conduct to prevent minors from obtaining tobacco. The Court noted that it presumed the law permitted retailers to display empty boxes for customers to inspect because the restriction was not intended to shield youth from the product packaging but rather from being able to obtain tobacco products themselves.[42] Therefore, the Court upheld the restriction. The lesson is that the government can regulate the placement of products for reasons unrelated to the suppression of expression consistent with the First Amendment.[43]

In commercial speech cases, the Court not infrequently recommends various conduct-regulations as constitutionally viable alternatives to the restriction of speech. Thus, numerous non-speech-restrictive avenues for regulation exist. For example, in *44 Liquormart v. Rhode Island*, the state sought to prohibit the advertisement of retail prices of alcoholic beverages. The state asserted an interest in reducing alcohol consumption, but the Court disapproved of bans on truthful advertising that sought "to keep people in the dark for what the government perceives to be their own good."[44] The Court struck down the regulation as violating the commercial speakers' First Amendment rights and suggested alternative forms of regulation that would not involve any restriction on speech but would likely achieve the state's goal of promoting "temperance:"

> [H]igher prices can be maintained either by direct regulation or by increased taxation. Per capita purchases could be limited as is the case with prescription drugs. Even educational campaigns focused on the problems of excessive, or even moderate, drinking might prove to be more effective.[45]

Additional suggestions made by the Court or members of the Court in separate opinions include: limiting the quantity of a harmful ingredient permitted in the food or beverages,[46] banning the product,[47] or prohibiting its purchase, possession, or use by minors.[48]

---

[40] *United States v. O'Brien*, 391 U.S. 367 (1968).

[41] *Lorillard v. Reilly*, 533 U.S. 525, 569 (2001).

[42] *Lorillard v. Reilly*, 533 U.S. 525, 570 (2001).

[43] *Lorillard Tobacco Co. v. Reilly*, 533 U.S. 525, 569-570 (2001).

[44] *44 Liquormart v. Rhode Island*, 517 U.S. 484, 503 (1996).

[45] *44 Liquormart v. Rhode Island*, 517 U.S. 484, 507.

[46] *Rubin* v. *Coors Brewing Co.*, 514 U.S. 476, 490-491 (1995).

[47] *44 Liquormart*, 517 U.S. at 524 (Justice Thomas, concurring in part and concurring in judgment).

[48] *Lorillard Tobacco Co. v. Reilly*, 533 U.S. 525, 586 (2001) (Justice Thomas, concurring in part and concurring in the judgment).

State and local governments have attempted to address the food environment by enacting some of the aforementioned suggested regulations of conduct. Price increases and educational campaigns will be discussed below. There has not been an attempt to restrict the per capita purchase of food products. However, several jurisdictions including New York City,[49] Philadelphia,[50] and California[51] passed a ban on the use of trans fat (from partially hydrogenated oils) as an ingredient in foods served in food service establishments and mobile food vending units. (These bans occurred prior to the FDA's trans fat regulation discussed in Chapter 5.)

It is rare for the government to ban a food item or to enact age limits on minors' purchase or use of products outside of alcohol and tobacco. However, in the context of energy drinks, state and local governments have been stepping in to protect their citizens. Energy drinks are marketed as producing increased energy in consumers through the addition of caffeine, sugar, and novel ingredients not typically found in other beverages.[52] They have been blamed for health problems, spikes in emergency room visits, and death in children.[53] The FDA has not directly regulated energy drinks or the amount of caffeine permitted in them. One county in New York banned the sale of energy drinks in county parks to youth younger than 18 years,[54] and several state legislators have proposed bills to prohibit their sale to minors in their states.[55,56] Other products, namely caffeinated alcoholic drinks, are a mix between alcoholic beverages and energy drinks. Some states, including Washington and Michigan, banned these products outright for sale in their state, while other states negotiated with manufacturers to halt sales in their state.[57] After these state-level actions, the FDA sent Warning Letters to manufacturers warning them that the addition of

---

[49] New York City Department of Health and Mental Hygiene. The Regulation to Phase Out Artificial Trans Fat. February 2007. http://www.nyc.gov/html/doh/downloads/pdf/cardio/cardio-transfat-bro.pdf

[50] Philadelphia. Trans fat information packet. December 2007. http://www.phila.gov/health/pdfs/Trans_Fat.pdf

[51] California. Trans Fat Ban Guidelines. January 2010. https://www.acgov.org/aceh/documents/TransFatBanGuidelines2010-01-07.pdf

[52] J. L. Pomeranz, C. Munsell, and J. L. Harris. Energy Drinks: An Emerging Public Health Hazard for Youth. *Journal of Public Health Policy*. 2013;34(2):254–271.

[53] Daniel J. DeNoon. FDA: 5 Death Reports for Monster Energy Drink. WebMD Health News. October 23, 2012. http://www.webmd.com/food-recipes/news/20121023/death-reports-monster-energy-drink

[54] NY SC Res 1086—Concerning sale of energy drinks to minors

[55] IL HB 2379—Prohibition to sell energy drinks to minors

[56] John Henrehan. Maryland. Considers Banning Sale of Energy Drinks to Minors. Fox DC News. March 7, 2014. http://www.myfoxdc.com/story/24914384/maryland-to-consider-banning-energy-drinks-sales-to-minors

[57] Angela Carter. *New Haven Register.* November 16, 2010. http://www.nhregister.com/general-news/20101116/updated-alcohol-laced-energy-drinks-including-four-loko-to-fade-from-conn-store-shelves

caffeine to alcohol was an "unsafe food additive," and thus the products were adulterated.[58]

Cities have experimented with other regulations of conduct more or less successfully. New York City unsuccessfully passed a cap on the serving size of sugary beverages sold in the city's food retail establishments; this is discussed in Box 9.1. Two cities in California placed a restriction on toys provided with children's meals. In 2010, Santa Clara, California was the first location to prohibit the distribution of a toy with food and beverages that did not meet specified minimum nutrition standards.[59] One year later, San Francisco enacted a Healthy Food Incentive Ordinance with the same intent. In order to bypass the San Francisco ordinance, however, McDonald's began selling the toy with its Happy Meals for ten cents.[60] Jack in the Box ceased providing toys with its kids' meals around this time, although it said its decision was not in response to the ordinance but rather part of an effort to increase the healthfulness of its products.[61] There was negative media backlash from these efforts and other municipalities have not followed suit.

Addressing Retail Food Prices

The relative price of unhealthy foods such as commercially processed baked goods, sweets, and sugary drinks is cheaper than fruits and vegetables in much of the United States.[62,63] Research indicates that food prices are one of the primary drivers of food selection and that higher quality diets are generally higher in cost.[64] There is cause for concern when a healthy diet is more expensive than an unhealthy diet and people of lower socioeconomic means cannot afford food that is not detrimental to their health.[65]

---

[58] Food and Drug Administration. Public Health Focus. Update on Caffeinated Alcoholic Beverages. http://www.fda.gov/NewsEvents/PublicHealthFocus/ucm234900.htm

[59] Justin Berton. Santa Clara County says no to fast-food toys. *SF Gate*. April 28, 2010. http://www.sfgate.com/bayarea/article/Santa-Clara-County-says-no-to-fast-food-toys-3266181.php

[60] San Francisco Happy Meal Toy Ban Takes Effect, Sidestepped By McDonald's. Huffington Post. November 30, 2011. http://www.huffingtonpost.com/2011/11/30/san-francisco-happy-meal-ban_n_1121186.html

[61] Anika Anand. Jack in the Box Stops Offering Toys in Kids' Meal. NBC News. 6/21/2011. http://www.nbcnews.com/id/43483446/ns/business-retail/t/jack-box-stop-offering-toys-kids-meals/#.U9EHEkCuCi1

[62] Adam Drewnowski, The Cost of US Foods as Related to Their Nutritive Value. 92 American Journal of Clinical Nutrition. 2010; 1181, 1187.

[63] K. D. Brownell and K. R. Frieden. Ounces of Prevention—The Public Policy Case for Taxes on Sugared Beverages. *New England Journal of Medicine*. 2009;360(18):1805–1808.

[64] C. D. Rehm, P. Monsivais, and A. Drewnowski. The Quality and Monetary Value of Diets Consumed by Adults in the United States. *American Journal of Clinical Nutrition*. 2011;94(5):1333–1339.

[65] Report submitted by the Special Rapporteur on the right to food, Olivier De Schutter. Human Rights Council. United Nations General Assembly. December 26, 2011. http://www.srfood.org/images/stories/pdf/officialreports/20120306_nutrition_en.pdf

BOX 9.1

New York City Sugary Beverage Serving Size Cap

The New York City Department of Health and Mental Hygiene, an administrative agency in the executive branch of the city government, proposed an ordinance establishing sixteen ounces as the maximum size for sugary drinks permitted to be sold in the city's food service establishments. The Department based the restriction on the science that large portions of sugary beverages are linked to obesity, diabetes, and heart disease, all of which were problems in the city at the time of passage. The ordinance had exceptions for milk-based drinks because the science was not as strong for these products, and the ordinance did not apply to retailers designated as grocery stores because they are regulated by New York State. The Department held a notice and comment period and accepted both written and oral comments. In 2012, the New York City Board of Health adopted the ordinance.

The proposed regulation was controversial in no small part because the media called the measure a "soda ban" and characterized Mayor Bloomberg, whose administration passed the ordinance, as a "nanny."[a] Moreover, the American Beverage Association created a coalition called New Yorkers for Beverage Choices to mimic a grassroots movement opposing the measure.[b] Such a fake grassroots movement has been termed "astroturfing." But many citizens, in fact, did oppose the measure as did several city council members. The National Restaurant Association, American Beverage Association, small business owners, their parent organizations, and others sued the city to prevent enforcement of the restriction. The case made its way to the state's highest court.

The plaintiffs argued that the New York City Board of Health did not have the authority to enact the serving size restriction and that the ordinance itself was irrational. The first complaint in the litigation was that the Board of Health had exceeded the authority granted to it by City Charter, and thus, was improperly acting in a legislative capacity. This is a separation of powers argument. As an administrative agency, the Board of Health can act only within the parameters set forth by the legislative body, and thus, it can only make rules according to the powers and duties delegated to it. The majority opinion in the case found that the Board had exceeded this authority. The court found, that because the portion cap rule restricts "activities preferred by large numbers of people" it raised "difficult, intricate and controversial issues of social policy" beyond the preservation of health and safety that rendered it a form of "policy-making, not rule-making."[c]

It is noteworthy that the court added that it would have come to the same conclusion if the Board had enacted an "outright prohibition of sugary beverages."[d] This is not to say that the government cannot ban sugary beverages, which would be contrary to the Supreme Court's statements above, but rather that the Board of Health was not granted authority to make such determinations. Regulatory agencies can enact regulations to carry out the intent of the legislator, but they cannot create new policy.

The second argument in the lawsuit was that the ordinance itself was not rational but rather was "arbitrary and capricious."[e] State and local governments have the discretion to use their police power to enact laws and regulations to protect, preserve, and promote the health, safety, and welfare of their population as long as the regulation rests upon a rational basis within the knowledge and expertise of the government body.[f] The court majority did not reach this question because it struck down the law on the separation of powers issue. The dissenting opinion in the case, however, found that the "Rule easily passes this test." It is noteworthy that no lower court found that regulating

(*continued*)

BOX 9.1
Continued

large portions of sugary beverages was irrational. The trial court found that the exceptions in the rule (for milk-based drinks and grocers) were arbitrary, and the intermediate appellate court did not reach the issue, stating that the "deleterious effects (e.g., obesity) associated with excessive soda consumption are well-known."[g] The legally binding outcome of the portion cap case is that health agencies in New York State cannot pass such a regulation without a legislative mandate. The New York City Council or state legislature could still pass this measure, as could any legislature in the country. Thus, while local governments might be granted police power authority by their states, health agencies must still be granted the authority to act on a particular issue. Political feasibility is a separate matter that likely has deterred future efforts in this arena. As the dissent noted, the rule was "unpopular."

[a]Brad Hamilton. Bloomberg's Ban Prohibits 2-liter Soda with Your Pizza and Some Nightclub Mixers. *New York Post*. February 24, 2013. http://nypost.com/2013/02/24/bloombergs-ban-prohibits-2-liter-soda-with-your-pizza-and-some-nightclub-mixers/

[b]Reihan Salam. Brief Note on the Soda Ban, Astroturf, and Subsidizing Political Participation. National Review Online. July 12, 2012. http://www.nationalreview.com/agenda/309249/brief-note-soda-ban-astroturf-and-subsidizing-political-participation-reihan-salam

[c]*In the Matter of New York Statewide Coalition of Hispanic Chambers of Commerce v. The New York City Department of Health and Mental Hygiene*, Case No. 134 New York Court of Appeals (June 26, 2014).

[d]*In the Matter of New York Statewide Coalition of Hispanic Chambers of Commerce v. The New York City Department of Health and Mental Hygiene*, Case No. 134 New York Court of Appeals (June 26, 2014).

[e]*In the Matter of New York Statewide Coalition of Hispanic Chambers of Commerce v. The New York City Department of Health and Mental Hygiene*, Case No. 134 New York Court of Appeals (June 26, 2014).

[f]*Jacobson v. Massachusetts*, 197 U.S. 11 (1905).

[g]*New York Statewide Coalition of Hispanic Chambers of Commerce v. New York City Dept. of Health & Mental Hygiene*, 110 A.D.3d 1 (NY App. 1st Dept 2013).

The most straightforward method for government to alter the price of unhealthy products would be to enact a tax. All state governments have the power to enact taxes, but this authority varies widely among local governments. Taxes can be instituted for a variety of purposes, including raising revenue and deterring consumption. The U.S. Supreme Court explained, "a tax does not cease to be valid merely because it regulates, discourages, or even definitely deters the activities taxed. The principle applies even if the revenue obtained is negligible, or the revenue purpose of the tax is secondary."[66]

A legislature would have to decide between enacting a sales tax or an excise tax. Sales taxes are levied as a percentage of the retail price and are added upon check-out. For example, as of 2014, 34 states plus the District of Columbia tax soda sold in retail establishments, while 39 states plus Washington, DC tax soda sold in vending machines, both at an average of 5%.[67] It is unclear whether these

[66] *United States v. Sanchez*, 340 U.S. 42, 44 (1950).

[67] Bridging the Gap. 2014 State-by-State Soda Tax Rates http://www.bridgingthegapresearch.org/_asset/s2b5pb/BTG_soda_tax_fact_sheet_April2014.pdf

sales taxes appreciably reduce consumption, but they are not generally passed for this purpose.[68] Further, if sales taxes are considered by consumers, they may encourage bulk purchases or the purchase of less expensive brands of the same item.[69]

An excise tax, on the other hand, is "a duty or impost levied upon the manufacture, sale, or consumption of commodities."[70] They are levied at the manufacturer level and if the manufacturer passes the tax on to consumers as intended, it raises the base price of the product. For example, all states have an excise tax on cigarettes and these are passed through to consumers, increasing the price of such tobacco products by the taxed amount. These excise taxes have been found to reduce tobacco consumption.[71] Researchers have found that an excise tax on food products would similarly reduce consumption of the taxed product.[72] Some states have business-related excise taxes on sugary beverages for the purpose of raising revenue.[73] Although about half of the states and several cities have proposed bills to pass higher excise taxes specifically to deter consumption of sugary beverages,[74] as of the date of publication, only the city of Berkeley, California, successfully passed a tax for this purpose, discussed further below.

The most common food-related tax proposal by state and city legislatures is for an excise tax on sugary beverages. Such a tax would be levied on the syrup or beverage manufacturer in order to increase the base price of the product. These vary on the percent mark-up, but the majority of bills call for one cent tax per ounce of beverage.[75] A side benefit of excise taxes as opposed to sales taxes is that the revenue can be earmarked, or dedicated, to a specific purpose. Many bills posit that the revenue could be earmarked for programs encouraging positive health, such as subsidizing fruits and vegetables.

Although taxing sugary beverages is the most commonly proposed food tax for the dual purposes of reducing consumption and raising revenue, other taxation

---

[68] Roland Sturm et al., Soda Taxes, Soft Drink Consumption, and Children's Body Mass Index. 29 *Health Affairs*. 2010;1052, 1057–1058.

[69] K. D. Brownell and K. R. Frieden. Ounces of Prevention—The Public Policy Case for Taxes On Sugared Beverages. *New England Journal of Medicine*. 2009;360(18):1805–1808.

[70] CCH Editorial Staff Publication. Introduction. In D. Becker (Ed.) *U.S. Master Excise Tax Guide* (6th ed.). Chicago, IL: Author; 2008, p. 26.

[71] Frank J. Chaloupka et al., Tax, Price and Cigarette Smoking: Evidence from the Tobacco Documents and Implications for Tobacco Company Marketing Strategies. *Tobacco Control*. 2002;11(Suppl 1):I62–I72.

[72] T. Andreyeva , M. W. Long, and K. D. Brownell. The Impact of Food Prices on Consumption: A Systematic Review of Research on Price Elasticity of Demand for Food. *American Journal of Public Health*. 2010;100(2):216–222.

[73] Berkeley Media Studies Group for the California Center for Public Health Advocacy. Kick the Can. FAQ about Soda Taxes. 2011. www.kickthecan.info/document/258

[74] Rudd Center for Food Policy & Obesity. Rudd Report. Sugared Sweetened Beverage Taxes: An Updated Policy Brief. October 2012. http://www.yaleruddcenter.org/resources/upload/docs/what/reports/Rudd_Policy_Brief_Sugar_Sweetened_Beverage_Taxes.pdf

[75] T. Andreyeva, F. J. Chaloupka, and K. D. Brownell. Estimating the Potential of Taxes on Sugar-sweetened Beverages to Reduce Consumption and Generate Revenue. *Preventive Medicine*. 2011;52(6):413–416.

methods have been discussed, including taxing specific ingredients such as added sugar;[76] taxing categories of food such as junk food,[77] fast food,[78] or highly processed food;[79] or taxing food considered unhealthy according to specific definitions, such as foods high in saturated fats, trans-fatty acids, sodium, and sugar.[80] At this juncture, it has been difficult for state and local governments to pass food or beverage-related taxes due to opposition and heavy lobbying by the food industry and other political barriers.[81] Support for such taxes varies around the country but increases when the tax is paired with a plan to earmark the revenue for positive health programs.

Not all local governments have the power to levy taxes. For example, New York State's constitution declares that the power to tax is held by the state, with specific limited exceptions, and only permits local governments to issue taxes if the legislature grants an exemption.[82] The lack of state permission is why New York City, which famously sought to address high consumption of sugary beverages through various different means , did not pass a sugary beverage tax. Conversely, Chicago does have such authority and has instituted its own soft drink "occupation tax," which is imposed on persons who sell canned or bottled soft drinks at retail establishments in the city.[83] Unlike the Berkeley tax, this was not instituted to additionally deter consumption. Chicago does have its own excise tax on cigarettes which does have that purpose.[84]

In California, local governments can only pass a business license tax, which is a form of excise tax, through the electorate.[85] The local government entity must first get the tax proposal on the ballot and the electorate must vote for the measure. Two cities, Richmond and Del Monte, placed a sugary beverage tax on

---

[76] Zhen Miao et al. Taxing Sweets: Sweetener Input Tax or Final Consumption Tax?, *Contemporary Economic Policy.* 2011;30: 344–361.

[77] C. Franck, S. M. Grandi, and M. J. Eisenberg. Taxing junk food to counter obesity. *American Journal of Public Health.* 2013;103(11):1949–1953.

[78] L. M. Powell, J. F. Chriqui, T. Khan, R. Wada, and F. J. Chaloupka. Assessing the Potential Effectiveness of Food and Beverage Taxes and Subsidies For Improving Public Health: A Systematic Review of Prices, Demand and Body Weight Outcomes. *Obesity Review.* 2013;14(2):110–128.

[79] J. L. Pomeranz. Taxing Food and Beverage Products: A Public Health Perspective and a New Strategy for Prevention. *University of Michigan Journal of Law Reform.* 2013;46(3):999–1027.

[80] Report submitted by the Special Rapporteur on the right to food, Olivier De Schutter. Human Rights Council. United Nations General Assembly. December 26, 2011. http://www.srfood.org/images/stories/pdf/officialreports/20120306_nutrition_en.pdf

[81] Duane D. Stanford. Anti-Obesity Soda Tax Fails as Lobbyists Spend Millions: Retail. Bloomberg. March 13, 2012 http://www.bloomberg.com/news/2012-03-13/anti-obesity-soda-tax-fails-as-lobbyists-spend-millions-retail.html

[82] NY CLS Const Art XVI, § 1. Powers of taxation; exemptions from taxation.

[83] The Chicago Home Rule Municipal Soft Drink Occupation Tax, 65 ILCS 5/8-11-6b. http://tax.illinois.gov/Businesses/TaxInformation/Sales/softdrink.htm

[84] Cigarette Tax Hike in Chicago Makes a Pack of Smokes in The Windy City the Priciest in the Nation. Huffington Post. November 26, 2013. http://www.huffingtonpost.com/2013/11/26/cigarette-tax-chicago_n_4344651.html

[85] Public Health Law & Policy. Local Taxes on Sugar-Sweetened Beverages in California. http://changelabsolutions.org/sites/default/files/Local-Taxes-SSBs-CA_Legal_Memo-20130513.pdf

the ballot in 2012, but the voters overwhelmingly rejected these. San Francisco and Berkeley also attempted to pass sugary beverage excise taxes by putting the measure on the ballot in 2014, but only Berkeley was successful. The San Francisco proposal would have placed a two cents per ounce "special" tax on sugary beverages. It would have earmarked the revenue for school nutrition and physical education programs and for installation of water fountains in the city.[86] A special tax under California law is a tax imposed for a specific purpose. Because the San Francisco tax was a special tax, the city could earmark the funds, but San Francisco needed a two-thirds vote to pass the measure.[87] The measure garnered approximately 55% of the vote so the tax did not pass.[88] Conversely, Berkeley proposed a penny per ounce "general" tax, imposed for a general government purpose, with the revenue going to the general treasury, and thus it only needed a majority of voters to pass.[89] The Berkeley tax passed, garnering approximately 75% percent of the vote.[90] The Berkeley soda-tax ballot measure was one of the best organized advocacy efforts in food policy history. Local news reports noted that one of the distinguishing factors in getting the tax passed, besides Berkeley's history of activism, was the powerful use of social media.[91]

In addition to taxes, other mechanisms exist to increase the price of unhealthy food or beverage products. Recall that in the case discussed above, *44 Liquormart*, the Supreme Court's principal opinion stated that, "higher prices can be maintained either by direct regulation or by increased taxation."[92] The concurring opinion explained this could be accomplished by establishing minimum prices.[93] Minimum price laws have not been utilized in the food context, but approximately 25 states have them for cigarettes. These laws require the addition of a minimum percentage markup to be added to the retail or wholesale price.[94] Although minimum price laws were originally enacted in the 1940s and 1950s to protect tobacco retailers from predatory business practices, they are now

---

[86] Randy Shaw. 2/3 Vote Could Doom SF Soda Tax. BeyondChron. July 28, 2014. http://beyondchron.org/23-vote-doom-sf-soda-tax/

[87] Public Health Law & Policy. Local Taxes on Sugar-Sweetened Beverages in California. http://changelabsolutions.org/sites/default/files/Local-Taxes-SSBs-CA_Legal_Memo-20130513.pdf

[88] Frances Dinkelspiel. Why Berkeley Passed a Soda Tax While Other Cities Failed. *Berkeleyside*. November 5, 2014. http://www.berkeleyside.com/2014/11/05/why-berkeley-passed-a-soda-tax-where-others-failed/

[89] Dana Woldow. Soda Tax Myths: Is A New Tax "The Last Thing" Berkeley Needs? BeyondChron. June 30, 2014. http://beyondchron.org/soda-tax-myths-is-a-new-tax-the-last-thing-berkeley-needs/

[90] Frances Dinkelspiel. Why Berkeley Passed a Soda Tax While Other Cities Failed. *Berkeleyside*. November 5, 2014. http://www.berkeleyside.com/2014/11/05/why-berkeley-passed-a-soda-tax-where-others-failed/

[91] http://www.beyondchron.org/social-media-helped-defeat-big-soda/

[92] *44 Liquormart v. Rhode Island*, 517 U.S. 484, 507 (1996); see also, *National Association of Tobacco Outlets, Inc. v. City of Providence*, 731 F.3d 71, 77 (1st Cir. 2013).

[93] *44 Liquormart v. Rhode Island*, 517 U.S. 484, 530 (1996); see also, *National Association of Tobacco Outlets, Inc. v. City of Providence*, 731 F.3d 71, 77 (1st Cir. 2013).

[94] Centers for Disease Control and Prevention. State Cigarette Minimum Price Laws—United States, 2009. *MMWR. Morbidity and Mortality Weekly Report*. 2010;59(13):386–392.

considered a potential method of maintaining higher cigarette prices to deter consumption. The retailers, rather than the government as in the case of taxes, benefit from the increased price requirement.

A second method of directly regulating prices is to prohibit the redemption of coupons or multipack discounts.[95] Examples of multipack discounts in the context of sugary beverages would be when the retailer sells a case of soda for a reduced price or offers two-for-one deals on liters. Retailers accept coupons or offer multipack discounts that have the potential to decrease the price of products in general, or to pre-tax levels, or to below the minimum price instituted by a law. This would nullify the effect of a tax or minimum price law, or in the absence of these, still decrease the price of a product to encourage increased purchase. Again, this strategy has not been implemented yet for food or beverage, but courts have upheld such laws in the context of cigarettes.[96] For example, Providence, Rhode Island requires all tobacco retailers to obtain a license in order to operate. It subsequently prohibited such license holders from accepting or redeeming coupons or from selling tobacco products through multipack or other discounts.[97] This was upheld by the First Circuit as "an appropriate regulation of pricing."[98]

Increasing Access to Healthy Food

Besides increasing the price of unhealthy food to deter consumption, other strategies include offering financial incentives or creating other programs to foster a healthy food environment. As discussed in the context of sugary beverage taxes above, many of the proposed tax laws would additionally earmark the revenue for positive health-related programs, such as subsidizing fruits and vegetables. The government can subsidize healthy food without the imposition of a tax, however. For example, some states, such as Florida, appropriate money to support the operation of farmers' markets.[99] Other locations offer financial incentives to specific populations to purchase produce. For example, Rhode Island and New York City both have programs to provide SNAP recipients with $2.00 extra money for every $5.00 they spend at a farmers' market.[100] Another method utilized to

---

[95] J. L. Pomeranz. Using Lessons Learned from Tobacco to Inform Sugary Beverage Tax Policy. *American Journal of Public Health*. 2014;104(3):e13–e15.

[96] *National Association of Tobacco Outlets, Inc. v. City of Providence*, 731 F.3d 71 (1st Cir. 2013); see also *National Association of Tobacco Outlets v. City of New York*, 2014 U.S. Dist. LEXIS 83058 (SD NY June 18, 2014).

[97] *National Association of Tobacco Outlets, Inc. v. City of Providence*, 731 F.3d 71 (1st Cir. 2013).

[98] *National Association of Tobacco Outlets, Inc. v. City of Providence*, 731 F.3d 71 (1st Cir. 2013). at 85.

[99] FL Chapter No. 2012-118 (enacted 2012).

[100] RI SNAP / EBT and Credit Cards at RI Farmers Markets. http://www.farmfresh.org/markets/freshbucks.php; see also NYC Health Bucks and EBT. http://www.grownyc.org/greenmarket/ebt/healthbucks

address disparities in access to produce is by offering permits to vendors who sell produce in neighborhoods in need. For example, New York City's Green Carts program provides licenses to vendors to operate a cart to sell fruit or vegetables in communities where there is low access to fresh produce.[101] The District of Columbia piloted a similar program in underserved communities and modeled it after the Green Carts program.[102]

Sometimes local governments and non-government organizations create voluntary programs to work with businesses to support a healthful food retail environment. Voluntary initiatives do not have the force of law so the government cannot penalize noncompliance, but it can provide rewards, technical assistance, or supplies to encourage participation. An example of a public–private voluntary partnership was the Health Vending pilot program in Minneapolis, Minnesota parks.[103] The Minneapolis Health Department partnered with both the city parks and the vending machine operators and gave participating parks and vendors small stipends. The department provided the vendor with resources and technical assistance to improve sales, including lists of healthy and popular products, and pricing and product placement strategies.

A national example of a public–private partnership is the National Salt Reduction Initiative, which is coordinated by the New York City Department of Health and Mental Hygiene and under which over 90 state and local health departments and national health organizations partner with packaged and restaurant food companies to reduce the amount of salt in the food supply.[104] Participating companies are publically applauded for pursuing the sodium reduction targets.

An example of a public–private partnership run by a nonprofit organization is the Philadelphia Healthy Corner Store Network developed by the nonprofit Food Trust, and run in partnership with the Philadelphia Department of Public Health.[105] The Food Trust conducted trainings for corner store owners to assist them in selling healthy products. It also provided financial assistance for infrastructural changes such as shelving and small refrigeration units. Over 600 Philadelphia stores joined the network to improve the healthfulness of the foods offered in the city.

State and local governments also can create and abide by their own food procurement policies and nutritional guidelines for foods provided in government buildings (e.g., worksite vending machines, hospital cafeterias) and through

---

[101] NYC Green Cart. http://www.nyc.gov/html/doh/html/living/greencarts.shtml

[102] D.C. Municipal Regulation 1909 (enacted 2012).

[103] Minneapolis Health Department. Healthy Vending in Parks. http://www.minneapolismn.gov/health/living/parks

[104] New York City Department of Health and Mental Hygiene. National Salt Reduction Initiative. http://www.nyc.gov/html/doh/html/diseases/salt.shtml

[105] Philadelphia's Healthy Corner Store Initiative. 2010–2012. http://foodtrust-prod.punkave.net/uploads/media_items/hcsi-y2report-final.original.pdf

government programs (such as elderly feeding programs). For example, in 2009, the Massachusetts governor signed an executive order launching a statewide food procurement policy that applies to all executive branch state agencies, including all offices, boards, commissions, departments, divisions, councils, and bureaus.[106] The order requires all food purchased or served to comply with nutrition guidelines established by the Massachusetts Department of Public Health. Such a procurement policy also could be enacted through state or local legislation and an individual agency may be able to pass a regulation for its own food procurement policy if permitted by its authorizing legislation.

Finally, although not based on law or government edicts, some organizations engage in self-regulatory approaches to positively change the food environment on their own. For example, the nonprofit network of hospitals, Providence Health & Services, voluntarily decided to remove sugary beverages from their dining areas, vending machines, catering, and gift shops in all of their Oregon-based hospitals.[107]

Providing Information

Although the Supreme Court stated in *44 Liquormart* that, "educational campaigns focused on the problems of excessive, or even moderate, drinking might prove to be more effective" than prohibiting the advertisement of retail alcohol prices,[108] there is little evidence that information alone, without other environmental changes or individual level support, is sufficient to alter health-related behaviors.[109] Consider an educational campaign that suggests eating an apple a day. If a person with reduced means lives in a community with little access to fresh produce or the apples that are available are $1 each, and across the street is a fast food establishment that can provide more sustenance from their Dollar Menu, how effective can the information be at creating change? Although the dissemination of information alone might not create positive public health outcomes by itself, the provision of factual information is still vitally important.

It is crucial that public health researchers disseminate their results and that governments use educational campaigns to provide people with accurate information about health and wellness. This is especially important when many people get

---

[106] By His Excellency Deval L. Patrick. Governor Executive Order No. 509. Establishing Nutrition Standards for Food Purchased and Served by State Agencies. January 7, 2009. http://www.mass.gov/governor/legislationeexecorder/executiveorder/executive-order-no-509.html

[107] Theron Park. Providence is Switching to Healthier Drinks in 2015. December 16, 2014. http://oregon.providence.org/news-and-events/news/2014/12/providence-is-switching-to-healthier-drinks-in-2015/

[108] *44 Liquormart v. RI*, at 507.

[109] Robert Crawford. You Are Dangerous to Your Health: The Ideology and Politics of Victim Blaming. In *Embodying Inequality Epidemiologic Perspectives*. Nancy Krieger, Ed. Amityville, NY: Baywood Publishing Company, Inc.; 2005.

a great deal of information about unhealthy food through marketing campaigns initiated by food companies or obtain false information on Internet websites.

Local governments provide information to their citizens through various methods. For example, the Boston Public Health Commission created a Healthy Beverage Toolkit with a sign that retailers can voluntarily display at the point of purchase, which categorizes beverages in a stop-light fashion: red to drink rarely, such as soda; yellow to drink occasionally, such as 100% juice; and green to drink plenty of, such as water.[110] Howard County, Maryland created a Better Beverage Finder website that ranks the healthfulness of hundreds of drinks and provides additional information such as whether it is good for children, or contains caffeine or artificial ingredients.[111]

Menu Labeling and Preemption

The primary informational strategy utilized in the food retail environment is the enactment of menu labeling laws. The goal of menu labeling laws is to provide consumers with nutrition information at the point of purchase. Many state and local jurisdictions passed menu labeling laws, predominantly requiring calorie content to be displayed on the menu, menu board, or drive-through at chain restaurants, which have standardized menu items across outlets. (As discussed in Chapter 6, a federal menu labeling law was passed as part of the Patient Protection and Affordable Care Act in 2010.)

When state and local governments began to pass menu labeling ordinances around the country, the restaurant industry initially responded by suing the governments. After it became clear that litigation was not going to effectively stop menu labeling, the industry began lobbying sympathetic state legislatures to preempt the ability of local jurisdictions to pass such laws. For purposes of state and local control, this fight for preemption is quite informative. Preemption is an important issue for state and local governments. As discussed in Chapter 2, it occurs when a higher level of government restricts or trumps the authority of a lower level of government to address a specific issue.

In 2006, New York City became the first jurisdiction to pass a menu labeling law. The New York State Restaurant Association sued the city in federal district court to prevent enforcement of the law, arguing that the law was preempted by the federal Food, Drug, and Cosmetic Act and that it violated the First Amendment. Based on the wording of the original ordinance, the court found that the ordinance was, in fact, preempted by federal law. The city revised

---

[110] BPHC. Healthy Beverage Toolkit. http://www.bphc.org/whatwedo/healthy-eating-active-living/healthy-beverages/Documents/HealthyBeverageToolkitFinal.pdf.

[111] Howard County Unsweetened Better Beverage Finder. http://www.betterbeveragefinder.org/results?sort=ra

the ordinance to correct the preemption violation and adopted the revised menu label law in 2008.[112] This required that the total calorie count of standard menu items be displayed on menu boards alongside the item. The restaurant industry sued the city again, arguing the same constitutional violations, but this time the city prevailed in court. In the meantime, San Francisco and Santa Clara, California passed menu labeling laws, and both were sued by the restaurant industry. The state of California subsequently passed a menu label law that preempted local efforts, making the ordinances passed in San Francisco and Santa Clara unenforceable, thereby nullifying the lawsuit. Other jurisdictions passed menu labeling laws, including Seattle Kings County, Washington and Philadelphia, Pennsylvania.

In addition to lawsuits arguing for preemption, the restaurant industry campaigned for states to use preemption as a tool to withdraw the ability of local governments to pass menu labeling laws. It was successful in Georgia, where the legislature passed a law that was signed by the governor in 2008 and prohibited local legislatures and local boards of health from passing a law that requires food service establishments to provide nutrition information about their products.[113] Perhaps the most disappointing case of preemption from a public health perspective occurred in Tennessee. In 2009, the Metropolitan Board of Health of Nashville and Davidson County passed a menu labeling ordinance that was popular in the jurisdiction.[114] Tennessee legislators disagreed with the provision and passed a law prohibiting nonelected government bodies (i.e., boards of health) from enacting regulations "pertaining to the provision of food nutritional information or otherwise regulate menus at food service establishments."[115] The governor actually vetoed the preemptive law but the legislature overrode the governor's veto, nullifying the previously passed menu labeling law and preempting all other boards of health in the state from enacting the same.

Preemptive legislation has broad reaching consequences. The higher level of government simultaneously withdraws powers from lower levels of governments to adopt innovative solutions to public health problems and respond to the needs of their distinct constituents, but it also increases its own authority by concentrating power at the state and federal capitals.[116] In addition, preemption negatively affects grassroots movements, which are organized efforts to address

---

[112] New York City, NY, Health Code § 81.50.

[113] OCGA §26-2-370 (July 1, 2008).

[114] J. L. Pomeranz. The Unique Authority of State and Local Health Departments to Address Obesity. *American Journal of Public Health*. 2011;101(7):1192–1197.

[115] 2010 Tenn ALS 614, An Act to Amend Tennessee Code Annotated, Section 68-14-303.

[116] M. Pertschuk, J. L. Pomeranz, J. Ralston Aoki, M. A. Larkin, and M. Paloma. Assessing the Impact of Federal and State Preemption in Public Health: A Framework for Decision Makers. *Journal of Public Health Management and Practice*. 2013;19(3):213–219.

threats to the health and safety of a community, led by activated citizens and organizations that devote time and resources to building grassroots capacity.[117] Grassroots movements often are built around a single issue, such as an innovative solution to a public health problem. Grassroots movements may help to educate the public about a policy initiative or rally around a policymaker who champions their cause. When legislation preempts the ability of lawmakers to pass the policy around which the movement was formed, the grassroots movement may disband and die out.[118]

Questions and Exercises for Classroom Discussion

What do you think about the legal feasibility of a state restricting food and beverages permitted to be sold in a supermarket check-out aisle to those that meet strict nutritional standards? Why do you think companies place junk food items in the check-out aisles? Is there a communicative component to placing items near cash registers?

Can you think of innovative solutions to the unhealthy food environment that a state or local government could champion under their police power?

What might be some benefits and drawbacks of grassroots movements' ability to create policy change?

What are some arguments for and against state or local governments passing taxes on foods, including unhealthy foods? As noted, Berkeley's success in passing the sugary beverage tax was partially attributed to an effective social media campaign. A difficult aspect of advocating for evidence-based policies is concisely and effectively conveying one's message. Pick a food policy topic and craft an effective 'tweet' to promote it.

---

[117] M. Pertschuk, J. L. Pomeranz, J. Ralston Aoki, M. A. Larkin, and M. Paloma. Assessing the Impact of Federal and State Preemption in Public Health: A Framework for Decision Makers. *Journal of Public Health Management and Practice*. 2013;19(3):213–219.

[118] M. Pertschuk, J. L. Pomeranz, J. Ralston Aoki, M. A. Larkin, and M. Paloma. Assessing the Impact of Federal and State Preemption in Public Health: A Framework for Decision Makers. *Journal of Public Health Management and Practice*. 2013;19(3):213–219.

INDEX

Page numbers in *italics* indicate tables or boxed discussions.

G

H

www.ingramcontent.com/pod-product-compliance
Lightning Source LLC
Chambersburg PA
CBHW020239090126
37977CB00042B/770
9780190227258